# ONE IN A THOUSAND

# ONE IN A THOUSAND

*The Life and Death of Captain Eddie McKay,*
*Royal Flying Corps*

GRAHAM BROAD

UNIVERSITY OF TORONTO PRESS

Higher Education Division

www.utppublishing.com

Library and Archives Canada Cataloguing in Publication

Broad, Graham, 1970–, author

   One in a thousand : the life and death of Captain Eddie McKay, Royal Flying Corps / Graham Broad.

Includes bibliographical references and index.
Issued in print and electronic formats.

ISBN 978-1-4875-9341-4 (cloth).—ISBN 978-1-4426-0746-0 (paper).
—ISBN 978-1-4426-0747-7 (pdf).—ISBN 978-1-4426-0748-4 (html).

   1. McKay, Eddie, 1892–1917. 2. McKay, Eddie, 1892–1917—Death and burial.
3. Great Britain. Royal Flying Corps—Biography. 4. Fighter pilots—Canada—
Biography. 5. World War, 1914–1918—Aerial operations, Canadian. 6. World War, 1914–1918—Aerial operations, British. I. Title.

D607.C2B76 2017  940.4'4971092  C2016-905197-8

              C2016-905198-6

We welcome comments and suggestions regarding any aspect of our publications—please feel free to contact us at news@utphighereducation.com or visit our Internet site at www.utppublishing.com.

*North America*
5201 Dufferin Street
North York, Ontario, Canada, M3H 5T8

2250 Military Road
Tonawanda, New York, USA, 14150

ORDERS PHONE: 1-800-565-9523
ORDERS FAX: 1-800-221-9985
ORDERS E-MAIL: utpbooks@utpress.utoronto.ca

*UK, Ireland, and continental Europe*
NBN International
Estover Road
Plymouth, PL6 7PY, UK

ORDERS PHONE: 44 (0) 1752 202301
ORDERS FAX: 44 (0) 1752 202333
ORDERS E-MAIL: enquiries@nbn
international.com

The University of Toronto Press acknowledges the financial support for its publishing activities of the Government of Canada through the Canada Book Fund.

Printed in the United States of America.

But I should blush
To face the men and long-rob'd dames of Troy,
If, like a coward, I could shun the fight.

*Iliad,* Book VI

I cannot tell you how much I feel his loss, as he was one in a thousand, and by far the best man I had, and the one that I could least spare.

*Letter from Major Arthur Bryant to Joe McKay, 29 December 1917*

# CONTENTS

*Acknowledgements*   ix

*Timeline*   xiii

*Introduction*   xv
Historians and Their Sources   xxvii

CHAPTER ONE
*To Western and to War: 1892–1916*
1
Historians and Fact Finding
32

CHAPTER TWO
*Over the Somme: July–October 1916*
41
Triangulation and Reading Against the Grain
70

CHAPTER THREE
*The Battle, October 28, 1916—March 14, 1917*
77
*Mentalité* and the Military Past
94

CHAPTER FOUR
*The Choice: March 15–December 28, 1917*
105
Thinking about Thoughts: The Past as a Foreign Country
121

CHAPTER FIVE
*The Letter: January 1918–July 31, 1932*
131
Historians, Historical Ethics, and the End of History
139


APPENDIX: THE MYSTERIES   149

SELECTED BIBLIOGRAPHY   157

INDEX   163

# ACKNOWLEDGEMENTS

I tell my students to avoid clichés, but sometimes they are inescapable. Searching for Eddie McKay was like trying to find a needle in a haystack—and occasionally a needle in a stack of needles. The difficulties would have been insurmountable without the help of friends, students, colleagues, librarians, archivists, an array of aviation historians in several countries, and members of McKay's extended family.

The first order of thanks is due to the students of my 2006–07 "Canada in the World Wars" seminar at King's University College, Western University. Their class project on Eddie McKay, which culminated in a bronze marker placed on campus in his honour, laid the groundwork for this book. At a time when there is growing concern about student disengagement, these exceptional young scholars demonstrated conclusively that the good students are as good as they ever were. Thanks especially to Courtney Everrett, Kerri Gibb, Chris Miller, and Dave Poisson for their sustained interest in Eddie's life.

Few historians know more about Canada in the First World War than Jonathan Vance and Tim Cook, who were generous with their time, ideas, and encouragement, helping to ease a Second World War historian into the Byzantine world of Great War historiography and record keeping. Mike Bechthold, John Edwards, Barrington Gray, Trevor Henshaw, Richard Holt, Peter Kilduff, Alex Revell, Ed Roach, and Amy Shaw offered their expertise to the finished work's advantage. I owe a particular debt to Stewart K. Taylor, who for decades conducted diligent and careful research into Canadian aviators who served in the British flying services. Stewart shared his research on McKay with me in several letters and phone conversations. He also gave me the remarkable photo of McKay taken by his squadron-mate George Trudeau just days before McKay was killed in action.

I spent many hours either working with or in correspondence with archivists and historians at institutions in six different countries. Among many others were Tom Belton and Theresa Regnier at Western University's Archives and Research Collection Centre; George de Zwaan at the sadly beleaguered Library and Archives of Canada; Peter Hart at the Imperial War Museum; John Armstrong at Wright State University Archives; Ross Mahoney at the Royal Air Force Museum; Patrizia Nava of the Eugene McDermott Library at the University of Texas at Dallas; Carol Reid at the Canadian War Museum; several volunteers at the Oxford County Archives and Oxford Genealogy Society; Carol Waggoner-Angleton at the Reese Library of Georgia Regents University; and Pam McKenzie at the Western Canada Aviation Museum. Historians and aviation enthusiasts on several Internet sites, most notably Mike Meech on aerodrome.com, were patient in answering the tedious technical questions of a newcomer. Of particular note is the work of Andrew Pentland, whose astonishingly comprehensive database (air-history.org.uk) of British aviators and their airplanes in the First World War led me in new and fruitful directions.

Some distant relations of Eddie McKay, including Eugene Kittmer, Robert Mackay, and Donald Vannatter, were of great value to this project. Mr. Kittmer had retained McKay's logbook, which until the eleventh hour I had believed to be lost. The logbook illuminated whole swaths of McKay's flying career, and its importance to this project cannot be overstated. Further thanks are due to Glenn Hislop of Stratford, Ontario, whose efforts led to McKay's name being added to the Stratford cenotaph, and Brian Shypula of the *Stratford Beacon Herald*, whose articles in 2006–07 concerning my class's project helped me make initial contact with some of the people mentioned above. In addition, family members of pilots McKay served with were generous with their time. These include Carol Nicholson, niece of Roy Brown; and Dr. Peter Saundby, son of Air Marshal Sir Robert Saundby, who among other things went to the trouble of transcribing a very rare paper by his father for me.

Internal research grants from King's University College at the University of Western Ontario eased the financial burden of travel and other research costs. Friends and colleagues at King's, including Claudia Clausius, Dorotea Gucciardo, Erin Hannah, Andrea Lawlor, Kristin Lozanski, Marcie Penner-Wilger, Renée Soulodre-La France, and Robert Ventresca have been allies and intellectual tutors, while my dogged research assistants Leonie Fleischmann, Caitlin McCuaig, Katrina Pasierbek, and Dave Poisson have never let me down. Thanks also to Chris Doris, who provided me with essential workspace during my sabbatical. I look forward to further collaborations with Natalie Fingerhut of the University of Toronto Press, who was with this project from its inception and whose enthusiasm helped sustain me through occasional periods of ennui. My copy editor, Karen Taylor, improved the work and saved me from several embarrassing errors.

This, my second book, is half the length of the first. Inexplicably, it has imposed twice the burden on my wife, Amanda Green. No words can serve as even partial recompense for the debt I have incurred. For over two years, she has shared our home with a long dead aviator, and has more than earned the right to pillory me with the biographical details of the medieval figures who are the focus of her scholarly interest.

Writing this book required me to travel by airplane to several destinations in Canada and the UK. I always did so while reflecting on the extraordinary difference between flying today and in Eddie McKay's time, partly to reassure myself that the statistics are true and that airplanes are now very safe. My father, David Broad, was for several decades a private pilot, and his help in interpreting the technical jargon in McKay's logbook was invaluable. Growing up, I went flying with him from time to time but was never comfortable or confident in the air, and neither was my late mother, Marilyn Broad (1936–2005), florist, art collector, and bookworm. Respectively, they taught me that problems have practical and imaginative solutions, and I dedicate this book to them with love and gratitude.

# TIMELINE

| | |
|---|---|
| *December 27, 1892* | Alfred Edwin McKay born in Brussels, ON |
| *1893–1908* | Childhood in West Zorra Township, south of Stratford, ON |
| *c. 1909–1910* | Moves to nearby London, ON, to live with his oldest brother, Alexander (Sandy); subsequently becomes noted local athlete |
| *May 25, 1912* | First flight of an aeroplane over London, ON |
| *August 4, 1914* | United Kingdom declares war on Germany; Canada automatically at war |
| *September 1914* | Registers as a student in the faculty of arts at the Western University of London Ontario |
| *November 1914* | Western wins the Dominion Junior Rugby Championship with McKay as one of the leading players on the team |
| *June 1915* | After passing exams at Western, takes commission as lieutenant in the 33rd Huron Regiment (Canadian Militia) |
| *November 1, 1915–January 27, 1916* | Civilian flight training at Wright Flying School, Dayton, OH, and Augusta, GA; earns Aero Club of America cert. #401 |
| *February 14, 1916* | Seconded to the Royal Flying Corps (RFC) as 2nd lieutenant |
| *March 13, 1916* | Arrives in UK; commences additional training with the RFC |
| *June 19 or 21, 1916* | Appointed flying officer |

| | |
|---|---|
| *July 3, 1916* | Posted to No. 24 Squadron at Bertangles, France |
| *July 20, 1916* | Scores first of approximately ten aerial victories |
| *October 28, 1916* | Leading German ace Oswald Boelcke dies in aerial collision while in combat with McKay and Arthur Knight |
| *March 14, 1917* | Posted to the Central Flying School, Upavon, as an instructor |
| *April 1, 1917* | Promoted to lieutenant |
| *April 26, 1917* | Promoted to temporary captain and flight leader |
| *October 28, 1917* | Voluntarily returns to France, serving as "A" Flight leader in No. 23 Squadron on the Ypres salient |
| *December 28/29, 1917* | Killed in action (or subsequently dies of wounds in German captivity); listed as missing by the RFC |
| *May 2, 1918* | Officially declared dead |

# INTRODUCTION

*For I dipt into the future, far as human eye could see,*
*Saw the Vision of the world, and all the wonder that would be;*

*Saw the heavens fill with commerce, argosies of magic sails,*
*Pilots of the purple twilight, dropping down with costly bales;*

*Heard the heavens fill with shouting, and there rain'd a ghastly dew*
*From the nations' airy navies grappling in the central blue.*

—Tennyson, *Locksley Hall*

This is a story about Eddie McKay, a First World War flying ace from Canada, but it is not a biography in the usual sense of the word. McKay lived 25 years, all but three in the obscurity imposed by everyday life in late-nineteenth- and early-twentieth-century Ontario.[1] He was not unimportant, but for most of his life he was ordinary, and ordinary people seldom anticipate the needs of future historians. The handful of records that survive from his youth provide only the crudest sketch of his life until his twenty-second year. It is only then, in 1914, when he enrolled at the Western University of London, Ontario, that a fuller portrait begins to take shape. Even so, with the passage of the intervening century, he might easily have been forgotten altogether, reduced by the ebb of time to no more than a name on a monument or gravestone, possibly in one of the hundreds of military cemeteries in Belgium or France. In 1915, however, McKay made a fateful decision.

---

1  I call my subject "Eddie" until he leaves university and generally by his surname thereafter, except to avoid confusion when other McKays are mentioned.

He decided to enlist in Britain's fledgling Royal Flying Corps (RFC), at a time when pilots were rare and most Canadians had never seen an aeroplane. In so doing, he secured himself a small place in the history books.

Throughout the First World War, the dashing figure of the aviator captured the imagination of a public yearning for heroes at a time when mass warfare had rendered most soldiers mute and anonymous. Technology may have obliterated chivalry in the trenches, but in the eyes of many it had restored it above them. Soaring fearlessly above the battlefield in his machine, the aviator both heralded the future and embodied an era of legend, when champions drawn from opposing armies would clash in single combat. "Every flight is a romance; every report is an epic. They are the knighthood of this war, without fear and without reproach," British Prime Minister David Lloyd George enthused in 1917. "They recall the old legends of chivalry, not merely by the daring of their exploits, but by the nobility of their spirit."[2]

Romantic notions such as these often bore no more resemblance to the grisly reality of aerial combat than tales of chivalry did to the brutality of medieval warfare, but that was beside the point. What mattered was that the reading public, politicians, journalists, propagandists, and idealistic recruits embraced and espoused this ideal. If anything, the achievements of the "Knights of the Air" were thought to have exceeded those of their medieval forbearers. When RFC veteran Alan McLeod, a recipient of the Victoria Cross, died of influenza at the age of 19 in Winnipeg in November 1918, his minister reflected in the local paper that he had been

> the finest flower of chivalry. The old days of knighthood are over, but for the very fairest blossoms of the spirit of knighthood the world has had to wait till the 20th century. It was these dauntless boys who have saved civilization. The heroism of the Crusades pales before the incredible and quiet courage of such boys who gave us a new interpretation of Calvary. I saw Alan within a few hours of his death. He faced the last enemy with the same joyous confidence with which he started on what he called the very happiest part of his life.[3]

Like most such tales, the myth of the Knights of the Air was not without some semblance of reality. With rare exceptions, the pilots of the British flying services were officers, but they differed from other officers in one crucial respect. Generals

---

2  Quoted in David Lloyd George, *The Great Crusade: Extracts from Speeches Delivered during the War* (London: George H. Doran Company, 1918), 212.

3  Quoted in George A. Drew, *Canada's Fighting Airmen* (Toronto: Maclean Publishing Company, 1930), 233.

might send men into battle and lieutenants might lead them into battle, but pilots carried the entire burden of battle itself. How readily, then, was the pilot transformed into knight, his aeroplane into his steed, his machine gun into his lance. And though the pilots themselves, having witnessed first hand how cruel the air war could be, often baulked at such idealized depictions of their trade, they were not above employing them when the occasion suited. Arthur Gould Lee, an RFC pilot who survived the First World War to rise to the rank of air vice-marshal in the Second World War, reflected in his memoir *No Parachute,*

> This was a time when air combat could indeed be tinged with something of the knightly chivalry of old, when a pilot, perhaps still in his teens, might inwardly salute his antagonist, even wave to him as they circled each other, seeking the chance to fire. And having killed, could feel pity for a fellow flyer, or, if he had gone down in flames, remorse for inflicting so gruesome an end. For now was a period, not to last long, when enemies in the air could fight without mercy but without hate, could even respect and admire each other's skill and valour.[4]

As this came five decades after the fact, it might be tempting to argue that time had dulled Lee's memory, that the horror of aerial warfare had given way to what the historian C.P. Stacey, in a different context, called "the golden haze of historical romance."[5] But *No Parachute* and its companion, *Open Cockpit,* are remarkably frank in their depictions of violent death in the sky and highly critical of the RFC's senior leadership. Much the same can be said of the most acclaimed of all First World War pilot memoirs, Cecil Lewis's *Sagittarius Rising,* first published in 1936. Yet Lewis, too, could not resist musing in lyrical and indeed often quixotic tones about his terrible vocation. Aerial combat was, he wrote, "the only sphere of modern warfare where there was chivalry and honour."

> Besides, there is, as everybody who has fought knows, a strong magnetic attraction between two men who are matched against one another. I have felt this magnetism, engaging an enemy scout three miles above the earth. I have wheeled and circled, watching how he flew, taking the power and speed of his machine, seen him, fifty yards away, eyeing me, calculating, watching for an opening, each of us wary, keyed up to the last pitch of skill

---

4 Arthur Gould Lee, *No Parachute: A Fighter Pilot in World War One* (London: Jarrolds, 1968), xiii.
5 C.P. Stacey, "Generals and Generalship before Quebec, 1759–1760," *Canadian Historical Association Report* 38, no. 1 (1959): 1.

and endeavour. And if at last he went down, a falling rocket of smoke and flame, what a glorious and heroic death! What a brave man! It might just as well have been me. For what have I been spared? To die, diseased, in bed? Sometimes it seems a pity.[6]

Dreadful though the air war could be, some pilots really did maintain certain chivalrous affectations. When Oswald Boelcke, the dean of German military aviation, died in a collision over the Western Front in October 1916, RFC pilots dropped a wreath expressing condolences into German lines.[7] When his protégé, Manfred von Richthofen, the famous "Red Baron," slayer of dozens of British pilots, was shot down over British lines in April 1918, the comrades of men he had killed buried him beside their most important aerodrome with an extravagant display of full military honours.[8] McKay himself was a posthumous recipient of one such gesture in February 1918, when a German machine crossed British lines and dropped a note, informing the British that their missing pilot was dead.[9] There are innumerable examples. Such high-minded ideals, coupled with the public's longing for a just and civilized war, were part of what propelled young men such as Eddie McKay into prominence. In the last two years of his life, he attained a degree of notoriety that most of those who served never did. Excerpts from letters written by or about him were published in the local papers, while hyperbolic, half-truthful, and even entirely confected stories breathlessly recounted his exploits overseas, praising his humility, resolve, and courage as traits of an exemplary manhood. For a brief moment in November 1916, because of a claim that he himself never made, McKay became nationally famous, well before Canadians had ever heard of Billy Bishop, Raymond Collishaw, Roy Brown, or any of the other heroic aces who heralded from Britain's most senior dominion. His fame rapidly would be forgotten, eclipsed by greater pilots who accomplished greater things, but for that moment he was Canada's foremost aviator.

---

6 Cecil Lewis, *Sagittarius Rising* (1936; repr., New York: Penguin, 2014), 35.

7 Johannes Werner, *Knight of Germany*, translated by Claud W. Sykes (1933; Philadelphia: Casement, 2009), 267. The first English edition (1933) is a translation of the standard biography of Boelcke, published in German in 1932. Werner's biography is also a work of National Socialist propaganda and should be regarded with some suspicion.

8 On von Richthofen, see Peter Kilduff, *The Red Baron: Beyond the Legend* (London: Cassell, 1999).

9 National Archives (NA) of the United Kingdom (UK), War Office (WO), Officer's Service Files, Captain Alfred Edwin McKay, Royal Flying Corps, WO 339/62435, Letter: War Office to J. D. McKay, February 5, 1918. McKay's fragmentary War Office file deals almost entirely with correspondence regarding his death and the disposition of his back pay. Hereafter cited as McKay, WO Service File, item description, and date.

McKay's service with the RFC, which ended when he was killed in action at the end of 1917, was commendable though not exceptionally distinguished. He was never decorated (perhaps because of an ill-considered joke he made in November 1916), but he did attain the rank of captain and flight leader. He also can be credited with roughly ten aerial "victories" according to the RFC's peculiar standards, which I discuss later in this introduction.[10] He merits a brief mention in most major histories of the air war, although almost always in relation to a single event, alluded to already and discussed in detail in Chapter Three. This book is by far the fullest study of his life, and the reader may well wonder why an entire work about him is justified. My rather idealistic response is that works of history contain their own justification. We study history to satisfy our curiosity, after all, so any good effort to illuminate the past has inherent value, from picture books about material objects to sweeping social-scientific analyses written by and for specialists. McKay's service as a pilot compels me for a number of reasons, not least of all because he was among the first Canadians to fly, hailed from my hometown, and was a student at my alma mater. But there is more to it than that, even. Historians of the air war have shared the wartime public's fascination with those pilots that Arthur Gould Lee called "a constellation of champions of glittering valour and deadly talent": the great aces, including Germany's Oswald Boelcke and Manfred von Richthofen; Britain's Albert Ball and Mick Mannock; and a host of Canadians, including Billy Bishop, whose visage appears on Canadian passports and after whom Toronto's island airport is named.[11] Alongside perhaps a score of others, the great aces fascinate precisely because they were so extraordinary—and so extraordinarily rare. By the time the war ended, about 100,000 men had served or were training as pilots in the combatant nations' respective air services. Of those, a mere 12 are credited with 50 aerial victories or more, and just 3 with more than 70. By contrast, the great majority of pilots never shot down another plane at all, often because it was not their job to do so. The principal task of airpower in the First World War was photographic reconnaissance and the related task of artillery observation. Fighter pilots seized the limelight and had laurels showered upon them, but theirs was the supporting role, engaging enemy machines so that their own observation aircraft could work unmolested. McKay was himself a fighter pilot, but he rose no higher than perhaps the third tier of wartime aces. He is of

---

10  Christopher Shores, Norman Franks, and Russell Guest, *Above the Trenches: A Complete Record of the Fighter Aces and Units of the British Empire Air Forces, 1915–1920* (Stoney Creek, ON: Fortress Publications, 1990) contains a list of British flying aces of the First World War, compiled from "Combats in the Air" reports, squadron record books, and similar documents; it credits McKay with ten victories. See discussion below.

11  Lee, *No Parachute*, xiv.

interest partly because his service is more representative of the average pilot. I have situated him at the centre of a story about that extraordinary air war, the first in history, so that his tale might shed light on aspects of that conflict and on other young men, especially Canadians, who fought in it. Students of the air war will find much of what follows familiar, but I hope that they will be intrigued to see the story refracted through the lens of Eddie McKay's life.

This book might be called a "pedagogical microhistory," one of several published in recent years by the University of Toronto Press. Microhistory emerged as a genre of historical writing in the 1970s. While mid-century social historians had often favoured broadly conceived studies, writing sweeping accounts of people across decades or even centuries, microhistorians asked big questions about small things, placing sharply defined topics under the microscope. They invited readers to consider these topics in their larger historical context but also to test the limits of the conclusions reached by historians of bigger historical topics by revealing exceptions to the norm.[12] In a similar fashion, this book examines the last three years of McKay's life, focusing in particular on the period for which by far the best sources exist: the nine months from July 1916 to March 1917, when he served with No. 24 Squadron in France. As a *pedagogical* history, this book also offers students an unusual reading experience. I am telling parallel stories here: one about history and one about historiography, or the methods historians use to study the past. In many academic disciplines, it is taken for granted that scholarly publications must include a discussion of methodology. History is methodologically more sophisticated than is usually appreciated, but it seldom is methodologically transparent. In most works of history, methods operate in the background, largely undetected by readers, the way that movies conceal the tremendous effort that goes into their production. Admittedly, some ambitious readers will plunge into a book's footnotes, endnotes, or bibliographical essays, just as some curious moviegoers will stay to the end of the credits. In the past two generations, it has become obligatory for academic historians to leave an evidentiary trail, in the form of citations, for readers to follow if they choose to do so. But citations do not by themselves tell us much about methodology, let alone about what theories underpinned the methods that led an historian to make a discovery or draw certain conclusions from it. By contrast, this book lays bare the theoretical and practical considerations I made when researching and writing McKay's story. To that end,

12 See the discussion from one of the founders of the field: Carlo Ginzburg, "Microhistory: Two or Three Things I Know about It," translated by John and Anne C. Tedeschi, *Critical Inquiry* 20, no. 1 (Autumn 1993): 10–35; see also Steven Bednarski, "On Microhistory and Pedagogy," in *A Poisoned Past* (Toronto: University of Toronto Press, 2014), 23–52.

the reader will find methodological discussions at the end of each chapter, including one prefatory discussion, below. These interludes employ examples from my research as a means of introducing historical theory and methods and of examining the strengths and considering the limitations of my approach. Although these sections are aimed at students of history, I have tried to write them in a way that will engage anyone who is interested in the practice and profession of history. It is possible to read this book without delving into that material, but I hope that readers who have come for the history will stay for the historiography. As a further enticement, I will reveal now that there are surprises about Eddie McKay in those sections, including several mysteries that I could not solve.

I do not purport to have written an original work on the philosophy of history. Contemporary philosophy of history is a broad-ranging, controversial, and immensely complex body of ideas. In its scope and sophistication, it is daunting even to professional historians, many of whom carry on their work unconcerned with such things.[13] Having said that, there is no doubt that the historical profession has changed a good deal in the past 50 years. Historians today study a broader range of subjects and are, in many respects, more self-reflective, critical, and skeptical, both of their sources and of the received wisdom of the past. At its core, however, the discipline remains an empirical one. Open any academic journal of history today and you will find historians writing about new topics but for the most part using familiar methods to do it. They may sometimes employ formidable new terminology; they are undoubtedly more open to utilizing theoretical insights derived from other disciplines, but fundamentally, most of them are doing what historians have done for centuries: telling stories and making arguments about the past based on an accumulation of hard evidence. In its methodological interludes, this book concerns itself with exactly that: the pragmatic problem-solving and evidence-based methods I used to write it. These methods occasionally relate to the more esoteric interests of philosophers and theorists (just as a pilot's struggle to keep his machine airborne related to broader questions of physics), but they are not my foremost concern. Instead, I hope to explain in prosaic terms how I have attempted to illuminate parts of a world that no longer exists. In expressing this hope, I am revealing the position I take regarding the view, held by some theorists, that historians cannot illuminate the past, only the sources it leaves behind. This is a view I find logically incoherent and inconsistently applied even by those who profess to believe it.

---

13  For a discussion of the practical impact (or lack thereof) of the philosophy of history on the historical profession, at least as matters stood in the late 1990s, see Richard J. Evans, *In Defense of History* (London: Granata Books, 1997), 9–13.

Unapologetically, I have written a story, one that I believe to be true. For centuries, if not millennia, this was the essence of what historians did. Only in the past few decades have some historians argued that the profession is better served by analytic approaches of the kind favoured in the social sciences. I do not object to social scientific writing, but I do reject the suggestion, sometimes made, that good stories, told as narratives, must necessarily lack conceptual depth and academic rigour. I will concede that the story I have told about McKay is not the only one that could be told, nor is this narrative the only way of telling it. I have included certain facts, excluded others, and there are some things about which I cannot be certain. Part of what follows is McKay's story; part is the story of how I wrote it. It is my sincere hope that students of history will find my methods to be rather old-fashioned, and refreshingly so.

## Sources and Terminology

Most of the surviving records of Britain's First World War flying services are held by the National Archives (formerly the Public Records Office) in the UK. While researching *Canadian Airmen and the First World War* (1980), the first volume of the official history of the Royal Canadian Air Force, a team of historians led by S.F. Wise photocopied material relevant to Canadians from the Air Ministry records. These copies are now held by the Library and Archives of Canada (LAC) in Ottawa. For the sake of transparency, I have indicated whether the Air Ministry records were cited from the National Archives (UK) or the LAC, even when the same record is held by both. Regrettably, the Air Ministry records as a whole are in a decrepit state. They were in the first place badly kept, in part because the rapid growth of the flying services outpaced their capacity to keep accurate records. They have suffered grievously since through loss, accidental and otherwise. In the Second World War, German bombing destroyed a large portion of the records of the flying services. Archival mismanagement and neglect has accounted for other losses. To cite one example, in 1960 the Royal Air Force (RAF) intentionally destroyed thousands of unclaimed First World War logbooks, furthering the project that the Luftwaffe had begun 20 years earlier.[14] The historian Denis Winter estimates that "well over" 90 per cent of the records used in the writing of Britain's six-volume official history of the air war have subsequently been lost.[15] Although this is almost certainly an overestimate, it is nonetheless true that the operational

---

14  Royal Air Force Museum, Aircrew Logbooks, accessed July 20, 2015, http://www.rafmuseum.org.uk/research/default/archive-collection/aircrew-logbooks.aspx.

15  Denis Winter, *The First of the Few: Fighter Pilots of the First World War* (New York: Penguin, 1983), 217.

and routine orders of most RFC units are only partially intact, while the files of many personnel, the record books of whole squadrons, and the great majority of documents relating to the training establishment no longer exist. Writing about a pilot who was not famous posed a number of additional challenges. McKay was killed nearly a century ago, and no living person remembers him. He kept no diary, and very few of his letters have survived, though by very great fortune his logbook was returned with his personal effects and was kept by his descendants.[16] This proved to be the single most valuable source for this study. For clues about what kind of person he was, I have had to rely on contemporary newspaper articles and the published or recorded recollections of his squadron-mates. He was, by all accounts, athletic, amiable, brash, funny though sometimes arrogant, and possessed of a "deadly talent," too, it seems. In addition, there is a substantial body of published and unpublished memoir literature by First World War pilots, some of whom flew with McKay. These and other such sources have allowed me to infer, plausibly, if somewhat generally, what McKay's experiences in the RFC would have been like. Inevitably, however, there remains a great deal about his life that is lost to history. In particular, many of the intimate and personal details of his life have eluded me.

A few remarks regarding terminology are required. For several years prior to joining the RFC, McKay resided in London, Ontario. To avoid confusion, I usually refer to that city as "London" and the capital of the United Kingdom as London, England. In 1914, McKay enrolled as a student at the Western University of London, Ontario. In 1923, that institution was renamed the University of Western Ontario (UWO). I note the distinction because, very recently, UWO "rebranded" as "Western University," its original name, and I do not wish Canadian readers to think I am using the name anachronistically. At Western, McKay emerged as one of the school's star rugby-football players. That sport was also referred to simply as "rugby" (despite having slightly different rules) and just "football," the latter not to be confused with either "American football" or "association football" (soccer). In addition, my use of excerpts from various works of literature as introductory quotations in chapters is not pretension. McKay studied those books and poems in school. My quotations from the *Iliad* are from the 1867 translation by Edward, Earl of Derby, as this was in all likelihood the one used in classrooms at Western. The curriculum at the time even required students to commit some of these passages to memory, a reminder of a quaint and unscientific era when teachers laboured under the impression that sustained attention was worth cultivating.

---

16  A digital copy and an annotated transcription of McKay's logbook are available on the website Wartime Canada (http://wartimecanada.ca/).

The Royal Flying Corps, founded in 1912, comprised a "military" wing, attached to the British army, and a naval wing. From the outset, the two branches operated more or less independently of one another. The naval wing, dubbed the Royal Naval Air Service (RNAS), came fully under the direction of the Admiralty in August 1915. The two services had a poor working relationship, competing for pilots, planes, and other scarce resources. This unsatisfactory state of affairs was remedied in April 1918, when the RFC and the RNAS were amalgamated into a new independent service, the Royal Air Force (RAF). I have used the term "flying services" when referring to two or more of them at once. RFC pilots who completed their training were said to have earned their "wings" (which included the right to sew the RFC's distinctive wing-shaped badge onto their uniform) and were appointed "flying officers." This was a job description, not the formal rank it subsequently became in the RAF. Pilots were sometimes referred to as "airmen," but this, too, was a colloquialism rather than a formal rank. It should also be noted that not all RFC pilots were officers. In exceptional cases, non-commissioned officers could also become pilots, although they usually were promoted from the ranks shortly thereafter.

Hardly anyone anticipated aerial combat when the war erupted in August 1914. Most aircraft in 1914 were two-seaters, with a pilot and an observer flying in tandem. The British called single-seat machines "scouts," a name that stuck even after they were armed with machine guns and tasked with shooting down enemy planes. Not until the early 1920s did the term "fighter" supplant "scout" as the standard term for single-seat aircraft designed for aerial combat, although it was occasionally used before then. In 1915, French newspapers began using the term "l'As" (ace) to describe pilots who had brought down five or more enemy aircraft. The term had no official standing and seldom appears in English-language newspapers prior to 1918.[17] Historian Christopher Shores has even speculated that many pilots did not even know the term until late in the war, although he acknowledges that it appears in the 1918 memoir of Canada's famous and controversial pilot Billy Bishop.[18] In my opinion, the fixation on aces and verifying their "scores," a marked trait in the community of First World War aviation writers, can convey a distorted impression of how and why airpower was deployed throughout the war. It bears repeating that, for the British and French, at least, the unglamorous but crucial work of photographic

---

17 A review of the *Globe and Mail* database reveals only about half a dozen uses of the word "ace" to describe military pilots prior to 1917. For a discussion, see Shores, Franks, and Guest, *Above the Trenches*.

18 Shores, Franks, and Guest, *Above the Trenches*, 9–10.

reconnaissance and artillery cooperation was the flying services' reason for being. As I have discussed, McKay can be credited with about ten "victories"— the term itself is highly problematic, as I will argue—but it is important to realize that the British kept no master list of aerial victories by pilot. Thus, an enemy machine was reported as having been driven down, out of control, by 2nd Lt. A.E. McKay on July 20, 1916, but the RFC did not keep his "score." Citations for decorations sometimes gave an approximation of the recipient's total victories based on combat reports, but the claim, often made, that such-and-such a British pilot was "officially credited" with 72, 60, 57, or 10 "victories" is something of a misnomer. The lists one finds in various published works and Internet pages were, for the most part, cobbled together from surviving combat records in the postwar period by historians and by the community of aviation history enthusiasts.

The system that the British flying services used to report combat in the air evolved over time. There was also no centralized victory claim authority, so both reporting and verification practices were at times quite subjective, varying some-what from unit to unit. Generally speaking, however, in 1915 and 1916, Combats in the Air reports, filed by squadron commanders and then submitted to higher headquarters for verification, recorded enemy machines "destroyed," "driven down out of control" (OOC), "driven down damaged," and "forced to land" (even if on their own side of the lines), along with the names of the pilots responsible. All of these are referred to colloquially as "victories," even though they might refer to radically different outcomes. In these early days of aerial combat, the "moral victory" of driving an enemy machine off or down was a significant accomplishment. On occasion, reports were filed even when no enemy machine was lost through deliberate action, as was the case in the most famous combat in which Eddie McKay was involved—that of October 28, 1916, which I discuss in Chapter Three. As the number of aerial combats grew by leaps and bounds in 1917 and the lethality of aircraft increased proportionately, the claim system was revised. Now "victories" were counted only in cases where an enemy machine was destroyed, captured, or driven down out of control in such a manner that was likely to result in its destruction, with higher headquarters generally requiring a higher standard of verification, especially for OOC claims.[19]

---

19 The revised Combats in the Air forms included a field to record enemy machines "driven down" (but not OOC), but these were not generally considered victories after mid-1917. Verification came in the form of a given claim being ruled "decisive" or "indecisive" at higher headquarters, with only the former being considered a victory.

A few additional remarks about this system are required. For reasons I will discuss, the vast majority of aerial combats fought by the British were on the German side of the lines. Without wreckage to examine or friendly eyewitnesses, British authorities were often at a loss to confirm definitively the majority of pilots' victory claims. Postwar historians who have attempted to verify Allied victories in German archives have been confounded by records in a far worse state of completeness than even those of the British air services. Nonetheless, what survives demonstrates that the pilots of many German machines reported OOC—a category unique to the British—almost certainly made it back to their own aerodromes by some combination of luck or skill.[20] The lack of corroborating evidence has led to accusations of intentional fraud against certain British pilots, Canada's Billy Bishop being the most notable and perhaps justifiable example.[21] This is not to suggest that pilots lied as a matter of routine: aerial combat was fast, confusing, and dangerous. Honest errors in reporting were inevitable. In brief, then, the British claim system was unique, changed over time, and was always subjective and fraught with the very great possibility of error. Attempting to establish with certainty any given pilot's "score" is probably a forlorn endeavour. Ranking British aces over time, or against their rivals in other services, is an endeavour of the apples-and-oranges variety.

A final word about terminology: I have tried to avoid other anachronisms by retaining the nomenclature and measurement preferences of the time: hence *aeroplane* or *machine* in place of "airplane" (although the word "plane" very occasionally was used during the war), and my use of imperial measurements is in keeping with the British practice of measuring speed in miles per hour, altitudes in feet, gun calibre in inches, temperatures in degrees Fahrenheit, and so on. One partial exception relates to the names of aircraft. Pilots often had their own names and nicknames for the types of machines they flew. For the majority of his front-line service, McKay piloted an aeroplane called the DH 2, but like his squadron-mates he called it the "De Havilland scout," "DeHav," or just "DH." Pilots also had nicknames for German machines, whose official names were usually unknown to them, and they often innocently misidentified enemy aircraft they encountered in the air. In the interests of consistency and clarity, I have generally

---

20 For a fuller discussion of the British claim system, see Shores, Guest, and Franks, *Above the Trenches*, 6–10.

21 Controversy over Bishop's claims has raged for decades. For a negative view, see Brereton Greenhous, *The Making of Billy Bishop* (Toronto: Dundurn, 2002). For a less critical assessment, built around an examination of surviving German records, see Peter Kilduff, *Billy Bishop VC—Lone Wolf Hunter: The RAF Ace Re-examined* (London: Grub Street, 2014).

referred to aircraft by their official names or those arrived at by the consensus of aviation historians.

## Historians and Their Sources

So what is a historian, then? The word "history" comes to us from the ancient Greek *historia*, meaning "inquiry" or "research," so, simply put, we might say that a historian is a person who conducts research into the past. In the modern period, professional historians, who "do" history for a living, tend to have advanced degrees and publish the results of their research with academic presses, although this is not a strict requirement to earn the title. There have been enormously influential works of history written by people without formal training as historians and published by trade or non-academic presses, in addition to important documentary films and the like. If the question of what constitutes a historian is comparatively easy to answer, the question of what history itself is and how to go about researching and writing about it are not. These matters are highly controversial, and different schools of thought are constantly at odds with one another over them. Surprisingly, however, there is one counterintuitive idea about which there seems to be a consensus across the discipline. That idea is that *history changes.*

Think of this book as a small object, placed in the path of the tide of history. The tide will flow over it, knock it about a bit, but ultimately the tide will, in its ebb and flow, be changed, perhaps imperceptibly, but changed nonetheless. Now picture ten such objects. A hundred. A thousand. The tide churns and breaks against them. History changes. It can be a difficult concept to grasp. Everyone who teaches history has had to endure a ribbing about having the easiest job in the world: you write your lectures once and then coast for the rest of your career. But this is to mistake history for the past, and they are not the same. "They swim miles apart," is how one philosopher of history put it.[22] The past is everything that happened before us, immutable and often dark. History is what we write about it. Historiography, or the methods historians use to write history, is the shaft of light we shine on the remnants of the past, which we call sources.[23] We can widen, narrow, brighten, or shift the beam of light, illuminating sources in different ways. This is what happens when historians devise new theories, employ new methods,

---

22  Keith Jenkins, *Rethinking History* (New York: Routledge, 1991), 77.
23  The term "historiography" is also used to refer to evolving historical interpretations of a topic, as in, for example, the "historiography" of the First World War.

ask new questions, make new discoveries, and revise or reject old ones. But we can only shed light on fragments of the past, not on its entirety. Much of it will forever remain in the darkness. It is for all these reasons that historians' conclusions must necessarily be regarded as imperfect, partial, and provisional. It is equally true, however, that there is no warrant for succumbing to the intellectual despair that was so fashionable in the humanities not long ago. Just because we do not know for certain what happened in the past does not mean that all claims about it are equal, or that we cannot adjudicate between one claim about history and another. It just means that we have to be careful about judging.

So history is not the past, nor even the sources that the past leaves in its wake. History results from the proper use of sources: the true stories we write using sources or the discussions and disputes we have about them.[24] A source, in turn, can be many things, from written records to oral testimony to material objects. I researched Eddie McKay's life in sources including birth and death records; census data; probate files; city directories; contemporary newspaper and magazine articles; church, grade school, and university records; official documents from multiple government agencies, armed forces, and private businesses; published and unpublished diaries and memoirs; private correspondence; transcripts and audio recordings of interviews; poetry, photographs, paintings, films, and physical artefacts; and through visits to some of the places he lived. (I will say nothing of the several hours I spent in a forlorn attempt to fly a startlingly realistic First World War flight simulator on my computer.) In addition, I read extensively in secondary literature, following in the footsteps of historians who went before me but blazing a new trail where I departed from them. Contemporary historiography is like that. As the interests of historians have diversified over the past several decades, they have found it necessary to use a proportionately broad range of sources. Historical research begins there: not with interpreting sources but with locating them in the first place. By itself, this enterprise can be enormously time consuming and laborious. It requires extensive reading (often in more than one language), patience, diligence, creativity, consultation with experts, and a significant degree of luck. For instance, what remains of the official records of the RFC are located primarily in the National Archives in the United Kingdom, where they are divided between two major collections, one belonging to the Air Ministry and one to the War Office. There are also major collections at the Imperial War Museum, the Royal Air Force Museum, and, where Canadian flyers are concerned, at

*Historiography*

---

24 For the term "true stories," I have been influenced by John Arnold, *History: A Brief Introduction* (Oxford: Oxford University Press, 2000).

the Library and Archives of Canada in Ottawa. In addition, letters, diaries, photo albums, and memorabilia belonging to RFC pilots remain in the hands of families or have over the past century been deposited in various archives throughout the British Commonwealth and even in the United States, reflecting the multinational character of the RFC. In attempting to track down sources about McKay or created by people who knew him, I corresponded with historians, archivists, and descendants of his squadron-mates in Canada, the United Kingdom, the United States, Australia, New Zealand, Ireland, France, South Africa, Germany, and Switzerland. I note this to illustrate the enormity of the task of historical research and the lengths to which historians must go in order to live up to the evidentiary standards of their profession.

Despite our best efforts, most of the past is lost to us irrevocably, never having been recorded in the first place, while many of the records that once existed are now lost. What are we to do with the inevitable gaps in the evidentiary record? These gaps present historians with a paradox. On the one hand, they render much of the past unknowable. On the other, they make historical research more manageable because too much source material can be as paralyzing as too little. Modern bureaucracies have produced a quantity of source material that historians of the premodern period, such as medievalists and classicists, find enviable. For historians in those fields, researching history is like working on a jigsaw puzzle that is missing many pieces. A picture might gradually emerge—especially with the discovery of new pieces or with new ways of interpreting existing ones—but the whole picture will continue to be elusive. Historians of the twentieth century often face a different problem. Imagine a dump truck of puzzle pieces, with some that fit where they do not belong, all of them imperfect, each subject to varying uses and interpretations depending on the abilities and interests of the puzzle maker, each posing questions even as they provide answers, and yet still not enough to complete the whole picture. Of course, even if it were possible to fill in all the pieces, the result would still be subject to interpretation and argument. What does it mean? How can we understand it? Are we certain the pieces are precisely where they are supposed to go? How does this relate to other pictures from the same time? Consider the origins of the First World War. Historians have a gigantic body of source material originating from several countries on the topic but, even a century later, are no closer to consensus about its causes than they ever were.

Whether few or many, whether clear or defiantly inscrutable, sources are the stuff from which history is constructed. People are sometimes uneasy with the idea that history is "constructed." They think this implies that history is untrue, or easily malleable, shifting to and fro as the political and cultural winds do. But why? Are airplanes somehow not real because they are constructed? Quite the opposite. History is not untrue because it is constructed: on the contrary, care-ful construction is what makes history true. Anyone can make a claim about the past; history happens when we can prove a claim. Proving it, in turn, is largely a question of assessing sources, deriving facts from them, and using those facts as evidence for the stories we want to tell or the arguments we want to make. For the sake of ease, I refer to such skills as "source criticism," or making proper use of sources. Among other things, sources and the facts extracted from them have to be authenticated, compared to one another, and understood in their historical context. Developing such an understanding is critical, lest we be misled by the preconceptions of our own era to an even greater extent than we inevitably will be. Although we must make a very great effort to understand what the creators of sources thought and intended, we can also interpret sources in ways that would surprise them. Early twentieth-century sports reporting in London's newspapers, for example, was not intended to support future historical research about social constructions of gender, but used properly, this reporting is an excellent source for precisely that. Also, though sources can invite many possible readings and interpretations, they do not invite an infinite variety of *valid* interpretations, as is sometimes claimed.[25] Eddie McKay's logbook may be a source for many things, but it is not a cookbook. This remark may strike some readers as being unduly glib, but, unfortunately, the academic clime is such that it needs to be made. Intel-lectual relativism abounds, from the soft form historians encounter in the class-room (e.g., "you weren't there, so you can't know for sure"; "there's no right or wrong answer"; "everyone has his or her own way of looking at things") to its more sophisticated academic variants, which at their most radical deny the possibility of discovering meaningful knowledge about the past at all. In my view, against careful and time-tested historiographical methods, popular and demeaning clichés such as "history is bunk" and their academic equivalents, fashionable in some circles today, wither to incoherence. Aeronautical engineers can build better airplanes and historians can produce better history.

---

25  For example, by Keith Jenkins in *Rethinking History*, 32.

CHAPTER ONE

# To Western and to War: 1892–1916

*Every man thinks meanly of himself for not having been a soldier ... were Socrates and Charles the Twelfth of Sweden both present in any company, and Socrates to say, "Follow me, and hear a lecture on philosophy"; and Charles, laying his hand on his sword, to say, "Follow me, and dethrone the Czar"; a man would be ashamed to follow Socrates.*
— Samuel Johnson, *Boswell: A Life*

He died in an aeroplane but was born in a world where no such thing existed, except in the imagination of science-fiction writers and a handful of eccentric inventors. On December 27, 1892, Alfred Edwin became William and Mary McKay's eighth child and fifth son. Scottish by descent but born in Canada, the McKays were farmers in southwestern Ontario's West Zorra Township, where they lived in a tiny crossroads hamlet called Harrington near a dozen or more families also named McKay.[1] The Scots intermingled with an even greater number of Irish immigrants, who dubbed the area "Little Ireland."[2]

Theirs was a Canada barely a quarter century old, populated by fewer than 5 million people, a small but surprisingly diverse population of English- and French-speaking Canadians, Indigenous peoples, and immigrants from a dozen or more countries.[3] Except for those who spoke French, they called themselves

---

1 Ancestry.com, *Ontario, Canada Births, 1869–1913* [database online]. Provo, UT, USA: Ancestry.com Operations Inc, 2010. Original source: Archives of Ontario. Registrations of Births and Stillbirths—1869–1909. MS 929; Reel 110. Although the McKay family farm was in West Zorra Township, Eddie was born in the village of Brussels, Ontario, about 40 miles east. His father probably worked there as a plasterer in the winter season. See also W.A. Ross, *History of Zorra and Embro: Pioneer Sketches of Sixty Years Ago* (Embro: Embro Courier Office, 1909), 14–15.

2 Ross, *History of Zorra and Embro*, 14.

3 Canadian population from M.C. Urquhart and K.A.H. Buckley, eds., *Historical Statistics of Canada*, Estimated Population of Canada, 1867 to 1977, Series A1–247.

Canadians, if they called themselves Canadians, colloquially and as matter of con-
venience. Legally, they were British subjects and Canadian citizenship lay half a
century in the future. Although the country was autonomous in terms of its internal affairs, on the world stage the British Empire spoke in one voice: the voice
of Westminster. Not many argued the point, and few who spoke English would
have doubted that the empire was an instrument of civilization and progress. Indeed, for many of British descent, the wellspring of the pride they felt in being
Canadian was the country's position of honour as the empire's senior dominion.[4]
Yet for most Canadians, living in small towns or on farms, doing their best to eke
out a living in hot but short growing seasons bound by long and sometimes cruel
winters, such matters as national identity and Canada's constitutional status were
probably of little day-to-day concern or consequence. Hard work, thrift, sobriety, reverence for family, and quiet, unobtrusive religiosity: these were the cardi-
nal virtues, the anchor points of personal identity, and the source of respect one
earned in the eyes of the community. Eddie McKay grew up in a society governed
by such values and circumscribed by the distance one's feet or horse and buggy
might carry you in a day. His was a tiny cosmos comprised of small farms and
small towns, of school days spent learning by rote (except when the snow was too
deep to get away from home), of Saturdays spent in farm work and chores, and
Sundays in the stern Presbyterian church.[5] We can well imagine the summers of
his childhood, too: tending to animals, chopping wood, and, when he was older,
working the fields; humid, buggy evenings spent down by pond, singing, playing
games with neighbouring children and his younger brother, Sidney, born in 1894.[6]
How inexplicable, extraordinary, and wonderful that he would one day soar in a
machine 10,000 feet above Belgium and France. How horrifying that he would be
killed there.

Eddie's mother, Mary, had nine children over a span of 20 years.[7] In April 1900,
she lost a son, Angus, age 21, in a grisly railroad accident. Just over a year later,
William, her husband of 27 years and one of the local community's stalwarts,
died of blood poisoning, brought on by a condition his obituary called "multiple

---

4  On early Canadian identity and imperialist sentiment, see Carl Berger, *A Sense of Power: Studies in
   the Ideas of Canadian Imperialism, 1867–1914* (Toronto: University of Toronto Press, 1970).
5  The McKays attended the Harrington Presbyterian Church, where they placed a stained glass
   window in Eddie's memory after the war. On the church and its place in the community, see William A. Ross, *One Hundred Years in the Harrington Presbyterian Church, 1857–1957* (Tillsonburg:
   McCready's Print, Co., 1957).
6  For Sidney McKay's birth, see Ancestry.com, Ontario, Canada, Births, 1969–1909. Original source:
   Archives of Ontario. Registrations of Births and Stillbirths—1869–1909. MS 929, Reel 121.
7  Details on Mary McKay's nine children are derived from Ancestry.com, Canada, Births, 1969–1909
   and the *Census of Canada*, 1881–1911.

abscesses on the knee."[8] No doubt these were painful blows for the family and for young Eddie, but the sudden death of people who were not old, in that era before modern safety standards, widespread vaccination, antibiotics, and clean drinking water, was something to which that generation was far more accustomed than our own. In 1901, Mary McKay and those children still at home in addition to Eddie (Joe, age 21; Garfield, 14; Mary, 11; and Sidney, 7) moved for a time to the nearby town of Stratford.[9] By 1908, for reasons that are unclear, Eddie had moved to nearby London, southwestern Ontario's biggest city, where he lived with his oldest brother, Sandy, a plasterer, 17 years his senior.[10] With just over 50,000 people, London must have seemed like a metropolis in comparison to the small towns and farm communities of Eddie's childhood.[11] Like its namesake in England, the city was situated on a forked river called the Thames. Its streets were named by people nostalgic for England and proud of their association with the empire: Richmond, Clarence, Oxford, York, and Talbot. In London, Eddie completed his secondary education at the Central Collegiate Institute, then worked as a clerk at Darch and Sons, a respected saddlery and manufacturer of steamer trunks, located in the core of the city adjacent the big farmer's market.[12] He was probably there, when, on Saturday, May 25, 1912, thousands of Londoners witnessed the first flight by an aeroplane over the city.

The early history of the aeroplane is marked by bitter rivalries, steady but incremental improvements to machines, and the quest for a practical application of the new technology. Starry-eyed futurists proclaimed the transcendent days to come when humans would master the air and travel effortlessly between distant locations, but the more mundane reality was that the flimsily constructed and mechanically unsound machines of the day could do little more than demonstrate the principle of flight. For the enthusiastic crowds who thronged to fairs and festivals to witness these marvels of the modern age (often flown by men who had more in common with P.T. Barnum than Orville or Wilbur Wright), it was more than good enough. Pioneering pilots were accorded the sort of celebrity status that, 50 years later, would be showered on the first

---

8   William McKay, Death Notice, *Ingersoll Chronicle*, June 20, 1901, 1. The story of Angus McKay's death is recounted in William McKay's death notice.

9   Ancestry.com, *Census of Canada*, 1901: Stratford, Perth, Ontario, 9.

10  *Vernon's City of London, Ontario, Miscellaneous, Business, Alphabetical and Street Directory* (Hamilton, ON: H. Vernon & Son), issues for 1910–12.

11  1914 population figures from *City of London Municipal Yearbook*, 1920, 99.

12  Central Collegiate, Student Index Card, Edwin McKay, copy in the author's personal collection via staff at Central Secondary School, London, Ontario. My thanks to Dave Poisson for locating this record for me. On London on the eve of the First World War, see H.W. Gardiner, *London 1914: A Presentation of Her Resources Achievements and Possibilities* (London, ON: London Printing Company, 1914). On Darch and Sons specifically, see page 57.

astronauts.[13] When the flamboyant American expatriate Samuel Cody, the first man to fly an aeroplane in Britain, was killed in an accident in 1913, tens of thousands of people lined the streets for his funeral procession.[14]

The pilot whom Londoners saw on May 25, 1912, was (in the estimation of the *London Advertiser*) the "daring" and "handsome" 22-year-old Beckwith Haven of the Curtis Aviation Company.[15] Haven had planned his flight for the day before, to coincide with Victoria Day celebrations, but thunderstorms had grounded his machine. The weather on May 25 proved more amenable. Preparing for take-off on a farm east of the city, he admonished curious onlookers to stay back 50 feet or more: "If you stand too close to the machine when I start the propeller," he warned, "you will be knocked head over heels by the wind and may be killed." "Those who were in the line of the wind were soon shown that the birdman knew what he was talking about," the *London Advertiser* noted sagely. Minutes later, the Curtis biplane droned over the core of the city at 2,000 feet, bringing business to a halt. "Crowds of people rushed out of the stores to witness the sight," the *Advertiser* recounted. "Out a Richmond street barber shop rushed a man with his face covered in lather, and the towels still about his neck," while one woman in a shoe store "rushed out ... forgetting for the moment she had only one shoe on."[16] Eddie's employer, Darch and Sons, was in the very core of the city. Haven's flyer would have passed directly overhead. It is not difficult to imagine that Eddie was among the gawkers, transfixed by the brief flight. Did it leave an impression? Many early First World War aviators recounted being "air minded" from youth, fascinated by the development of early aviation technology, collecting aviation journals, and seeking out every opportunity to witness demonstrations. We do not know, but something must have planted the idea of flight in his mind.

Well before he became one of Canada's earliest military pilots, Eddie was already known to the thousands of Londoners who followed local sports. An outstanding hockey, rugby, and lacrosse player, he became a fixture in the sports pages in the two years before the First World War, playing on several local teams and in a number of leagues. As in Britain, organized amateur sports had an important role to play in the lives of young men in late nineteenth- and early twentieth-century

13  On the early history of aviation in Canada, see Jonathan F. Vance, *High Flight: Aviation and the Canadian Imagination* (Toronto: Penguin Canada, 2002).

14  On early aviation in the UK, see Harold Penrose, *British Aviation: The Pioneer Years* (London: Putnam, 1967). On Samuel Cody, see G.A. Broomfield, *Pioneer of the Air, The Life and Times of Colonel SF Cody* (Aldershot, UK: Gale and Polden, 1953).

15  "3,000 Feet above the Earth, Aviator Flies over the City," *London Advertiser*, May 27, 1912, 1. Victoria Day is a Canadian holiday held on or near May 24 to mark the birthday of Queen Victoria.

16  "3,000 Feet," *London Advertiser*, 1.

Canada. Although many Canadians regarded professional sports as tainted by greed and crass commercialism, amateur athletics were thought to offer vital lessons for the larger game of life. The hockey rink, the rugby pitch, the lacrosse field—these were proving grounds on which young men in Canada learned the values of physical fitness, dedication, team work, fair play, and humility, virtues many social reformers feared were in decline.[17] Historians have often noted the late Victorian and Edwardian era's preoccupation with such matters, including what is sometimes called the "crisis of masculinity," a widespread fear of the supposedly emasculating influences of modern life. The rapid emergence of an urban and industrial society, with unhygienic living conditions, increasingly sedentary jobs for the middle class, and its soft materialist and secular vices would, it was feared, sap young men of the vigour, industriousness, and even piety of preceding generations. Sports became a surrogate for the strenuous life of old, a means of promoting physical fitness, manliness, and a "muscular Christianity."[18] The latter, described by one historian as "the transformation from religious asceticism to athleticism," was part of a general movement on the part of Protestant churches to adapt to the rapid changes of modernity, exemplified through such organizations at the Young Men's Christian Association, which took a lead in building gymnasiums and organizing amateur sports leagues in the United Kingdom, United States, and Canada.[19] In the decade before the First World War, such ideals were nowhere so clearly espoused as in the novels of Canada's most popular writer, Charles William Gordon. Gordon, a Presbyterian minister who wrote under the pen name Ralph Connor (and who grew up in West Zorra Township, very near the McKays) populated his enormously successful westerns with upstanding, self-reliant, pious, athletic men of high morals—exemplars for Canadian youth to emulate.[20] In a closely related fashion, some scholars have emphasized the role that formal education played in attempting to ameliorate the perceived crisis of masculinity. The anxiety about the physical and moral character of youth was part and parcel of a greater apprehension about the global status of the British Empire. The rise of Germany and the growth of American economic power and influence

---

17  Colin D. Howell, *Blood, Sweat, and Cheers: Sport and the Making of Modern Canada* (Toronto: University of Toronto Press, 2001), 49–50.

18  On Canadian sport generally in the late nineteenth and early twentieth century, see Don Morrow, *Sport in Canada: A History* (Toronto: Oxford University Press, 2005), especially chapters 4 and 5, 44–86.

19  Gerald Redmond, "Some Aspects of Organized Sport and Leisure in Nineteenth-Century Canada," in *Sports in Canada: Historical Readings*, ed. Morris Mott, 81–106 (Toronto: Copp Clark, 1989), 97.

20  Bruce Kidd, *The Struggle for Sport in Canada* (Toronto: University of Toronto Press, 1996), 36. On Gordon's life, see John Lennox, *Charles W. Gordon ("Ralph Connor") and His Works* (Toronto: ECW Press, 1989.)

were potential threats to Britain's global supremacy. Boys in the late Victorian and Edwardian era were brought up on a steady diet of toys, games, and literature that celebrated strenuous living, martial virtues, and Britain's glorious military past. In the opinion of some scholars, this cultural environment provided fertile ground for recruiting efforts when the First World War erupted in August 1914, and helps to explain the seemingly naïve enthusiasm for war felt by so many young men.[21] Indeed it might, but it would also be unwise to underestimate the extent to which Canadians were well informed by newspapers about events in Europe and shared the belief that Britain's cause was just. The initial "spark" in Sarajevo that ignited the "Balkan powder keg" at the end of June 1914 may have seemed remote and unimportant to many in Canada, but Germany's invasion of France through neutral Belgium in August did not. It precipitated Britain's declaration of war and the entry of the whole British Empire, including Canada, into the war against Germany.

Although 70 per cent of the first Canadian contingent to go overseas consisted of immigrants from the British Isles, thousands of young men born in Canada also enlisted, and the majority of officers were Canadian.[22] Certainly Eddie would have had friends, teammates, and relatives who answered the call in August and September. Did he feel a twinge of envy, or even shame, for not going with them? Doubtless he felt all these pressures and many more. But as Europe descended into flames and thousands of young men rushed to the recruiting stations, he chose a remarkably different path. In September 1914, he registered as a student in the faculty of arts at the Western University of London Ontario. Now one of Canada's biggest universities, in 1914, "Western" was an undistinguished institution so small that it had no established campus of its own. The two faculties, arts and medicine, comprising fewer than 20 professors and 200 students, made do by renting space from Huron College, an Anglican divinity school with which the university had a longstanding affiliation.[23] By the time Eddie enrolled at the end of September, the male student body had already been diminished by enlistment. In 1914, for what was almost certainly the first time in the school's history, the incoming class had an almost even number of men and women.[24]

---

21  Mark Moss, *Manliness and Militarism: Educating Young Boys in Ontario for War* (Toronto: University of Toronto Press, 2001) discusses this in detail.

22  Terry Copp, "The Military Effort" in *Canada and the First World War*, ed. David Mackenzie, 35–61 (Toronto: University of Toronto Press, 2005), 37–38.

23  On Western's early history, see William Ferguson Tamblyn, *These Sixty Years* (London: University of Western Ontario, 1938) and James John Talman and Ruth Davis Talman, *Western: 1878–1953* (London: University of Western Ontario, 1953).

24  Western University of London, Ontario, *Arts Department Calendar for the Year 1915–1916*, 66–67.

At 22, Eddie was slightly older than most of his classmates. He had enrolled as a special student, taking classes in the faculty of arts but not initially pursuing a degree. It was a typical arts program for the time: mathematics, literature, composition, and languages, of which he initially chose French, not wanting to contend with Latin in his first year, apparently. Later, probably based on satisfactory performance in his January exams, he seems to have been admitted in full to the faculty of arts. By the reckoning of the student paper, the *Gazette*, he was affable and well liked at Western. Apart from being a stellar athlete, he was chair of the freshman social committee and class treasurer. More than once, the souvenir publication for the 1914 Freshmans' Banquet makes good-natured fun of him (and his considerable appetite), such as in the following snippet:

"Did you see how much Eddie McKay ate last night?"
   "Yes. He's been working on the boats all summer. He's what you call a stow-away."[25]

His final grades indicate that he was a solid though not stellar student; he earned the very respectable averages of "C" in algebra, geometry, and English literature, and a strong "B" in French. His exceptional and rare grade of "A" in English composition, a course that required him to submit regular original works of writing, is further cause for regret that he did not survive to write his memoirs. Canada produced many aces, but few with literary ability.[26] Whatever his academic standing, Eddie's real passion and preoccupation was sport. He was not alone in prioritizing athletics. Indeed, it would be difficult to overstate the importance of sport to campus life. In November 1915, when Western's president invited the minister of militia, Sir Sam Hughes, to speak on campus, he forewarned the minister that the speech would have to conclude by 2:30 PM, there being a rugby game set to commence shortly thereafter.[27]

Eddie played wing on Western's excellent 1914 rugby-football team. At 5'6" and just a shade over 140 pounds, he was the smallest player on the team, slight even for his time. The biggest player, the predictably nicknamed "Tiny" Sage, tipped the scale at a monstrous 255 pounds.[28] Eddie compensated with speed, technical

---

25  *The Freshman Inaugural Banquet, 1914* (London: Western University, 1914), 25.
26  Examination Record of A.E. McKay, 1915. Many thanks to the Office of the Registrar at Western University for providing me with this record.
27  Archives and Regional Collections Centre (ARCC), University of Western Ontario, Braithwaite Papers AFC40 / 41 1914–1918, General Correspondence Series, M, Letter: Braithwaite to Sam Hughes, November 20, 1914.
28  "Some Gridiron Ballast," *London Free Press*, November 14, 1914, 10.

proficiency, and perfectly timed aggression. The local sports reporters described him as quick, fleet-footed, lithe, and cool under pressure. Opposing players, said the *Advertiser's* Bert Perry (later to serve in the Royal Flying Corps himself), did "not have the chance of a snowball in summer of getting away" from him.[29] He seems to have positively revelled on the rugby pitch, never happier than when putting his heart on the line against bigger men and bringing them down. With McKay as one of its outstanding players, the team had a stellar year, bringing home the Dominion Junior Championship in November. It was a grandiose title for a league consisting of half a dozen Ontario teams, none further away than Toronto, about a three-hour trip by train. Nonetheless, the victory in the championship game was exalted in the local sports news and with a celebratory banquet and dance at Western, attended by 200 guests, including all members of the faculty and the board of governors.[30]

In the imagination of social reformers, amateur sport taught the virtues of fair play and gentlemanly conduct. On the pitch itself, play was rough, tough, and often dirty. Fights on the field, the sidelines, and in the stands broke out so frequently that the papers always saw fit to mention when they did not. Foul language ("French lessons," one local sports reporter called it) was obligatory in both practice and play, with Eddie being singled out for his particular virtuosity in its use. "Eddie McKay declares he would rather miss a meal than a French lesson," said the *Advertiser's* roving sports reporter.[31] Well liked though he was by his own teammates, there was a distinct streak of brashness or even arrogance in his character. In one game, some jibe he made set off an opposing player, and Eddie was met with a flurry of punches.[32] Asked by a reporter before the championship match how he thought Western would do, he replied, "If everyone else plays as well as I know I'm going to, we'll be okay."[33] The entire student body and hundreds of local spectators attended the home games; hundreds travelled by train when the team was visiting. Yet through all these thrilling matches, the war surely could never have been far from anyone's mind, even if Canadians were not yet fighting. Matters hung in a dramatic balance overseas, and hundreds of thousands had already fallen. During one playoff game, McKay cried out, "Vive la France!" as he and his teammates barrelled down the field. It was November 1914, and those words meant something.[34]

---

29  "Western All Ready for Final Game of District in Petrolia," *London Advertiser*, 6 November 1914, 8.
30  The event is described in "The Rugby Dinner," *Gazette*, January 1914, 93.
31  "Football News," *London Advertiser*, November 10, 1914, 6.
32  "Parkdale Fails to Stop Western's Rush," *London Advertiser*, November 16, 1914, 6.
33  "Western Certain to Win Is Opinion of the Players," November 28, 1914, 8.
34  Recounted in the UWO *Gazette*, "Notes," January 1915, 113.

FIGURE I.I: Eddie McKay of Western. *Eddie McKay in Western University's rugby team uniform, fall 1914. A solid if unexceptional academic performer, he possessed enormous athletic gifts. Educators considered sports integral to young men's physical and moral development. (Courtesy J.P. Metras Sports Museum, Western University.)*

Why had he enrolled at Western? It was not an obvious choice. University graduates were very rare in prewar Canada, with barely one person in a hundred pursuing an undergraduate degree at the time. Eddie came from a family of farmers and labourers, none of whom had attended university. Only his brother Joe, an insurance broker who had struck it rich in the northern mining town of Cobalt, Ontario, had a "white collar" profession. We can only speculate about his motives and intentions. Family lore has it that he was interested in becoming a dentist.[35] Or perhaps he was considering a career in teaching or in the church (one of his nephews would later become a minister), although surely in 1914 all that seemed very remote given the war. One possible answer is that he knew a year's higher education would help him secure an officer's commission when he enlisted, but in September 1914, he may very well have believed that the war would be over before the academic year was. Indeed, Western as a whole made very few gestures

---

35  Telephone interview with Eugene Kittmer, March 13, 2015.

FIGURE I.2: *Newspaper Cartoon. Western's rugby-football team won the Dominion Junior Championships in 1914. Amateur sport was praised for teaching the virtues of fair play, teamwork, good sportsmanship, and gentlemanly conduct. Real play was rough and tough. (London Advertiser, 7 December 1914, 8.)*

in support of the war effort in 1914, except to organize a campus contingent of the Canadian Officers Training Corps (COTC) to give male students some rudimentary instruction in military law and drill.[36]

Western's exam period began on April 28, 1915.[37] The papers had just begun to announce that the 1st Canadian Division had come through heavy fighting in the salient around the strategically important Belgian town of Ypres. For the next week, the picture of the Second Battle of Ypres came into sharper focus in a succession of front-page articles in the papers. The Canadian Division, in action for the first time, had gallantly held the line in the face of a massive German assault. For three days, the two sides mauled each other terribly, with the Germans

---

36  A nominal roll for Western's COTC is located in the Archives and Regional Collection Centre, Western University.

37  Western University, *Arts Department Calendar for the Year 1915–1916.*

unleashing poisoned gas for the first time on the Western Front.[38] In the opinion of some historians, Canadian newspapers in wartime were largely propaganda sheets, with censors concealing the terrible reality of the war from the public.[39] Even a brief glance at the headlines over the coming weeks, however, reveals that the Canadian press was remarkably frank in its depiction of the horrors of the war. Articles in the London Free Press referred to "desperate fighting" with "frightful" losses and recounted thousands of unburied corpses marking the battlefield. On May 3, the paper's headline declared "Canada Lost 6,000 Men at the Battle of Ypres." In graphic detail, first-hand accounts described the annihilation of whole battalions, of men "blown to fragments," of scores of dead and suffering horses lin-ing the roads. The Toronto Globe, read by many Londoners, recounted the "pain-ful and lingering death" many had suffered from poison gas.[40] Appalling though these losses were, the papers strove to frame them as gallant sacrifices that had resulted in a great victory against a cruel and implacable foe. As if to illustrate the point about the inhumanity of that foe and the necessity of fighting, news broke just days later that the famed liner Lusitania had been torpedoed, drowning over a thousand passengers. A "murderous deed of German pirates," the London Free Press raged.[41] Coverage lasted for days.

It was in the shadow of these shattering events that Eddie McKay completed his first and only year of university. Arguably, there had been a certain patriotic naiveté about the initial rush to enlist in August 1914. By May 1915, no one in Canada could be called naïve about the nature of modern warfare, yet they contin-ued to enlist nonetheless. Enlistment in the Canadian Expeditionary Force (CEF) doubled between April and July.[42] McKay was a second generation Canadian of Scottish descent, educated, exceptionally fit, upright, churchgoing, and 22 years old—exactly the sort of man to serve as a junior officer in the CEF. No doubt, in the wake of the events of April and early May, he felt enormous pressure to enlist and "do his bit" overseas. He probably genuinely desired to do so. Nothing less than his manhood was at stake, and the respect he had earned in the eyes of the community. But he did not enlist in the expeditionary force. Instead, in June, he took a commission as lieutenant in the 33rd Huron Regiment, a militia

38  On the 1st Canadian Division at the Second Battle of Ypres, see Tim Cook, At the Sharp End: Canadians Fighting the Great War (Toronto: Viking, 2007), 101–70.

39  See, for instance, Jeffrey Keshen, Propaganda and Censorship During Canada's Great War (Edmonton: University of Alberta Press, 1996).

40  "Retaliation Possible in Use of Poison Gas," Globe, May 5, 1915, 7.

41  "Official Announcement of Murderous Deed," London Free Press, May 7, 1915, 1.

42  G.W.L. Nicholson, Official History of the Canadian Army in the First World War: Canadian Expe-ditionary Force, 1914–1918 (Ottawa: Queen's Printer, 1962), 546.

unit, following the successful completion of a training course at the Provisional School of Instruction in London.[43] Apart from parade-ground training, the course would have familiarized him with the rudiments of military law, small unit tactics, map reading, and musketry, some of which he would already have learned while a member of Western's COTC.[44] Periodic training and a longer summer "camp" would have followed. Like his decision to enroll at Western, McKay's enlistment in the Hurons seems curious at first glance. As a militia unit, the 33rd was assigned home-front duties, and its members were not obligated to serve overseas. This was not the sort of thing that won young men Victoria Crosses, enduring fame, and the respect of their peers. In the early years of the war, thousands of young men, eager for action, had resigned from the militia to join the CEF. Militia ranks swelled with men who were too old, unfit, or unwilling to go to France. Yet nothing about his subsequent career in the Royal Flying Corps (RFC) would lead us to question McKay's bravery or desire to get into the fight. So why did he join?

The answer to both that question and the one concerning McKay's decision to attend Western may lie in a remark made in a 1920 retrospective on his athletic career. According to the author of the article, "As soon as the war broke out, Eddie McKay announced his intention of joining the Flying Corps."[45] But joining required overcoming several serious obstacles first. Canada had no air service of its own, and, in 1914, the RFC had no recruiting mission in Canada. Indeed, the RFC hardly recruited at all in 1914. Most authorities expected that the war would be a short one, and the tiny RFC was only supposed to find, not fight, the enemy, so its casualties would be low. As the writer Denis Winter put it, the RFC's senior officers believed that "gentlemen weekend fliers would keep the supply topped up."[46] By early 1915, however, there was sufficient demand for pilots and interest from prospective applicants in Canada that the Royal Naval Air Service (RNAS) began small-scale recruitment efforts in Toronto. In June, the RFC established a small office of its own in Toronto, initially headed up by a Captain Alec Ross-Hume, a flying officer who had broken both legs in a crash in France.[47] Hume neither wanted to be in Canada nor was terribly impressed with what he found. He and his successor,

---

43 Canada, Department of Militia and Defence, *Quarterly Militia List of the Dominion of Canada* [corrected to July 1, 1916] (Ottawa: King's Printer, 1916), 295; Canada, Department of Militia and Defence, *Militia Orders*, No. 432 to 438 (Ottawa: King's Printer, September 27, 1915), 3.

44 Provisional School of Instruction syllabus: LAC RG9, vol. 5064, file 986, War Diaries, Provisional School of Instruction, Military District No. 7.

45 C.S. Grafton, "The Eddie McKay Memorial Cup," *London Advertiser*, April 10, 1920, 8.

46 Denis Winter, *The First of the Few: The Fighter Pilots of the First World War* (New York: Penguin Books, 1983), 19.

47 LAC, Air Ministry (UK), MG 40 D1, vol. 15, AIR 1/721/48/4, "Memorandum on the Development of the Royal Flying Corps in Canada." Burke succeeded Ross-Hume in Canada in November 1915.

Lt. Colonel C.J. "Percy" Burke, preferred, if possible, to have a face-to-face meeting with potential applicants, and it is likely that McKay, living a mere two hours' train ride away, met with one of them sometime in the summer of 1915. At the very least, he would have corresponded with them, though no letter survives.

The guidelines they established for recruits in Canada were modelled after the ones used in the UK, but they tended to be, as the Canadian official history notes, confusing and frequently changing.[48] In September 1915, they stipulated that candidates should be British, an officer in some branch of the Canadian armed forces, between the ages of 18 and 30, certified by a medical board to be in good health and of good character, and, crucially, already in possession of a civilian aviator's certificate. Candidates who met these requirements would have their passage paid to the UK for advanced flight instruction.[49] These were guidelines, not regulations, as exceptions to nearly all of them can be found. Two of them bear further examination. The stipulation that recruits should already be officers was in response to concerns from CEF authorities that completely untrained men were being fobbed off on them in cases where they washed out of pilot training. Accordingly, Canadians who wished to join the RFC were often advised to seek a commission in the CEF and then apply for a transfer once overseas, but there was no guarantee that such a request would be granted. This made the militia, which did not entail overseas commitments, the preferred option for early Canadian recruits and may explain McKay's decision to join the Hurons. The stipulation that applicants from Canada must have a civilian aviator's certificate prior to joining the RFC or RNAS seems to have been taken somewhat seriously, even if it was not observed with perfect fidelity. This reflected prewar practice in the RFC, whose Central Flying School did not typically provide *ab initio* flight training but instead turned civilian pilots into professional military aviators.[50] The certificates—known universally as one's "ticket"—were issued under the auspices of national flying clubs, including the Royal Aero Club in the UK and the Aero Club of America, on behalf of their governing body, the Fédération Aéronautique Internationale (FAI). As the training establishment expanded, the RFC amended its rules to permit men to receive their certificate as part of their military flight training (and, in mid-1916, dropped the requirement altogether), but officials in Canada remained wary of the expense

---

48   S.F. Wise, *Canadian Airmen and the First World War*, vol. 1 of *The Official History of the Royal Canadian Air Force* (Toronto: University of Toronto Press, 1980), 30. Wise discusses recruitment in Canada in detail 23–45.
49   Requirements for Canadian applicants to the RFC: LAC RG 25, Colonial Office Canada House Records, vol. 151, File C 9/91.
50   On the Central Flying School, see John Taylor, *C.F.S. Birthplace of Airpower* (London: Putnam, 1958).

of sending untrained applicants overseas only to discover that they were completely unsuitable as pilots.[51]

For many prospective Canadian applicants in 1915 and early 1916, this requirement posed a problem that may have been insurmountable. There was only one flight school in the entire country, the Curtiss School at Long Branch, just west of Toronto, and, in common with such schools everywhere, instruction was exceedingly expensive. The school charged $400 for 400 minutes of flight instruction, easily half a year's wages for a day labourer or clerk. This did not include cost of living expenses for students from out of town, many of whom had given up their jobs. To offset the cost of training, the RFC and RNAS offered a stipend of £75 (or about $375) to recruits who completed their training, but the problem of raising the money in advance remained.[52] It was more than McKay, a militia officer with a clerk's job, was likely to save. Moreover, the Curtiss School was having severe teething problems. Managed by John McCurdy, Canada's first pilot, the school had commenced operations in April using flying boats operating from Hanlan's Point in the Toronto Islands. In July, it opened its main training facility at Long Branch, west of the city, on a former militia rifle range, but the school had too many students and too few aeroplanes.[53] Worse still, heavy rain that summer turned the field into what the Toronto *Globe* described as a "quagmire."[54] In a report to his superiors, Colonel Burke described the aerodrome as "the worst I have ever seen."[55] In August, hardly any students flew at all. Pessimistic articles in the Toronto papers detailed the plight of the school's frustrated students. By September, it had produced only a trickle of graduates, about 43 from an applicant pool five times that size.[56] In mid-September, with winter looming, McCurdy and British authorities considered moving the operation to Bermuda, but when those plans fell through, they closed the school altogether for the winter.[57]

---

51  LAC, RG 24, vol. 2032, RFC in Canada, Enlistment in RFC, file HQ-6978–2-85 indicates that, as late as August 1916, candidates in Canada were still required to obtain an FAI Certificate before beginning RFC / RNAS training.

52  LAC, RG 24, vol. 4331, WW1 Aviators for RFC, file 34-2-34, Letter: Curtiss Aeroplanes to James R. Maclean.

53  On the history of the Curtiss School: LAC, Curtiss School of Aviation Fonds, MG 28 III 65, "The Log of the Curtiss Flying School, 1915–1916."

54  "Toronto Flying School Will Go to Bermuda," *Globe*, September 14, 1915, 6.

55  LAC, Air Ministry (UK), MG 40 D1, vol. 35, AIR 2/13/058/4066, Burke to Director General Military Aeronautics, January 3, 1916.

56  "Canadian Aviators Need Financial Aid," *Globe*, October 8, 1915, 6.

57  LAC, Air Ministry (UK), MG 40 D1, vol. 15, AIR 1/656/17/122/552; MG 40 D1. vol. 35, AIR 2/13/058/4047, Stanton to Henderson, 1 November 1915. See also: "Canadian Aviators Complain of Treatment," *Globe*, November 6, 1915, 8. In addition, the RNAS enlisted a few dozen pupils who had been unable to complete their training before the school closed for the winter.

McKay's next nearest options, each about a day's trip by train, were the Curtiss School at Hammondsport, New York, and the Wright Brothers School of Aviation near Dayton, Ohio.[58] Hardly any administrative records from either school exist, and we can only speculate about why McKay chose one over the other. Like its counterpart in Toronto, lessons at Hammondsport's Curtiss School were a hefty $400, but at least the school returned 400 minutes of flying time versus the "two to three hours of actual practice in the air" promised by the Wrights in the brochure they sent to prospective applicants. The Wright School had advantages nonetheless. Not only did the name of the pioneering brothers still retain its epochal, even mythical status, but Orville Wright (Wilbur had died of typhoid fever in 1912), faced with increased competition, halved the cost of tuition in 1914. The new fee was $250, including insurance against damage to the machines. This sum was far more manageable for a militia officer and clerk, although he would also have to cover the estimated $10 per week cost of living in Dayton.[59] How did McKay raise the money? In May, Western's president furnished him with a letter of introduction to a member of the university's board who was also a director of the London and Port Stanley Railway.[60] Since the 1850s, the railway had linked London to the popular beachfront town on the north shore of Lake Erie, 25 miles due south. It is possible that McKay found more lucrative employment there, although the partially intact records of the firm provide no indication that he was ever hired. Another very strong possibility is that he secured a partial loan from his brother, Joe, with whom he seems to have had a special connection despite their 13-year difference in age. Eddie would list Joe as his next of kin with the RFC, although this may have been because Joe, an insurance broker, was uniquely qualified in the family to discharge the duties related to the position if it came to that. Joe was also a firm believer in the power of education, having for a time headed up the International Correspondence School in London and later helping to pay for his nieces' and nephews' education.[61] Interestingly, in 1919, after Eddie's death, the other family members waived all claims to the £150 ($750) back pay he was owed

---

58  The school was also called the Wright School of Aviation and the Wright Company School of Aviation. Howard J. Roach, *The Wright Company: From Invention to Industry* (Athens: Ohio University Press, 2014), 89.

59  Library of Congress (Washington, DC), Wilbur Wright and Orville Wright Papers, Wright Company School of Aviation, 1911–1916, Form Letter 1911; Pamphlet 1914.

60  ARCC, UWO, Braithwaite Papers AFC40 / 41 1914–1918, General Correspondence Series, M, Letter: Braithwaite to Pocock.

61  Telephone interview with Robert Mackay, March 15, 2015. That Joe operated the International Correspondence School is documented in "London Boy Sends Great German Flier to Death," *London Advertiser*, November 18, 1916, 4.

in favour of Joe.[62] This may have been for administrative purposes, but it may also have been in repayment for some outstanding debt owed. In any case, by whatever means, Eddie had the money in hand by the end of October. On Sunday, October 31, 1915, he crossed the border at Detroit. On his entry card, he declared $290 cash; his race as "Scotch"; and, no doubt with a measure of pride, his destination as the Wright Brothers Aviation School in Dayton, Ohio.[63]

In 1915, Dayton was a growing city with a population of about 120,000, but still recovering from a catastrophic flood of the Great Miami River that had killed 300 people and destroyed 20,000 homes two years earlier. McKay probably checked into the Algonquin, the city's biggest hotel, where some of the school's other students were residing. It was Halloween but also the sabbath, so he had probably arrived a day too late for the fun. He had just missed the Halloween dance at the YMCA, to which all the Wright students had been specially invited. As one of them, Lloyd Breadner of Carleton Place wrote in a letter home, "All week there has been a masquerade carnival going on and everyone is out in a comic costume of some sort."[64] McKay may have been surprised by the number of Canadians already there. In all, more than 40 had descended on the Wright School that year, and he found himself amidst a very large group of them either finishing up or just arriving. Among them were a number who went on to outstanding careers, particularly in the Royal Naval Air Service, including Daniel Galbraith, who received the Distinguished Service Order and Bar in 1917; Roy Brown, who would go down in history for being officially (though perhaps erroneously) credited with shooting down Manfred von Richthofen, Germany's infamous "Red Baron"; and Breadner himself, who survived the war to rise to the rank of Canada's air chief of staff in the Second World War. Most of the Canadians in Dayton intended to join the RNAS. Reputedly, it was the less dangerous of the two services, as its main duty was flying coastal patrols out of England rather than over the Western Front.[65] Brown's father had agreed to pay for his flight training only in exchange for a promise that Roy would join the RNAS.[66] McKay's decision to join the RFC despite its

62 Ontario Genealogical Society, Oxford Branch, Oxford County Wills (Estate Files), Alfred Edwin McKay, Reel 1645, Estate 6811.

63 Ancestry.com. *Detroit Border Crossings and Passenger and Crew Lists, 1905–1963* [database online]. Provo, UT, USA: Ancestry.com Operations Inc., 2006. Original source: *Selected Passenger and Crew Lists and Manifests*, The National Archives at Washington, DC.

64 Canadian War Museum, Lloyd S. Breadner Fonds, Breadner to Father (?) (first page missing), November 1, 1915. Breadner's letters indicate that many students of the Wright School stayed at the Algonquin.

65 The RNAS would later deploy several crack squadrons to the Western Front, where they served with distinction.

66 On Brown's early training, see Alan Bennett, *Captain Roy Brown: A True Story of the Great War, 1914–1918* (New York: Brick Tower Press, 2011), 1: 57–125.

reputation for greater risk and lower pay is therefore revealing. This was a young man who craved adventure and perhaps even danger.

The Wright School was situated just northeast of Dayton, on an 84-acre former cow pasture called Huffman Prairie. The brothers had conducted many of their pioneering experiments in aviation there in 1904 and 1905 and had returned to the field in 1910 to open the flying school. The Dayton-to-Columbus interurban railway made regular stops at Simms Station, adjacent the airfield, and it was a mere five-cent, half-hour ride by electric tram from Dayton.[67] When the weather was good, crowds still travelled from the city to watch the flyers do circuits of the field. The Wright School's pamphlets promised an average eight-to-ten day course of study, but if McKay had expected to complete his training that quickly his fellow pupils probably disabused him of any such notions. He arrived to find the school in total disarray. Wilbur's death had been a heavy blow to Orville, who had neither the interest nor the acumen to run the business himself. Only days before McKay's arrival, Orville sold the Wright Company to a group of investors in New York.[68] The school itself had a few dozen students—nearly all of them Canadians—but only two serviceable Wright Flyers, one having just been repaired after it was smashed up in a crash during Roy Brown's failed FAI test two weeks earlier.[69] When the other flyer was slightly damaged in another test a short time later, the new owners imposed an additional financial burden on the students: they had to pay a cash deposit of $500 before taking their test.[70] No doubt this resulted in McKay frantically writing home, probably to Joe, for additional financial support. Between the new requirement for a cash deposit, which no doubt many students could not meet, the shortage of flyers, and worsening weather, students had begun to quit, frustrated to find that the promised ten-day course of studies had extended into weeks. Breadner, eager to get overseas, complained to his father that in seven weeks in Dayton he had spent only about 80 minutes in the air. He took his complaint directly to Wright, who in turn blamed the instructors. He assured Breadner that things would be better when the school relocated to its winter campus in Augusta, but that would not occur until mid-December.[71]

McKay's own training would have begun in Dayton itself with a tour of the Wright factory and instruction in the assembly and service of the machines, vital

67  David McCullough, *The Wright Brothers* (New York: Simon and Schuster, 2015), 112–13.
68  Edward J. Roach, *The Wright Company: From Invention to Industry* (Athens: Ohio University Press, 2014), 57.
69  Alan Bennett, *Captain Roy Brown: A True Story of the Great War, 1914–1918* (New York: Brick Tower Press, 2011), 1: 88–89.
70  Bennett, *Captain Roy Brown*, 1: 92.
71  CWM, Lloyd S. Breadner Fonds, Breadner to Father, Friday (unintelligible) October 1915.

training in those early days of flight. The factory also housed the "preparatory balancing machine," a retired Flyer students used to learn the Wright machine's unduly complicated control system before actually flying at Huffman Prairie. The modified Wright Model "B" Flyer used for flight lessons sat two and had dual controls, with students sitting beside their instructors. Training flights consisted of low-altitude circuits and seldom lasted more than 15 minutes.[72] Far from completing the course of instruction in the promised two weeks, McKay was there for three before his first flight, which he took around November 20.[73] Such delays were so routine that some of the students took to calling themselves "Aviwaiters."[74] To pass the time, they watched their classmates fly, and when no one was flying they organized impromptu games of baseball and football, but they had come for flight instruction and were eager to secure their certificate and proceed overseas.[75] Sometime in early November, someone took a group photo of them at Simms Station. McKay stood in the back row, with Roy Brown, quite coincidentally, on his right. They could not possibly know that their names would inextricably be linked to the deaths of two of the most infamous German aces of the Great War: Oswald Boelcke and his protégé, Manfred von Richthofen. Both McKay and Brown are attired in suit and tie (in a subsequent photo, taken next to the flyer, McKay wears a handsome fedora), but, as historian John Edwards writes,

> Although many would-be pilots showed up ... nattily attired, their instructors quickly had them without boaters, ties, and coats, their sleeves rolled up to their elbows, their bodies reeking of perspiration and gasoline, and covered from head to shoe with dirt, engine oil, and grease. The Wright's promotion literature understandably made no mention of the ruts, hummocks, cow patties, and rattlesnakes to be found on the Simms Station flying site; nor, for that matter, of the daily grind of removing the flimsy biplanes from their hangar each morning and late afternoon for a takeoff.[76]

---

72  John Carver Edwards describes typical flight training at the Wright School in *Orville's Aviators: Outstanding Alumni of the Wright Flying School, 1910–1916* (Jefferson, NC: McFarland and Company, 2009), 5–10.

73  McKay wrote a brief narrative account of his flight training on the inside flap of his logbook under the title "Reference." He recollected his first flight as being "about" November 21, 1915. More probably, it was the day before or after, as November 21 was a Sunday and Wright forbade flying on the sabbath. Hereafter the Logbook of 2nd Lt. A.E. McKay, RFC will be referred to as Logbook, date or page. A copy is in author's personal collection via Eugene Kittmer.

74  Edwards, *Orville's Aviators*, 5.

75  Breadner mentions these in his November 1 letter.

76  Edwards, *Orville's Aviators*, 6.

In mid-December, the school relocated to its Augusta, Georgia, aerodrome, where it had wintered since 1911.[77] McKay and about a dozen other students arrived on the evening of December 16 with their instructor, Howard Rinehart, a lifelong adventurer who later, albeit very briefly, flew in the service of Pancho Villa.[78] The disassembled and crated Wright Flyers followed a day or two later. In a letter to Sandy, quoted very briefly in the *London Free Press*, McKay said that he was "delighted" with flying, though admittedly he had not done much of it.[79] It took another six weeks for him to complete his training, which probably amounted to not much more than three or four hours in the air. During that time, he returned home at least once, probably to fulfill militia duties. At the Provisional School of Instruction in London, he qualified for promotion to captain, although he was seconded to the RFC before attaining the rank.[80] Back in London once again in January, he even managed to sneak in a game of basketball with Western's team, and scored the highest number of hoops. As always, there were few sports he seemed incapable of mastering.[81] But his real goal was to get overseas, and the interminable delays must have been a source of immense frustration.

In Europe, the war in the air was about to enter a new phase, one in which air-to-air combat would emerge as a central feature. If war in the trenches presented generals with problems of tremendous complexity, the war in the air posed problems totally without precedent. When the war erupted in 1914, the aeroplane was still a new and experimental technology, and the principles of aeronautics were still poorly understood. No one had ever shot down an aeroplane; only a handful of men had ever discharged a weapon or taken a photograph in the air. Almost everything about military aviation had to be developed through an often fatal process of trial and error. To claim, as some historians of the air war have, that Britain's prewar military leaders were inordinately conservative and even timid about embracing the aeroplane fails to account for this dominating fact.[82] If we accept the Wright brothers' claim to having been "first in flight," the aeroplane had not yet had its eleventh birthday when the war broke out in 1914. In Europe, where experiments in aviation were insulated from developments in the United States, it was

---

77  "Aviation Pupils Got in Last Night," *Augusta Chronicle*, December 17, 1915, 7.

78  On Rinehart, see Edwards, *Orville's Aviators*, 123–56.

79  "Aviator McKay Returns," *London Free Press*, January 10, 1916, 8.

80  *Militia Orders*, No. 549–558, December 20, 1915, 2.

81  "Western University Beats London Y in O.B.A. Basketball," *London Free Press*, January 19, 1916, 10.

82  For examples of these claims, see Ian Mackersey, *No Empty Chairs: The Short and Heroic Lives of the Young Aviators Who Fought and Died in the First World War* (London: Weidenfeld and Nicolson, 2012), chap. 1; Ralph Barker, *A Brief History of the Royal Flying Corps in World War I* (London: Constable & Robinson, 2002), 9–10.

FIGURE I.3: *McKay at Wright School. Canadians at the Wright Flying School, Huffman Prairie, Ohio, early November 1915. McKay is fourth from the left in the top row. On his right is Roy Brown, later to gain fame when he was credited with downing Germany's infamous "Red Baron." (Courtesy Dayton History–Mayfield Collection.)*

newer still.[83] The first aeroplane flights in France had been flown in 1906; in England and Germany, in 1908. Like the Wright brothers' pioneering flights in December 1903, these and other aeroplane "firsts" were short-distance, low-altitude hops, demonstrations of the principle of flight not practical aviation. Distance records quickly fell, but no aeroplane carried a passenger until 1908; the English Channel was not surmounted until 1909; and, as late 1910, England's *Daily Mail* awarded the incredible sum of £10,000 to the French aviator Louis Paulhan when he successfully flew the 185 miles between London and Manchester in under 24 hours.[84] Expensive, unproven, short-ranged, flimsily constructed, mechanically unreliable, and often dangerous to fly, even the best aeroplanes at the end of the first decade of the twentieth century had little to recommend them as implements of war.

83  French aviators in particular were exceedingly skeptical that the Wrights had flown at all until the Wrights demonstrated their flyer in Europe in 1908.
84  On early flight in Europe, see Richard P. Hellion, *Taking Flight: Inventing the Aerial Age, From Antiquity through the First World War* (New York: Oxford University Press, 2003) and, for the UK in particular, W.A. Raleigh, *The War in the Air* (Oxford: Clarendon Press, 1922), 1: 110–45.

Nonetheless, despite some of the frequently quoted (and sometimes mis-quoted) remarks deprecating aviation attributed to senior British military leaders, there is good evidence that Britain's senior military commanders readily grasped about aeroplanes what they already knew to be true about balloons and airships: they had tremendous potential for the related tasks of reconnaissance and artillery cooperation.[85] The RFC was established in April 1912, fewer than four years after former Wild West showman Samuel Cody became the first man to fly an aeroplane in England, in a flight that lasted 27 seconds and ended in a crash.[86] On inception, the RFC was a minuscule service of barely more than a hundred officers and a few dozen flying machines, including kites and balloons. Undeniably, it was smaller and more poorly funded than the air services of France and Germany. The military wing deployed to France in mid-August 1914 with 60 machines out of its total of about twice that many, while the increasingly autonomous naval wing had only about 600 personnel and 90 planes in total.[87] Often forgotten, however, is that the RFC's primary mission was cooperation with the army and Britain's volunteer army was simply much smaller than those of its continental rivals. In August 1914, the RFC deployed half as many aircraft on the Western Front as France's Armée de l'air, but the British Expeditionary Force (BEF) was less than a tenth the size of the French Army. Some aviation historians have criticized General Douglas Haig, later commander in chief of the BEF, for remarking in his memoirs that these early aircraft were of "true value" as "ancillaries to infantry, artillery, and cavalry," but this was no more than an accurate description of the flying services' intended function.[88] It bears repeating that the exploits of the fighter aces may have captivated the imagination of the public at the time and of aviation historians ever since, but theirs was the supporting role. The core function of airpower in the Great War was to carry out the unglamorous but essential tasks of photographic reconnaissance and artillery spotting. Historian Peter Hart argues,

*Historiography*

> The shape of every aerial battle was driven and dominated almost entirely by what was happening to the troops on the ground. That was why the missions were flown, lives risked and casualties accepted. On the Western Front, no British offensive could have any real chance of success without

---

85  See Andrew Whitmarsh, "British Army Manoeuvres and the Development of Military Aviation, 1910–1913," *War in History* 14, no. 3 (July 2007): 325–46.

86  On the founding of the RFC, see Barker, *A Brief History*, 12–13. For a full account, see Raleigh, *The War in the Air*, 1: 198–276. On Cody's first flight, see M.J.H. Taylor and David Mondey, *Milestones of Flight* (London: Janes, 1983).

87  On the RFC's deployment to France, see Raleigh, *The War in the Air*, 1: 411–12. On the RNAS, see Raleigh, *The War in the Air*, 1: 357–58.

88  For example, Winter, *The First of the Few*, 11–12.

harnessing the awesome destructive power of the Royal Artillery ... the RFC existed primarily to serve those guns by aerial photography and artillery observation.[89]

Military historians might differ in their assessment of the RFC's efficacy in these roles, but Britain's senior political and military leaders clearly considered airpower a vital asset. One indication of this fact is that tremendous resources were allocated to the expansion of airpower over the course of the war. In August 1914, the naval and military wings of the RFC had a combined manpower just over 2,000 officers and men and about 120 aircraft. By war's end, this number had increased to over 290,000 personnel and 22,000 aircraft.[90] Although the RAF comprised only about three per cent of British military personnel at the end of the war, it accounted for half the value of the Ministry of Munition's production orders.[91]

Combat in the air developed organically rather than by design. When the RFC deployed to France in August 1914, none of its aeroplanes was armed. In the opening weeks of the war, pilots and observers on opposing sides began to fight one another with small arms and eventually with mounted machine guns. By necessity, these had a limited field of fire so as to prevent damage to one's own aircraft. In mid-1915, the Germans gained a decisive albeit temporary advantage by fielding synchronization equipment that permitted a machine gun, mounted directly in front of the pilot, to fire through the propeller arc without striking the moving blades. During the summer of 1915, Germany's single-seat Fokker monoplanes, equipped with this device, shifted the balance of the air war in favour of the Central Powers. Still struggling to develop reliable synchronization gear of their own, the British and French services countered the "Fokker scourge" with a variety of machines, some of which had been under development for some time. French Nieuport scouts mounted a machine gun above the top wing, permitting the pilot to fire over the propeller. The RFC's two-seat FE 2 and single-seat De Havilland scout (officially called the DH 2) were "pushers," with the engine and propeller to the rear of the pilot. This design was known to be less aeronautically efficient than the "tractor" layout with its frontward engine, but it had the advantage of giving the pilot or gunner an unobstructed field of fire. Most of these British and French

---

89  Peter Hart, *Bloody April: Slaughter in the Skies in Arras 1917* (London: George Weidenfeld and Nicholson, 2005), 11–12.

90  H.A. Jones, "Appendix XXXV: Strength of British Air Personnel August 1914 and November 1918" and "Appendix XXXI: British Aircraft Produced and Labour Employed, August 1914 to November 1918," in *The War in the Air*, 6 vols. and appendices (1922–1937; repr., Uckfield: Naval and Military Press and the Imperial War Museum, 2002), appendices: 160, 154–55.

91  Peter Dye, *The Bridge to Airpower: Logistics Support for Royal Flying Corps. Operations on the Western Front, 1914–1918* (Annapolis: Naval Institute Press, 2015), 14.

machines were not deployed until 1916, however, and even in late 1915, the age of single-seat "fighters," duelling in the sky, had barely begun.[92] All this underscores the fact that McKay would have had little notion in late 1915 that he would one day engage in frenzied machine-gun battles in the sky. The era of the dogfight was yet to come. He would be there to see its inception.

His course at the Wright School finished at last, Eddie McKay took his FAI flight test on January 27, 1916, soloing on the Wright Flyer for the first and last time. This was the test's single greatest challenge and the cause of many failures. For most candidates, their flight test was also their first solo, and the aerodynamic qualities of the flimsy Wright Flyer (and its equivalent in other schools) changed significantly without the added weight of the instructor. The test itself consisted of two "distance" flights of about five kilometres each that had to be completed without touching down, an "altitude" flight in which the pilot was required to attain a height of 100 metres, and a series of figure-eights around the airfield.[93] He passed, as most pilots did. On February 2, McKay formally received Aero Club of America's Aviator's Certificate number 401.

McKay's place among the first 500 marks him as a relative pioneer. Certainly there could not have been more than a hundred or so Canadians among them. The certificate came in a leather billfold with his photograph. It included entreaties in a dozen languages to local authorities to offer assistance to the aviator should he require it, a reminder of a more genteel age that had passed, one in which airmen regarded each other as members in an international fraternity, as differing in nationality but bound together by the stronger ties of their pioneering pursuit of mastery over the air.[94] Now, the occasional fraternal or chivalrous nod aside, they were killing each other. McKay returned to London via Toronto, probably to present his credentials to military authorities there.[95] Within days, orders arrived at the small London home he shared with Sandy. He had been seconded as probationary 2nd lieutenant in the RFC and was to depart Saint John at the end of the month.[96]

One can only imagine the days of excitement and preparation that followed: the news shared with his mother, brothers, and sisters; the handshakes and hearty pats on the back from his former professors ("brave lad!"); the applause from members of his congregation at First St. Andrew's Presbyterian Church, whose hockey

---

92  The story of the first year of the air war has been recounted many times. See Barker, *A Brief History*, 22–56; 94–109.

93  ARCC, UWO, Beatrice Hitchins Memorial Collection of Aviation History, Box 4647, Aero Club Certificates.

94  The certificate is in the author's personal collection via Robert Mackay.

95  "McKay and [unintelligible] Home," *London Free Press*, February 12, 1916, 10.

96  LAC, RG 24, vol. 2022, HQ6978-2-92, Letter: Stanton to Gwatkin, February 11, 1916; Letter from Director of Supplies and Transport to Lt. A.E. McKay, February 17, 1916.

FIGURE 1.4: FAI Certificate. *McKay graduated from the Wright School at the end of January 1916 with about four hours' flying time. He received Aero Club of America certificate #401 on February 2, 1916. The certificate included appeals in half a dozen languages to local authorities to render assistance to the pilot, a reminder of a time when aviators conceived of themselves as an international fraternity. By 1916, they were killing each other in great numbers. (Courtesy Robert Mackay.)*

team would miss him the most; the goodbyes from humbled and perhaps envious classmates and teammates at Western. Then came packing (perhaps in a fine steamer trunk from Darch and Sons); donning the uniform he had been instructed to wear, that of a 2nd lieutenant in the infantry, which he already owned; the tear-ful farewell to his mother, whose youngest, Sid, had already departed—and a final moment, perhaps, with a sweetheart. We do not know.

Then the long train ride east, through famous and historic cities he had never seen and perhaps never expected to: Ottawa, Montreal, and Quebec. On Febru-ary 26, 1916, McKay departed Saint John, New Brunswick, with first-class passage aboard SS *Missanabie*.[97] A two-stack, 13,000-ton steamer owned by Canadian Pacific, *Missanabie* had entered service just as the war began and was at once pressed into use as a troopship. Under ideal conditions, it could complete a cross-ing in six days. McKay's took 16, with *Missanabie* making long, zigzagging legs across the North Atlantic to avoid German submarines. Around the time McKay arrived in England, the UWO *Gazette* announced his departure in the best tradi-tion of its hyperbolic sports reporting:

Eddie McKay ... has sailed for England to join the Imperial Flying Corps. If we were a German we would shiver in our clothes at this information. Eddie was one of the coolest heads the school ever turned out—perfectly at home in the air and what is best, careful. Besides, Eddie never missed the mark while at Western whether it was the 100 yards dash or a French exam. Germans in the trenches go bury yourselves! When Eddie starts handing you British souvenirs from the clouds you'll eat breakfast with the angels.[98]

Of the nearly half million Canadians who crossed the North Atlantic in the Great War, very few remembered the trip fondly. They endured seasickness, congested quarters, bad food, and stale air below decks. McKay, accorded first-class pas-sage by the RFC, might have been relieved of the worst of this but certainly not of the chief enemy: boredom. Vivian Ross, a Canadian pilot who crossed on the *Missanabie* the following year, recalled forlorn efforts to break the monotony with early morning exercise on deck followed by breakfast and then whole days spent playing poker and bridge without betting limits.[99] McKay disembarked at Plym-outh on Monday, March 13, amidst the bustle of nearly 2,000 officers and men of the Canadian Expeditionary Force and a small number, like him, bound for the air services. Ross recalled the scene at his own arrival a year later:

97  Date of departure from Logbook, "Reference." Name of McKay's ship from February 17 letter, cited above.
98  UWO *Gazette*, March 1916, n.p.
99  Vivian Ross, *Flying Minnows* (1935; repr., London: Arms and Armour Press, 1977), 60.

Valises were rolled and strapped, then unrolled again to have pyjamas and other forgotten articles crammed into them, officers in charge of men hurried to and fro shouting orders, and overhead cranes were rattling and groaning as they swung great nets containing officers' valises and men's kit-bags and other baggage ashore.[100]

In 1917, Ross received a week's leave upon arrival. McKay reported to No. 3 Reserve Squadron at Shoreham-by-Sea before the week was over.[101] Probably his first discovery at Shoreham was that his FAI certificate counted for very little. At the Wright School, he had learned only the very rudiments of piloting, and on an obsolete machine at that. In a letter home, Roy Brown, who had arrived overseas for training with the RNAS three months earlier, complained that the Wright Flyer was "a joke" compared to modern machines. "I wish I had never seen a Wright machine. Any machine is better to take a license on than that one."[102] As for the FAI certificate itself, it conveyed only one real advantage: trainees who had got to fly sooner than others.[103]

Prior to the war, the task of turning civilian aviators into military pilots had been vested in the Central Flying School at Upavon. Since August 1914, however, the flying services had grown dramatically. As early as January 1915, the War Office had recognized that "it is impossible to train the required number of pilots at the Central Flying School."[104] The demand for replacements and new pilots had quickly overwhelmed the capacity of the training establishment to provide them. One indication of the rapid growth in pilot training is that the Royal Aero Club, which granted FAI certificates in the UK, certified roughly as many pilots in 1915 as in all previous years of its existence.[105] To meet demand, the flying services absorbed civilian schools and established a growing number of training units they dubbed reserve squadrons.[106] Service squadrons in England, working up for deployment to France,

---

100  Ross, *Flying Minnows*, 61.

101  Logbook, "Reference"; NA (UK), AHB, AIR 1/1272/204/9/145, 7 Wing, RFC, Daily Routine Orders, March 17, 1916.

102  Roy Brown, Letter, February 4, 1916, quoted in Bennett, *Roy Brown*, 146.

103  Roy Brown, Letter, January 10, 1916, quoted in Bennett, *Roy Brown*, 139–40.

104  LAC, Air Ministry (UK), MG 40 D1, vol. 35, AIR 2/6/87/4469, Memo from Assistant Director of Military Aeronautics, January 6, 1915.

105  Royal Aero Club certifications are now available from ancestry.com. Later in 1916, the RFC and RNAS dropped the requirement that pilot recruits had to either have an FAI certificate beforehand or earn one as a condition of service.

106  Originally called Reserve Aeroplane Squadrons, they were renamed Reserve Squadrons in January 1916. Reserve Squadrons were numbered sequentially, like Service Squadrons, which can lead to confusion: there was, for example, a No. 1 (Service) Squadron and a No. 1 Reserve Squadron that bore no administrative relationship to one another. NA (UK), AHB, AIR 1/676/21/13/1773, Notes on Flying Training at Home, Part 1. For a discussion of the organization of RFC squadrons, see C.G. Jefford, *RAF Squadrons* (St. John's Hill: Airlife Publishing, 1988), 4–5.

offered more advanced instruction in aviation. Few records of the training establishment have survived, forcing historians to rely heavily on memoirs to assess its character and quality. Though it is not true, as is sometimes claimed, that the early training system lacked a proscribed curriculum—there were manuals and tests to teach to—pilots' memoirs almost invariably describe the quality of training, especially in the first three years of the war, as slapdash and even dangerously erratic. McKay's future squadron-mate Robert Saundby, who went on to a long and outstanding career with the RAF, was so disappointed with his training that he seriously considered returning to his former infantry regiment.[107] He later wrote,

> I have never found it necessary to modify the opinion which I formed at the time that, with the exception of the C.F.S. and one or two individuals, the standard of flying training was on the whole extremely bad. The instructor felt no responsibility for his pupils' flying and invariably explained away their crashes by reporting that they were hopeless idiots, better dead, of whom nothing could reasonably be expected.[108]

The shortage of qualified instructors that Saundby alluded to was probably the most serious problem the training establishment faced. In his postwar memoir, Arthur Gould Lee described his own terrifying introduction to flight training in August 1916. On his first day of instruction, a seething and truculent squadron major ordered Lee to take control of their machine. "I was petrified," Lee wrote. "I had no idea what to do." His sole experience in an aeroplane had been as a passenger on a joyride the day before. "I tried to explain that I'd not been given a single lesson, but he wouldn't listen." Lee did his best, nearly killed them both, was severely and profanely dressed down, and went on to rate the major as the best of his instructors! In many cases, instructors were pilots who had returned from a tour in France, sometimes wounded in both body and mind. Sent home for a rest, they were instead further exhausted by the nonstop routine of instruction and exposed to the psychological trauma of having to relinquish control of their machines to novices. Other instructors were newly appointed flying officers, tapped to teach having only just concluded their own training, sometimes because they were promising pilots but in other cases relegated to training because they had no promise at all.

---

107   R.H.M.S. Saundby, "Service Experiences," January 1928. My thanks to Dr. Peter Saundby for transcribing his father's unpublished account, given to the RAF Staff College in the 1920s. Saundby, later Air Marshal Sir Robert Saundby, served as deputy air officer commanding (AOC), Bomber Command, in the Second World War.
108   Saundby, "Service Experiences."

McKay's training at Shoreham began on French-designed biplanes called Maurice Farman "Shorthorns" and "Longhorns"—the "horns" being curved landing skids that protruded from the front of the machine. These were easy-flying but obsolete pushers that had been relegated to elementary flight training duties. "A queer sort of bus like an assemblage of bird-cages" is how the pilot and novelist Victor Yeates described the Shorthorn. "There did not seem to be any *a priori* reason why this structure should leave the ground," he wrote. "Flying with their antiquated controls was a mixture of playing a harmonium, working the village pump, and sculling a boat."[109] As in most trainers, student and instructor sat in tandem, communicating by shouting.[110] Apart from some brief periods of dual instruction on new types of machines, however, most of McKay's flying time in training was solo. Trainees, especially those who already had an FAI certificate, were encouraged to fly solo as quickly as possible and work out the kinks on their own. McKay's logbook indicates that he began flying solo on March 24, after a frighteningly meagre 1 hour and 40 minutes dual instruction.[111] In all, he flew eight different models of aircraft in four squadrons before leaving for France.[112] Subsequent generations would look aghast upon the open cockpit, flimsily constructed, and mechanically unreliable aeroplanes of the era, but to the pilots who flew them they were the technological marvels of the age. Even the Shorthorns and Longhorns flew faster and higher than the Wright Model B that McKay had flown stateside, while the obsolete Blériot monoplane (a version of which, piloted by Louis Blériot himself, became in 1909 the first aeroplane to fly the English Channel) outperformed it by far in many respects, especially manoeuvrability. Other machines McKay trained on included the Avro 504, a highly dependable trainer that served until the early 1930s, and the RFC's workhorse, the BE 2C reconnaissance plane. Training flights involved performing circuits of the aerodrome, take-offs and landings, and the occasional cross-country jaunt. They seldom lasted more than 20 or 30 minutes, and some as few as 10. This was still long enough for pilots to return sticky with engine oil and dirt when flying tractor-layout machines. Only once in just over a hundred training flights was McKay airborne longer than an hour and only twice at altitudes above 6,000 feet. In France, that summer, he routinely would fly patrols for twice as long and at twice

---

109  V.M. Yeates, *Winged Victory* (New York: H. Smith and R. Hass, 1934), 64–65.

110  The RFC later adopted a speaking tube, the "Gosport Tube" to facilitate communication in two-seaters.

111  McKay's arrival at Shoreham: NA (UK), AHB, AIR 1/1272/204/9/145, 7 Wing RFC Daily Routine Orders, Order No. 114, March 20, 1916; Logbook, "Reference." Date of first solo: Logbook, "Reference." Solo after 1 hour 40 minutes: Logbook, "Time Flown at Shoreham," n.d., p. 4. McKay began to date individual flights on April 20, 1916.

112  Logbook, March–June 1916. McKay trained with (in order) No. 3 RS; No. 28 Squadron; No. 1 RS; again, briefly with No. 28 Squadron; and No. 40 Squadron.

the altitude. His training would have involved virtually no practical instruction in formation flying or combat manoeuvres. Although he probably took a course of instruction in the use of the Lewis gun—the British army's mainstay light machine gun—he almost certainly never fired one in the air before deploying to France. Aerobatics, including fast turns, side slips, spins, and loops, were referred to by the derogatory term "stunting" and usually forbidden.[113] McKay did have a fortuitous encounter in mid-May while training with 1 RS at Gosport. In late 1917, Captain Robert Smith-Barry would become the driving force behind efforts to rationalize and improve the RFC's training system. In 1916, he was still elaborating his method, but he believed that trainees had to practice "stunting" under proper supervision if they were to survive at the front. McKay's logbook indicates that he had four training flights with Barry before the latter returned to France.[114] Brief though these were, they may have been the most important of his training.

Such rare exceptions aside, training in early 1916 vacillated between excessively cautious and exceedingly dangerous, often depending on the temperament of individual instructors or training squadron commanders. Minor smash-ups were a rite of passage for nearly every pilot. McKay suffered through engine failures, forced landings, and, late in his training, a sudden crosswind that slew his Blériot monoplane sideways on landing, tearing both wheels off the undercarriage.[115] Although there is no empirical support for the oft-stated claim that half of all pilots died in training, fatal accidents were nonetheless all too common, accounting for roughly one-fifth of all fatalities in the flying services over the course of the war.[116] Small wonder, then, that one historian has opined that pilot training amounted to "culpable, if not criminal negligence" on the part of RFC.[117] But this is a hindsight criticism, and careful historians will note that RFC authorities were not unaware of the shortcomings of their

---

113   The foregoing description was derived from a number of memoirs.
114   Logbook, May 12–14, 1916. McKay's May 12 entry expressly states "stunting." On Smith-Barry, see Frank D. Tredrey, *Pioneer Pilot: The Great Smith Barry Who Taught the World How to Fly* (London: P. Davies, 1976).
115   Logbook, April 23, April 28, May 22, June 14, 1916.
116   Precise figures for deaths in the flying services are difficult to establish. See Chris Hobson, *Airmen Died in the Great War, 1914–1918* (Suffolk: J.B. Hayward and Son, 1995), which gives a figure of 9,352 British "airmen" killed or died from all causes. Hobson estimates approximately 2,000 dead as a result of training accidents. There is no evidentiary support for the claim made by Winter in *The First of the Few*, repeated in other sources, that 8,000 pilots were killed in training (pp. 36–37) nor for the claim, repeated in several sources, that half of British pilot deaths were suffered in training (see, for instance, Edward Bujak's otherwise excellent *Reckless Fellows: The Gentlemen of the Royal Flying Corps* [London: I.B. Taurus, 2015], 6.) The exterior cover blurb on Ian Mackersey's popular history *No Empty Chairs* makes the further claim that *half of all* British pilots were killed in training in the war. The resultant figure, if true (it is not) would exceed total deaths in the air services from all causes.
117   Barker, *A Brief History*, 220.

pilots. Training establishment authorities made continual efforts to improve their standards. In December 1915, the RFC opened a ground school at Reading University called the School of Military Aeronautics (SMA). A second school opened at Oxford in mid-1916. In a course of study lasting about a month, the SMA taught students the theory of flight, navigation, wireless communication, and crucial aspects of aircraft and engine maintenance. The rapid growth of pilot training made it difficult to implement wholesale changes at once, however. Saundby was a member of the first class at Reading, and he later described the course of study as the only bright spot in his training.[118] His contemporary Willie Fry, with whom McKay would serve in late 1917, was pulled from the school along with his classmates and sent to their training squadrons before they were finished.[119] McKay did not attend Reading at all. He did, however, arrive in Shoreham just as the War Office issued a new directive, based on "serious complaints" from Hugh Trenchard "concerning the insufficient training of some of the pilots sent out as reinforcements." The directive stipulated that, to qualify as a flying officer, a trainee had to have a minimum of 15 hours solo, including experience on a service machine (i.e., a model actually used in front-line service); had to complete a cross-country flight of at least 60 miles; had to remain at the altitude of 6,000 feet for a minimum of 15 minutes; and had to complete 2 landings at night. In addition, the directive urged that pilots "be given every opportunity of gaining air experience." This included practice fighting and formation flying, although McKay's logbook contains no mention of his receiving either before his first tour in France. Trifling though they might seem in retrospect, these requirements were far more stringent than those mandated by the FAI for an Aero Club certificate. The directive fully acknowledged that these new regulations might create temporary bottlenecks in the training establishment but stressed that "the standard of efficiency must be improved."[120] These changes might explain why McKay's training—slapdash though it undeniably was at times—lasted longer than might have been expected. McKay departed for France in late June with 46 hours of flying under his belt. His contemporaries and future squadron-mates, Harry Wood of Toronto and Robert Saundby, had 52 and 60, respectively.[121]

---

118   Saundby, "Service Experiences."
119   William Fry, Air of Battle (London: Kimber, 1974).
120   LAC, Air Ministry (UK), MG 40 D1, AIR 1/131/15/40/218, "Pilots Sent to Expeditionary Force with Insufficient Training." See also AIR 1/131/15/40/218, "Notes of Flying Training at Home, Part 1."
121   RAF Museum, RHMS Saundby Papers, box 1, AC 72–12 Pilot's Logbook. An incomplete copy of Harry Wood's logbook (now apparently lost) is located in the University of Texas at Dallas, Eugene McDermott Library, George H. Williams Jr., World War One Aviation Library, Ola A. Slater Collection, box 11.

None of this is to suggest that the training regime of early 1916 was a good one, only that its deficiencies need to be understood in context. Moreover, it bears repeating that historians, reliant on memoir literature, have sometimes failed to recognize the steady improvement in the quality of training. The oft-repeated claim that the training regime was completely without a formal syllabus, for instance, is belied by the existence of standardized exams recruits were required to pass. The "A" examination, which McKay wrote in the officer's mess at Fort Grange on May 9, tested the candidate's knowledge on such matters as the theory of flight, cross-country flying, and cooperation with infantry and artillery. The "B" examination, which he took a week later, was a more practical test, taken at the Central Flying School in Upavon. Candidates had to demonstrate knowledge of engine mechanics, aircraft maintenance, the rigging of aircraft, map reading, identifying infantry, and Morse code.[122] The culminating "C" examination consisted of the night and cross-country flights to meet the requirements laid down in the March War Office memo.

McKay completed this final test early in the third week of June, his last in training. He began the week with two days flying FE 2Bs with 28 Squadron, performing his cross-country flight and night landings on his second day. He then spent three days with 40 Squadron flying DH 2s, the backbone of British scout machines in France.[123] The officer commanding 40 Squadron, McKay's last posting in training, was Major Robert Loraine, a well-known West End stage actor, friend of the playwright George Bernard Shaw, and a prewar aviator who had been the first man to fly the Irish Sea.[124] Loraine was talented, egotistical, severe, and disapproving. Before McKay departed, Loraine wrote a brief appraisal of his ability: "A steady pilot and a keen officer."[125] Coming from him, this was handsome, nearly gushing praise. McKay apparently valued this appraisal and kept it. A century later, it was discovered tucked between the pages of his logbook. His examinations passed and training complete, McKay had his status as a probationary 2nd lieutenant lifted. In the day's routine orders, Loraine noted that 2nd Lt. A.E. McKay was to

---

122  Dates of McKay's "A" and "B" examinations are from NA, Air Ministry, Air Historical Section, AHB, AIR 1/1273/204/9/149, Daily Routine Orders, RFC Station Gosport, May 6 and 13, 1916. Description of the "A" exam is from C.G. Jefford, *Observers and Navigators* (London: Grub Street, 2014), 46. A rubric for a "B" exam can be found in 7 Wing, RFC, Confidential Reports on Officers, AIR 1/1271/204/9/137.

123  Logbook, June 14–17, 1916. He completed his other requirements, stipulated in the March memorandum, on these machines.

124  On Loraine, see Winifred Loraine, *Robert Loraine: Soldier, Actor, Airman* (London: Collins, 1938) and Lanyard D. Liggera, *The Life of Robert Loraine: The Stage, the Sky, and George Bernard Shaw* (Newark: University of Delaware Press, 2013.) Loraine actually crashed a short distance from shore and swam the remaining distance to Ireland. It was good enough for the record.

125  No. 40 Squadron, Sixth Wing, assessment of A.E. McKay by Major R. Loraine, June 19, 1916. Author's collection via Eugene Kittmer.

report to 6th Brigade Headquarters, London, for posting overseas as a DH scout pilot.[126] Only the best pilots were deemed worthy to fly scouts, and McKay had been judged one of them, no doubt to his overwhelming joy. That day, he was appointed flying officer and earned his "wings," the RFC's distinctive, wing-shaped badge he was now entitled to sew onto his uniform. His orders received in London, he may have had time for celebration and a photographic portrait, and then he departed for France. He had come to the war at last.[127]

## Historians and Fact Finding

How do we know that the facts just recounted about Eddie McKay are true? It is not an easy question to answer. In 1961, the eminent English historian E.H. Carr published an influential book called *What Is History?* based on a series of lectures he gave at Cambridge. It was and is a controversial work, one that every student of history should read and think about. In part, Carr set out to challenge the idea that the historian could be an objective authority of the past. On the contrary, he argued, the historian cannot be dispassionately detached from the act of finding and interpreting sources because he is "of his own age, and is bound to it by the conditions of human existence."[128] Even the sources themselves do not come to us pure, Carr said, because they are "refracted through the mind of the recorder" and therefore laden with the same sorts of social and cultural biases that historians inevitably are.[129] Controversial though they were at the time, many of Carr's ideas were highly influential, especially among social historians on the political left who were suspicious of traditional historiography. Compared to the radical skepticism and relativism that would buffet the humanities in the decades that followed, Carr's views seem moderate today. In fact, he expressly renounced the extreme relativist position when he said, "It does not follow that, because a mountain appears to take on different shapes from different angles of vision, it has objectively either no shape at all or an infinity of shapes."[130] Nonetheless, some historians—especially those who persisted in thinking of history

---

126   NA (UK), AHB, AIR 1/1408/204/28/24, 40 Squadron RFC Daily Routine Orders, June 19, 1916.

127   NA (UK), Air Ministry and Royal Air Force Records, A.E. McKay, AIR 76/321/167. The Air Ministry kept short form service records of pilots detailing dates of postings, promotions, etc. These are distinct from officers' War Office service records. McKay's Air Ministry record is hereafter referred to as "McKay, Air Ministry service record." All others are Air Ministry Service Records, Name, File Number.

128   E.H. Carr, *What Is History?* (Harmondsworth, UK: Penguin Books, 1964), 24. Of course, Carr was a product of his time, before gender-neutral language was widely adopted.

129   Ibid., 22.

130   Ibid., 26–27.

in Rankean terms (after Leopold von Ranke, a nineteenth-century historian who advocated a scientific methodology)—considered Carr's work an affront to the profession. Another heavyweight historian, Geoffrey Elton, took such umbrage at *What Is History?* that he wrote an entire book, *The Practice of History*, in rebuttal.[131]

One particular point of contention between Carr and Elton was over the question of how to define a fact. Obviously, facts are derived from sources, but Carr distinguished between what he called "the facts of the past" and "the facts of history."[132] Not all of Carr's readers have agreed about what, precisely, he meant by this, and his terminology has not been widely used by historians. We might take it to mean the difference between mere information about the past and actual historical knowledge, the latter of which is the result of the correct use of historical method. The "facts of history," as Carr saw it, are those bits of information about the past that historians have agreed are true and important. In this sense, Carr's distinction is not unlike the one we noted earlier: the past is the totality of what occurred before us while history is what historians write about it. What was difficult for some critics to accept about Carr's argument was the implicit suggestion that, since historical facts resulted from the consensus of historians, the facts could change if historians changed their minds. Strict Rankeans found such notions troubling. In their view, facts were something historians discovered, so they had to be out there in the first place, like new elements or distant planets, waiting to be found. Although Carr's notions seemed to undermine this scientific conception of historiography, they may be more scientific than they appear at first glance. Consider the definition of a fact advanced in a well-known passage by the late scientist and popular writer Stephen Jay Gould. In science, Gould said, a fact is something "confirmed to such a degree that it would be perverse to withhold provisional assent."[133] Notice how Gould's definition of a scientific fact is similar to Carr's definition of a "fact of history": both hold that facts do not exist independently of confirmation. Moreover, this definition forces us to concede the possibility that what is factually established today might be overturned tomorrow by new discoveries. For instance, we might discover that our sources were inauthentic, unreliable, or had been interpreted incorrectly. Or we might discover new sources that force us to change our minds about things we once thought were true.

At this point, it is worth underscoring that just because facts *can* in principle lose their status is not evidence that they *will*. It certainly does not mean that every crackpot theory about the past is worthy of serious consideration. Regarding

131  G.R. Elton, *The Practice of History* (London: Collins, 1969).
132  Carr, *What Is History?* 11–13.
133  Stephen J. Gould, "Evolution as Fact and Theory," in *Hen's Teeth and Horse's Toes* (New York: W.W. Norton, 1980), 255.

various pseudoscientific ideas that bedevil the scientific community, Gould made the following analogy: "I suppose apples may start to rise tomorrow, but the possibility does not merit equal time in physics classrooms."[134] Much the same can be said for various outlandish conspiracy theories that inflict themselves on historians. Unsatisfied, perhaps, with the complex and often ambiguous nature of historical causality (there is no simple answer as to why the First World War erupted, for instance), many people prefer to believe that shadowy cabals, operating undetected or purposefully concealed by historians, are the operative force in human history. Generally speaking, conspiracy theorists have far lower evidentiary standards than most historians would consider acceptable, and their methodology—if it can be called that—is different, too. Historians, for instance, consider contrary evidence something that forces them to change their views (a willingness to do so is one definition of "objectivity"); conspiracy theorists see counter evidence as proof of how deep the conspiracy goes, thus confirming it further.[135]

However we define the term, it seems clear that history is constructed from facts and, more important, from the ideas that we form about them. Cultivating the skills of fact-finding and source criticism is therefore critical for students of history. Elaborate theorizing is often necessary, too, but this step must occur over a stable foundation of evidence. As I shall demonstrate, even establishing the bare-bones facts about Eddie McKay's life required hundreds of hours devoted just to locating sources. Reading, understanding, verifying, interpreting, and contextualizing those sources and the facts derived from them took much longer. Marshalling those facts into evidence on which to base McKay's story took longer still. Then I had to actually write that story, which was the most difficult thing of all. Consider this, however: I cannot possibly have established (or, if you prefer, have discovered) every fact there is to know about McKay's life. Most of the events in his life were not recorded in the first place, and many of the sources pertaining to those that were are lost irretrievably. I have only seven sources that refer directly to him prior to 1913: his birth registration, his family's entry in the census of 1901, an attendance book from his elementary school, an index card with his vital details from Central Collegiate Secondary School in London, two entries in London city directories, and an undated photograph of a teenage Eddie with an unknown London hockey team. Of those, one is slightly suspect. The card from Central Collegiate for Edwin McKay gives his date of birth as 1894. This could be a simple mistake, as errors occur frequently in old records. Or it may be that this

---

134  Gould, "Evolution," 255.
135  On this, see the introduction to David Aaronovitch, *Voodoo History: The Role of Conspiracy Theory in Shaping Modern History* (New York: Riverhead, 2010), 1–16.

Edwin McKay is another student altogether. I doubt this, because Eddie's name appears on the school's cenotaph and no other Edwin McKay died in the service of Canada. In any case, seven sources for 21 years is a very rickety foundation on which to build a biography. Might there be other sources waiting to be discovered? No doubt there are. Somewhere in archives and attics there are sources undiscovered: letters from him, to him, or about him; newspaper articles I missed; old photos, faded and curled, in which he appears; diaries in which he is mentioned; official documents that refer to him; and perhaps even things he owned.

In addition, I deliberately excluded certain sources when writing this biography, not to conceal anything but because I found them uninteresting. Eddie was a gifted athlete, and in 1913 and 1914 he was mentioned in dozens of newspaper articles covering London's sports scene. I decided against writing a detailed account of his athletic career, however, because time and space are at a premium, and I am more interested in Eddie the aviator than Eddie the athlete. But that is *my* interest. Someone else, writing a history of sports in Canada, might consider his wartime service a footnote to his outstanding amateur athletic career. It might also be a valid criticism of this work to argue that, in emphasizing McKay's service in the RFC, I have created a distorted impression of him, since he was a pilot for only about two of his 25 years. Finally, as Carr reminds us, how I interpret, understand, and write about the facts will necessarily be different, perhaps dramatically so, from how other historians would, because we are different people. An entire generation of social scientists and cultural theorists have expounded upon the same idea, often taking their conclusions to radical extremes: our understanding of the world is socially and historically conditioned because we are. Try as we might to be objective (which I define as a willingness to change one's mind when the evidence says that you should), it is inevitable that our personal worldview is going to inform—and to some degree prejudice—our view of the past. The belief that two historians, examining the same sources, inevitably will come to the same conclusion denies not only the accumulated evidence of centuries of historiography but also the humanity of the historians themselves.

It is worth reiterating that just locating sources and deriving facts from them can be a major undertaking. Sometimes, however, facts can be established with surprising ease. For example, when a claim made in one of our sources is uncontroversial, we tend to unconcernedly call it a fact. I have no particular reason to doubt that Eddie intercepted a pass in Western's rugby game against Sarnia in October 1914, even though I have only one source for the claim, a newspaper article written shortly after the game.[136] Given what I know about how inaccurate

*[margin, handwritten: You don't need to use every source you have!]*

---

136   Bert Perry, "Smith's Drop Kicking and Ross's Punting Give Western Victory over Sarnia," *London Advertiser*, October 26, 1914, 6.

that particular newspaper could be about his military service, perhaps I should not be so confident. Then again, I have no reason to think that a sports writer, actually present, would get such details wrong (surely fans of the losing team would correct him if he had been), and I consider it of no great consequence if he did. But my easy acceptance of this "fact" occurs partly because McKay's career as an athlete is of comparatively little importance to me. More careful historians, or ones more interested in sports, might seek out additional independent sources verifying this claim before calling it a fact, but they would also have to be historians with more time on their hands.

I want to pause for a moment to reflect on the rather glib remark I just made. Consider the following source, which I examined but did not use in writing McKay's story. Most of the records for the Canadian Militia prior to the First World War are lost. Among those that survive are some nominal roles for various militia regiments. In 1908, an "A. McKay" appears on one such role for the Perth Regiment.[137] Is this Alfred Edwin McKay? It might be. The Perth Regiment was the one nearest to where he grew up, and Eddie's younger brother, Sidney, served with the regiment for two years prior to enlisting in the CEF in 1915.[138] Furthermore, we know that, in the summer of 1915, Eddie enlisted in the militia, albeit with the 33rd Hurons, which might suggest that he had an affinity for the militia as an institution. So there are reasonable grounds for believing that this "A. McKay" might be our Eddie. On the other hand, in 1908, Eddie would have been a little young for militia service (though not impossibly so, if he had his mother's permission), and it was extremely unusual for him to sign his name as "A. McKay." Another source of doubt is that the handwriting on the nominal roll is not a match with Eddie's either. Or is it possible that someone else was filling out the ledger at roll call ("A. McKay?" "Here!"). Or maybe young Eddie simply signed his name differently than he did years later. Given the paucity of militia records from this period, how else might we discover whether this "A. McKay" is Eddie? We could explore smaller, local archives and museums in Perth County. Do they have any records relating to the regiment? A photograph, perhaps, from which he might be picked out? It might also be possible to investigate other names on the list. Through meticulous excavation of surviving sources and thorough genealogy (a highly specialized subfield of history devoted to the study of family lineages), we might find out more about other members of the Perth Regiment. Maybe some of them knew Eddie or were friends with him. Perhaps they corresponded with him or had their picture taken with him. After all that, we *might* find new sources and establish new facts

---

137   LAC, RG 9-II-F-6, Nominal Rolls and Paylists for the Volunteer Militia, 28th Regiment, Perth.
138   LAC, RG 150, accession 1992–93/166, box 6937–10, CEF Attestation Paper of SPR Sidney McKay.

that are important to the story we want to tell. At this point, however, we are confronted with a difficult question. Would it be worthwhile to spend hundreds of additional hours on such a task? In this case, I concluded that it was not. This was a choice based on a variety of factors, a cost-benefit analysis wherein I concluded that the huge expenditure of time involved was not worth it given the low probability of success and the comparatively minor pay-off even if I did discover something. By contrast, given that this book's focus is on McKay's career as a pilot, I thought it was an urgent task to compile lists of his squadron-mates in the RFC and to follow up on each of them. Did they write memoirs or keep diaries? Can their personal correspondence or photo albums be found? In all, I searched for records relating to over 90 pilots and other military personnel he served with. This sort of work is painstaking, the historian's equivalent of archaeological excavation, where progress is measured in centimetres of earth methodically sifted at dig sites. It yields few finds, and those it does are often no more than shards or fragments that present as many questions as they answer.

In the end, I decided against using the 1908 nominal roll as a source. If I had, I would have been justified in claiming only that there is some evidence that McKay might have served in the Perth Regiment before 1914. Now consider the following source, which I did decide to use. In Chapter One, we learned that McKay arrived in Augusta, Georgia, on December 16, 1916. My initial source for this claim was a newspaper article that appeared in the *Augusta Chronicle*. That article, however, does not say that Eddie McKay arrived that day, nor does it use any of the common variations of his name such as "Alfred," "Edward," or "MacKay." Rather, it reads as follows:

### Aviation Pupils Got In Last Night

Mr. H.M. Rinehart, one of the instructors of the Wright School of Aviation, which has been established in Augusta, arrived in the city last night, accompanied by his wife and thirteen pupils. The party of students are from different parts of the United States and Canada ... in the party arriving last night were H.M. Rinehart and his wife, Dayton; N.A. Moor and brother, Dayton; T.C. Wilkinson, R.S. Kennedy, and J.G. Ireland, Montreal, Canada; F.H. Petrie, Minneapolis, Minn.; **J.D. McKay**, C.N. Somerville, and Charles Willis, Dayton; W.H. Chisam and A.J. Shaw, Edmonton, Canada; A.H. Pearce, Vancouver and R.M. Wier of Toronto, Canada.[139]

---

139   "Aviation Pupils Got in Last Night," *Augusta Chronicle*, December 17, 1915, 7.

*J.D.* McKay, not *A.E.* Moreover, "Dayton" follows on the list in which his name appears, which we might take to mean that J.D. McKay was from there. Yet I have every confidence that the J.D. mentioned in this article is actually Eddie McKay. Sources often contain errors. It may be wise to proceed from the assumption that they invariably contain errors. With diligence and care, however, errors can often be detected. In this case, our suspicions might be aroused because "J" rhymes with "A" and "D" with "E"—it would be easy to mistake these letters for one another over the telephone, for instance. It was for this reason that a phonetic alphabet was developed for use in radio communication. By itself, however, this would not be sufficient evidence to factually establish that this J.D. McKay is our A.E. How else might we determine if it is?

We know for certain, from multiple sources (newspapers, correspondence, photographs, and secondary sources) that, in 1916, the Wright Flying School wintered in Augusta beginning in December. We also know, from multiple sources (McKay's Aero Club certificate, announcements in aviation journals, articles in London newspapers, the Aero Club's own annual publication) that McKay graduated from the Wright School at the end of January 1916. So he must have arrived in Augusta at some point in December 1915 or January 1916. By contrast, no records exist to show that a J.D. McKay graduated from the Wright School that winter, although it is possible that someone named J.D. McKay started to take the course but failed to complete it.

Can we learn anything from the other names on the list? Investigating them, we find that small errors in the *Augusta Chronicle* are quite common. A.J. Shaw, for instance, was probably J.A. (James Alexander) Shaw, who graduated in Augusta with Aero Club certificate 382 on Christmas Day, 1915; R.S. Kennedy was probably P.S. (Patrick Sylvester) Kennedy, who graduated on Boxing Day with certificate 383.[140] Or consider the name immediately following J.D. McKay in the article above: C.N. Somerville. In mid-January, an article appeared in the *Augusta Chronicle* with the headline, "Remains of Aviator Shipped to Canada: Mr. *S.N.* Somerville Died Following Surgical Operation."[141] In the next sentence, the article states that "The remains of Mr. *S.H.* Somerville, a student aviator at the Wright School of Aviation ... will be shipped to Georgetown, Canada." Georgetown, Ontario, is not far from Toronto. Checking, we find that an obituary for Somerville, whose actual name was Cavanagh N. Somerville, appeared in the *Toronto Daily Star* on January 17, 1916.[142]

---

140   Aero Club of America, *1917*, 77. See also cards for Shaw and Kennedy in the Royal Aero Club records, now available from ancestry.com (see *Great Britain, Royal Aero Club Aviators' Certificates, 1910–1950* [database online], Provo, UT, USA: Ancestry.com Operations Inc., 2008).
141   *Augusta Chronicle*, January 18, 1916, 18.
142   "Killed in Augusta, GA," *Toronto Daily Star*, January 17, 1916, 2.

What can we conclude about Eddie from these various sources? First, at least one of the people that the article implied was from Dayton actually *arrived from* Dayton. Second, accurate spelling of names was not the *Augusta Chronicle*'s forte. Third, we have overwhelming evidence that A.E. McKay travelled to Augusta for flight training and none at all that someone named J.D. McKay did. Given all this, we can reasonably conclude that the J.D. McKay in the article above is in fact our A.E. McKay. We cannot, based on this source alone, know with absolute certainty, *Emily* but historians seldom do. We deal in probabilities. As it turns out, our hunch *Dickson* in this case was correct after all. Midway through the writing of this biography, I located McKay's pilot's logbook. It includes a one-page summation, written by McKay himself, of his early flight training. In it, he says he arrived in Augusta on December 16, 1916.[143]

Social scientists often speak of "triangulation," a term borrowed from trigonometry and geometry and used in navigation. In those fields, triangulation refers specifically to establishing the location of a point by measuring angles to it from other points whose location is already known. In the social sciences, it tends to be used more generally, with triangulation referring to the importance of using multiple, independent sources to verify facts. If the foundation of historical method is to derive facts from reliable sources, then historians must necessarily repeat processes similar to this one hundreds of times. Unfortunately, there remains a widespread perception that history is nothing more than that, no more than an immutable bill of facts about the past, with certain facts ("When did the Battle of Vimy Ridge occur?" or "How many victories did Billy Bishop have?") to be committed to memory because of their importance. Teachers of history and authors of textbooks do neither their profession nor their students any favours when they succumb to the temptation to present history in such a fashion. History can be a story—a "narrative"—but such stories should never be unproblematic, never a mere recitation of facts, because history is not like that. It is not the past; it is not a bill of facts about the past. It is, as Carr put it, a never-ending process of engagement with those facts.[144] What we consider to be a fact can change; how we understand facts can change; and so history can change, too. It does not follow from this that all interpretations of the past are equally valid. Clearly, some ideas about history are better than others, for the same reason that some ways of building an airplane are better than others: because the preponderance of evidence and experience points in their direction. Some historians and philosophers of history have warned against "archival fetishism," arguing that imagination and intuition

---

143  Logbook, "Reference."
144  Carr, *What Is History?* 24.

are part of the historian's craft, too.[145] Indeed they are, as we shall discuss, but either historians have evidence for the things they believe to be true or they do not. We need theories, too, by which I mean ideas to explain facts, but as the great French historian Marc Bloch put it, nice theories are sometimes undermined by unpleasant facts.

---

145   For a discussion, see Richard J. Evans, *In Defense of History* (London: Granata, 1997), 84–86.

CHAPTER TWO

# Over the Somme:
# July–October 1916

In our halls is hung
Armoury of the invincible Knights of old:
We must be free or die, who speak the tongue
That Shakespeare spake; the faith and morals hold
Which Milton held.—In every thing we are sprung
Of Earth's first blood, have titles manifold.

—Wordsworth, *It Is Not to Be Thought Of*

There is a photograph taken at the Bertangles aerodrome in July 1916 of the officers and men of "B" Flight, No. 24 Squadron, posing with their machines. Captain Robin Hughes Chamberlain, their flight leader, is seated centre in a folding chair. Beside him, his pilots sit cross-legged on the ground like boys in summer camp: Evans, Manfield, Chapman, Tidmarsh, and Eddie McKay. On McKay's left is Watts, the squadron's equipment officer. Behind them, two dozen enlisted men, the flight's mechanics, riggers, and fitters, stand at attention.[1]

In mid-August, Hughes Chamberlain will be severely wounded in the foot and never return to the squadron. Henry Evans will fall to anti-aircraft gunfire on September 3 and Philip Manfield to the machine guns of the dreaded German ace Oswald Boelcke just six days later. David Tidmarsh, Hughes Chamberlain's successor as flight leader, will be shot down while serving with 48 Squadron the following April, survive, but spend the rest of the war in German captivity. Charles Chapman will rise to command 29 Squadron, only to die in Belgium at the beginning of

---

1  This photograph appears in several works. A copy is in the author's private collection via Stewart K. Taylor. Original source unknown.

October 1917 of wounds received during a German raid on his aerodrome. McKay will be killed just over two months later, diving on a German two-seater near Ypres.[2] One photograph: six pilots, six casualties, four of them fatal. There are many photos like it—of whole flights, sometimes whole squadrons, simply gone.

Eddie McKay set foot in France for the first time on June 21, 1916.[3] Pilots deploying from England sometimes flew, but McKay crossed the Channel by ship, probably landing at Boulogne-sur-Mer, one of the BEF's most important disembarkation ports. Intensive final preparations for the summer offensive were underway, and we can well imagine the sights he would have seen: ships disgorging columns of men and horses, officers shouting directions, trucks laden with supplies trundling by. Since its arrival in France in August 1914, the BEF had expanded tenfold to comprise five field armies and over 1.5 million men. Of those, barely 400 were pilots, serving in one of the RFC's 27 front line squadrons or pooled at higher headquarters.[4] The RFC "wings" on McKay's uniform therefore marked him as a breed apart: the rarest of the rare and, if not the bravest of the brave, certainly the most foolhardy. Yet his initial posting was the dullest imaginable, to the reserve pool of pilots that Hugh Trenchard maintained at the 1st Air Depot in St. Omer and the 2nd AD in Candas.[5] The depots served as the logistical backbone for RFC operations on the Western Front, providing stores, spare parts, pilots, and new and repaired machines to front-line squadrons.[6] Despite being hubs of BEF activity, St. Omer and Candas were otherwise small and rather charmless towns, offering scant amusements for bored and anxious reserve pool pilots who had little to do except wait and complain. "I must say I think France is a bit of a 'hole,' the decidedly unimpressed 2nd Lt. Gwilym Lewis groused to his parents from St. Omer at the end of May.[7] "The streets are nasty and dirty and

2 Service records for other members of "B" Flight: Air Ministry Service Records, Robert Hughes Chamberlain, AIR 76/91/92; David Mary Tidmarsh, AIR 76/507/52; C.M.G. Chapman, AIR 76/83/46; Henry Cope Evans, AIR 76/153/136; Neville Philip Manfield, AIR 76/332/36. For Manfield's death at Boelcke's hands, see Trevor Henshaw, *Sky Their Battlefield II* (London: Fetubi Books, 2014), 51.

3 The date of McKay's arrival in France is recorded in Logbook, "Reference." He records no flight in his logbook that day.

4 Number of pilots in France: LAC, Air Ministry (UK) Fonds, MG 40 D1, RFC Work Summary and Headquarters, June 22, 1916, AIR 1/762/204/4/164–170. The precise number of pilots according to the report dated the day after McKay's arrival was 398, of which 359 were flying with service squadrons. Number of squadrons in France: LAC, Air Ministry (UK) Fonds, MG 40 D1, AIR 1/1211/204/5/2625, Order of Battle, RFC on Somme.

5 Logbook, "Reference." See also NA (UK) Air Ministry, AHB, AIR 1/1723/204/125/18, 2nd Air Depot Weekly Field Returns, June 30, 1916.

6 On the 1st and 2nd ADs, see the official history: H.A. Jones, *The War in the Air* (London: Hamish Hamilton, 1928), 2: 188–89.

7 Gwilym Lewis, "Letter, 31 May 1916," in *Wings Over the Somme, 1916–1918*, 2nd edition, ed. Chaz Bowyer (Wrexham: Bridge Book, 1994), 35.

the people have a nasty habit of throwing all their refuse out into the streets to be taken away." His brother, Edmund, who would serve with McKay in 24 Squadron, complained about his own purgatory in the 2nd AD later that summer. "It is a miserable existence in many ways as we may move at any moment and yet may remain here weeks ... we have absolutely nothing to do and lead a most miserable life."[8] There were minor consolations to be had: the usual bevy of coffee, cards, tobacco, and drinking; visits to nearby squadrons; friendships to be made or renewed in the small fraternity of pilots; and tea with the nurses in the military hospitals. Those so inclined could also partake of the services offered by France's peculiar institution—the legal brothel. Among the "entirely new experiences," Arthur Gould Lee recollected these from his own first day in St. Omer a year later:

> long queues of British and Imperial troops waiting impatiently outside the licensed brothels: or the more refined officers' place, with a waiting room with out-of-date copies of *La Vie Parisienne*, right in the shadow of the Cathedral, which, as it was Sunday, was packed to the doors.[9]

But the days spent in the reserve pool mostly involved waiting, and compounding pilots' misery was the full realization of what they were waiting for. In mid-1916, there were fewer than 60 DH 2 pilots in France, and McKay could not expect a posting until one of them had to be replaced. Lee, in similar circumstances a year later, reflected in his diary, "It's an odd feeling, waiting. Somewhere, out in the squadrons, is a pilot who, today, tomorrow, will be shot down, killed, wounded, or taken prisoner, and into his place, maybe into his machine, I shall move."[10] McKay did manage to break the tedium by getting some flying in, ferrying BE 2Cs between the air depots and once to No. 8 Squadron on the Ypres salient. His inaugural flight in France was inauspicious. On June 25, in reasonably good weather, he managed to get lost on the one-hour, due-south hop between St. Omer and Candas.[11] He landed to get directions—feeling grateful, perhaps, for the "B" he had earned in French—and got underway again.[12]

The day before, to the east, the Royal Artillery commenced an immense, earth-rending artillery bombardment in preparation for the imminent offensive.

8  Edmund Lewis, "Letter, 29 September 1916," in Gwilym Lewis, *Wings Over the Somme*, 188–89. Edmund Lewis's letters appear in the 2nd edition of the work only.

9  Arthur Gould Lee, *Open Cockpit: A Pilot of the Royal Flying Corps* (London: Jarrolds, 1969), 95.

10  Arthur Gould Lee, Diary Entry, May 21, 1917, in *No Parachute: A Fighter Pilot in World War I*, by Arthur Gould Lee (London: Jarrolds, 1968), 8.

11  McKay seems to have remained at Candas until being posted to 24 Squadron on July 3, 1916. NA (UK), AHB, AIR 1–1723–204–125–18, 2 Air Depot Weekly Field Returns, June 30, 1916.

12  Logbook, June 25, 27, and 29, 1916.

Over the next week, the gunners fired over a million and a half shells, a hurricane of metal and high explosive intended to pulverize the German defences prior to the assault.

The Somme offensive had its genesis in December 1915, Allied leaders had agreed to launch coordinated offensives the following year, a succession of blows intended to bleed the Germans white.[13] After protracted and at times acrimonious discussion, BEF commander General Sir Douglas Haig and France's Marshall Joseph Joffre settled on a joint assault in which their armies would meet astride the upper reaches of the Somme River. But in February, the Germans unexpectedly struck first, launching a large-scale offensive of their own near the French town of Verdun. Drawn into an immense attritional battle he had not foreseen, Joffre was forced to reduce his initial commitment to the Somme offensive.[14] Now, the BEF's Fourth Army would deliver the opening blow, supported on its right by the French Sixth and on its left by a diversionary attack by the British Third. Air support for Fourth Army was provided by the RFC's IV Brigade, commanded by Brigadier General Edward "Splash" Ashmore. At the beginning of the battle, IV Brigade comprised six aeroplane squadrons with a nominal strength of 18 machines each and one squadron of tethered observation balloons. These in turn were organized into two wings. Third (Corps) Wing, consisting of No. 1 Kite Balloon Squadron and No. 3, 4, 9, and 15 squadrons (operating Morane "Parasols" and BE 2s), provided the Fourth Army's corps formations with photographic reconnaissance, artillery spotting, light bombing, and contact patrols.[15] Fourteenth (Army) Wing, flying from an aerodrome adjacent the tiny village of Bertangles, just north of Amiens, consisted of No. 22 and 24 squadrons, tasked with providing an airborne screen for the Fourth Army as a whole. Though the FE 2BS of 22 Squadron were intended for hybrid duties—aerial patrol, reconnaissance, and bombing as required—the DH 2s of 24 Squadron had one mission only: to

---

13  There is an enormous literature on the Battle of the Somme, though much of it inordinately focused on the disaster the British suffered the first day rather than on the many staged battles in the months that followed. That the battle was fought almost equally and with notable successes by the French has been often forgotten in English-language literature. For a balanced but ultimately negative assessment of British leadership, see Robin Prior and Trevor Wilson, *The Somme* (New Haven, CT: Yale University Press, 2005). Peter Liddle is less critical in *The 1916 Battle of the Somme: A Reappraisal* (London: L. Cooper, 1992), as is William Philpott in *Three Armies on the Somme* (New York: Alfred A. Knopf, 2010), a work that gives full consideration to the French and German armies in the great battle.

14  On Verdun, see Paul Jankowski, *Verdun: The Longest Battle of the Great War* (Oxford: Oxford University Press, 2013).

15  Contact patrols involved communicating the position of advancing infantry to headquarters, no easy feat given the crude wireless radio technology of the time. Obsolete by 1916, the Morane-Saulnier L, called the "Parasol" in the RFC, was a one- or two-seat monoplane used as a fighter and for reconnaissance.

establish air supremacy over the battle zone. In addition, RFC headquarters retained four squadrons of its own, designated Ninth (HQ) Wing, available for strategic reconnaissance and long-range bombing.[16] Impressive though they might
seem, these dispositions amounted to just 109 machines in direct support of the
Fourth Army, with an additional 58 held at RFC headquarters. Arrayed against
these, the Imperial German Flying corps units attached to the German 2nd Army
fielded about 129 machines, the majority of them two-seaters, and none that were
a one-on-one match for either the DH or FE at the beginning of the summer.[17]
The Germans were also forced to contend with roughly equal numbers of French
machines, which at intervals cooperated with their British opposite numbers to
lay down line patrols on their respective fronts.[18]

By the beginning of the battle, the corps machines of Third Wing had photo-
graphed the entirety of the German defensive system. Heavy rain and low cloud in
the last week before the attack, however, hamstrung RFC operations. When they
did get up, pilots were awestruck by the scene of devastation. The artillery had
transformed the landscape and reduced the towns that dotted the front to brick
and concrete nubs. As Cecil Lewis, flying with No. 3 Squadron, recalled,

> We went out in the afternoon. Clouds forced us down to two thousand
> feet. A terrific bombardment was in progress. The enemy lines, as far as
> we could see, were under a white drifting cloud of bursting high explosive.
> The shell-bursts were continuous, not only on the lines themselves, but on
> the support trenches and communications behind ... as the shells passed,
> above or below us, the wind eddies made by their motion flung the ma-
> chine up and down, as if in a gale.[19]

The Allied offensive on the Somme began on July 1. Along a 25-mile front west of
the medieval city of Amiens, over a hundred battalions of the Fourth Army hurled
themselves across no-man's land, supported on their flanks by elements of the
British Third and, to the south of the river Somme, the French Sixth. The week-
long bombardment had left the ground cratered like the surface of the moon, but
given the width of the front, the actual concentration of fire had been considerably less than in some of the BEF's earlier engagements.[20] All along the front,

---

16 Jones, *The War in the Air*, 2: 196–99. At the beginning of July, Ninth (HQ) Wing comprised No. 21,
   27, and 60 squadrons, as well as two flights of No. 70 Squadron.
17 NA (UK), AHB, AIR 1–1588–204–82–71, 4th Brigade RFC Operations Orders, July 3, 1916.
18 Jones, *The War in the Air*, 2: 200.
19 Cecil Lewis, *Sagittarius Rising* (London: Peter Davies, 1944), 72.
20 Prior and Wilson, *The Somme*, 115–18.

FIGURE 2.1:   DH 2. *Called the DH "scout" by pilots, the De Havilland 2 formed the backbone of the RFC's fighter strength in 1916. A pusher with the engine to the rear of the pilot, the DH 2 offered an unobstructed field of fire but was lightly armed and plagued with engine problems. By autumn 1916, it was outclassed by faster, more heavily armed German machines. (Courtesy Barrington Gray.)*

advancing infantry met uncut barbed wire and intact German defences. There were local successes, particularly by French units south of the river; but north of the Albert-Bapaume road, in particular, whole battalions were eviscerated by machine-gun and artillery fire, dying by their thousands in a forlorn effort to press forward.[21] High above, on the first clear day in over a week, the RFC struggled to maintain communication between the leading edge of the assault and higher headquarters. Whole squadrons had trained in air-ground cooperation for weeks; now, in the chaos and confusion of the day, the system more often than not broke down. "From our point of view an entire failure," a disappointed Cecil Lewis wrote in his logbook.[22] He was referring to his squadron's contact patrols, but more than a few of his contemporaries and subsequent historians reached the same conclusion about the day, and indeed about the Battle of the Somme as a whole.

McKay spent July 1 ensconced in the pilot pool at Candas, 20 miles behind the front.[23] Everyone knew the offensive had begun. No doubt the day was rife

21  See Martin Middlebrook, *The First Day on the Somme* (London: Allen Lane, 1971).
22  Lewis, *Sagittarius Rising*, 78.
23  Logbook, June 27, 1916, and July 3, 1916.

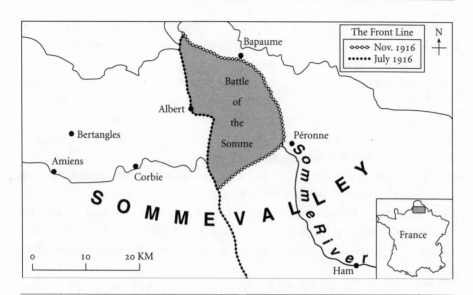

MAP 2.1  The Battle of the Somme

with rumour and the rumble of distant artillery. He certainly would have heard and felt the cacophonous eruption of at least some of the 19 British mines, packed with explosives, whose immense detonations near the German front lines marked the beginning of the infantry's assault. The detonation at La Bissell hurled earth nearly a mile into the air, imperilling nearby pilots.[24] Adding to the conflagration at the front were batteries of anti-aircraft guns capable of firing explosive shells to high altitudes. These pounded away incessantly at hostile aircraft and sometimes mistakenly at their own. RFC pilots called the explosive barrage "Archie," a term supposedly coined in 1914 by one Captain "Biffy" Borton. The story goes that Borton, showcasing the famous pluck and abandon of the RFC's pioneers, would sing out the refrain of the popular song, "Archibald, Certainly Not!" while dodging air bursts.[25] Archie was highly inaccurate but in its sheer intensity could be terrifying and sometimes deadly. Slow moving artillery spotters and reconnaissance machines, flying plodding orbits over the front, suffered the worst, but even scout pilots learned not to take it lightly.[26] It

---

24  Lewis, *Sagittarius Rising*, 77.

25  Barker, *A Brief History*, 48.

26  According to Henshaw (*The Sky Their Battlefield II*, 349), 21 per cent of casualties in artillery cooperation flights were the result of anti-aircraft gunnery (AA) and a further 15 per cent resulted from other ground fire. By comparison, AA accounted for less than 10 per cent of casualties on scout patrols.

forced them to fly at progressively higher altitudes, where they coped instead with frigid temperatures and low air pressure that dulled the senses and inflicted punishing headaches. Around 9:30 in the morning of July 3, a DH 2 piloted by Lt. Douglas Gray of No. 24 Squadron's "B" Flight was hit by anti-aircraft fire just north of the village of Puisieux, behind German lines. Gray's machine turned over and spun out of control from 11,000 feet.[27] His body was never recovered.[28] It was Hugh Trenchard's unyielding policy that fallen pilots were to be replaced without delay, not just for the sake of maintaining a squadron's strength but for the sake of its morale. "No empty chairs at breakfast," he insisted. "If as an ordinary pilot you see no vacant places around you, the tendency is to brood less on the fate of friends who have gone for ever. Instead your mind is taken up with buying drinks for the newcomers and making them feel at home."[29] The call went out to the pilot pool: Eddie McKay would fill Douglas Gray's empty chair in No. 24 Squadron.

Three squadrons in France flew DH 2s, but 24 Squadron was the prize, the most prestigious posting a pilot could hope for. Its commanding officer, Major Lanoe Hawker, was just 25 years old but already a legend in the RFC. A pioneer of military aviation, Hawker was Britain's first ace, and only the third pilot to have been awarded the Victoria Cross. When 24 had arrived in France in February, it had been the first squadron in the RFC equipped entirely with scouts. Stolid performers though they were, the DH 2s outclassed the best German machines at the beginning of the summer. In late May, while awaiting assignment at St. Omer, Gwilym Lewis had paid a visit to 24's aerodrome at Bertangles. "They have gained the genuine article," he reported in a letter to his parents, "supremacy of the air. They simply cannot find any Huns. If a Hun sees a De Hav he runs for his life."[30]

Sometime in the afternoon of the 3rd, McKay departed the air depot at Candas in a newly assembled DH 2. It was a fine summer day, warm with intermittent clouds, ideal weather for the leisurely flight at 3,000 feet to Bertangles,

27  There were two witnesses from 24 Squadron whose accounts are recorded in the squadron record book (see NA, Air Ministry, AHB, AIR 1/169/15/160/6, 24 Squadron RFC, Squadron Record Book, vol. 1, July 3, 1916). No. 24 Squadron's record books are in 12 volumes and are hereafter referred to as 24 Squadron Record Book, volume number, date. Note that the British Army did not use the 24-hour clock until 1918.

28  Gray's name is engraved on the Commonwealth War Graves Commission's Arras Flying Services Memorial, which commemorates missing pilots of the First World War. See CWGC website at www.cwgc.org.

29  Andrew Boyle, Trenchard: Man of Vision (London: Collins, 1962), 190.

30  Gwilym Lewis, "Letter, 31 May 1916," in Lewis, Wings Over the Somme, 33.

though his machine's badly vibrating engine might have spoiled an otherwise pleasant 15-minute hop.[31] A tiny village of about 200, Bertangles was situated 18 miles west of the front and just north of the medieval city of Amiens. Before the war, the villagers and local farmers had probably seldom heard a word of English spoken and never seen an aeroplane at all. Now their tiny hamlet was headquarters for both the 3rd and 14th air wings and the site of one of the RFC's most important aerodromes.[32] As McKay approached the southern end of the heavily wooded Bois de Bertangles, against which the village itself was nestled, the stately eighteenth-century chateau and its expansive grounds would have come into view. Just beyond that, surrounded by farms, he would have spotted the aerodrome itself, with its huts, hangars, and aeroplanes arrayed next to the grass strip. Between them, the aerodrome's two squadrons, No. 22 and 24 (inopportunely separated by a railway line), represented the greatest concentration of airborne might anywhere on the BEF's 60 miles of the Western Front.[33]

How did McKay's initiation into what Arthur Gould Lee called the "tight, self-contained cosmos of a squadron of fighter pilots" go?[34] As is often the case where the more personal details of his life are concerned, we have no record of McKay's experience on arrival. Later that year, while convalescing in hospital from a minor wound, his squadron-mate 2nd Lt. Robert Saundby mused about his own introduction to the squadron three weeks after McKay's. Using the pseudonym "Smith" and writing in the third person, Saundby wrote,

Smith was thinking of the squadron he was on his way to join—a scout squadron, the summit of his ambition. For months he had lived through this moment in anticipation, but now that it had arrived, he found himself unable to realize it. His mind was filled with a strange blend of curiosity

---

31  Weather from Gerald Gliddon, *Somme 1916: A Battlefield Companion* (Phoenix Mill: Sutton Publishing, 2006), 17–19. McKay's service record indicates that he was posted to 24 Squadron effective June 21, 1916, but his logbook and field returns from the 2nd AD make it clear that he spent nearly two weeks at 1st and 2nd AD before being posted to Bertangles. In all probability, the date of his posting was made retroactive to the date of his deployment to France on his service record. McKay ferried DH 2 7842 from Candas to Bertangles and flew the machine in action on a number of occasions. Logbook, July 3, 1916. For the movement of DH 2 7842, see NA (UK), Air Ministry, AHB, AIR 1/926/204/5914, Weekly Aircraft Returns: RFC Units in France.

32  Jones, *The War in the Air*, 2: 459.

33  On 22 Squadron, see W.F.J. Harvey, *'Pi' in the Sky: History of No. 22 Squadron, Royal Flying Corps and R.A.F. in the War of 1914–1918* (Leicester: Colin Houston, 1971). On the Bertangles aerodrome (sometimes referred to as two aerodromes), see Mike O'Connor, *Airfields and Airmen: Somme* (Barnsley, UK: Pen and Sword, 2002), 69–72.

34  Lee, *Open Cockpit*, xvi.

and apprehension ... he saw the Squadron office and, suddenly, all confidence deserted him. He walked up to the office feeling nervous and self
conscious. The Recording Officer was there, very busy with maps and papers, and he tried diffidently to attract his attention. The Recording Officer
looked up. "Oh," he said. "You are Smith! Come along to the Mess and have
some tea. We can fill up the forms afterwards." And they walked together to
the Mess. Almost before Smith realized what was happening, he was being
introduced to the CO. He was surprised to see how young he looked and
how full of energy and enthusiasm.[35]

Each squadron had a distinctive character, but this remarkably informal initiation was probably typical of the early and mid-war RFC, whose officers conceived of themselves as peers in a unique and storied profession. Many of the
British officers McKay had encountered so far were exemplars of the gentleman
pilots of the prewar RFC, members of an Edwardian social elite, "cavalrymen
and fox-hunting country gentlemen," in the words of historian Edward Bujak.[36]
They were graduates of England's elite public schools, had studied at Oxford
and Cambridge, and some were landed gentry. McKay's commanding officer in
28 Squadron, had been Lord George Wellesley, the great-grandson of Arthur
Wellesley, first Duke of Wellington, who had defeated Napoleon at Waterloo.
Officers, and therefore gentlemen almost by definition, they believed that their
prowess derived from their character and their character from the trappings of
their social status. It was a notion Sir Walter Raleigh, author of the first volume
of the official history of the air services, declaimed upon in 1922. The prewar
RFC, he reflected,

had a body of youth fitted by temperament for the work of the air, and
educated, as if by design, to take risks with a light heart—the boys of the
Public Schools of England. As soon as the opportunity came they offered
themselves in thousands for work which can never be done well when it
is done without zest, and which calls for some of the highest qualities of
character—fearlessness, self-dependence, and swift decision.[37]

McKay's year of university was a rare distinction in prewar Canada, but the fact
remained that he was a farmer's son, a British officer by wartime necessity and

---

35  Royal Air Force Museum, RHMS Saundby Papers AC 72/12. My thanks to Alex Revell for bringing
    the source of this quotation to my attention.
36  Bujak, *Reckless Fellows*, 1.
37  Raleigh, *The War in the Air*, 1: 111.

only temporarily. He was not truly a gentleman, yet he had joined the RFC at a time when many of his superiors and squadron-mates were. But the exponential growth of the flying services and the recruitment of thousands of Canadians, Australians, New Zealanders, South Africans, and men of various nationalities and social ranks from within the British Isles could not help but destabilize the RFC's social exclusivity. Whatever reservations we might harbour about ranking "aces" and their "scores," it is noteworthy nonetheless that of Britain's ten leading aces at war's end, four were Canadian, two were Irish, one South African, one Australian, and two English, only one of whom, Albert Ball, attended a public school, and even he was promoted from within the ranks. In their memoirs, surviving imperial pilots seldom recounted resistance to their *temporary* inclusion in the fraternity of officer gentlemen, even if they were regarded as a somewhat rough and rowdy sort. Canadians alone probably accounted for one RAF pilot in four by war's end. McKay was among the early Canadians to serve in the RFC, but when he arrived at Bertangles, he found that there were already three others in 24 Squadron. Two were former students of the University of Toronto: Arthur Gerald Knight, a graduate of the Curtis School of Aviation, and Harry Wood, who would become McKay's closest friend in the RFC. The other, with McKay in "B" Flight, was the 36-year-old, 6'3" Boer War veteran Henry Cope Evans of Alberta, a former fruit farmer, range rider, and sergeant in the Alberta Dragoons.[38]

Expansion may have undermined their prewar identity, but the pilots of the British flying services remained an elite of sorts, comparatively few in number, masters of the technological wonder of their age, and seeking to model themselves on the RFC's "aristocratic fox-hunting, cavalry officer originals" as Bujak puts it.[39] A portrait photograph of McKay taken sometime in the summer of 1916 illustrates the point. In it, he wears the distinctive "maternity" jacket of the RFC and sports the "wings" of a pilot, but the other accoutrements are those of a cavalry officer. The Sam Browne belt, tall riding breeches, swagger stick, and leather gloves, held in one hand, capture the dash and élan of a bygone age, kept alive in the form of the modern aviator.

---

38 Air Ministry Service Records, Arthur Gerald Knight, AIR 76/279/155; Harry Alison Wood, AIR 76/558/124; Henry Cope Evans, 76/153/136. On Evans, see also LAC RG 150, CEF Attestation Papers, accession 1992–93/166, box 2945–41 and "Casualties," *Flight*, June 7, 1917, 565, https://www.flightglobal.com/FlightPDFArchive/1917/1917-0565.PDF. Wood alone survived the war. He died in Montreal in 1959.

39 Bujak, *Reckless Fellows*, 6.

FIGURE 2.2: 2nd Lt. Alfred Edwin McKay, Royal Flying Corps. *McKay wears the distinctive "maternity" jacket and "wings" of an RFC pilot, but he also sports the accoutrements of a cavalry officer: breeches, swagger stick, and Sam Browne belt. Pilots were symbols of modernity but also captured the dash and élan of a bygone era. (Courtesy Eugene Kittmer.)*

With the Somme offensive barely two days old, McKay's own introduction to Hawker's squadron might have been considerably less casual than Saundby's. Non-stop patrol duties had stretched the squadron's resources to the limit, even with the addition of five pilots flying Bristol scouts and Morane

"Bullets" temporarily attached from Third Wing.[40] But if 24 was the squadron McKay wanted, McKay was precisely the pilot that Hawker needed. Trenchard estimated that newly deployed pilots usually required anywhere from ten days to four weeks of additional training before they were ready to cross the enemy line.[41] Normally, new arrivals would spend this time under the tutelage of the squadron commander or their flight leader, flying circuits near the aerodrome, fixing the bad habits they had picked up in training, learning the lay of the land, and only gradually advancing to offensive patrols.[42] Hawker had no time for that now. Since the opening of the offensive, 24 had been flying sweeps along the entirety of the Fourth Army's front and into the French Sixth Army's zone of operations, a 20-mile line stretching from Gommecourt in the north to as far south as Péronne.[43] Between them, the squadron's pilots had flown more than a hundred patrols in the two days since the offensive began. Hawker himself had defied Trenchard's prohibition on squadron.[44] With about 50 hours under his belt, McKay arrived ready to fly. Furthermore, he had just over eight hours on DH 2s, so at least he knew one end of the machine from the other, and he brought with him the positive appraisal written by Loraine, whom Hawker surely knew.[45]

Like all RFC service squadrons in mid-1916, 24's machines were organized into three flights of six each. McKay assumed Gray's former place in the roster of "B" Flight, under the command of Captain Robin Hughes Chamberlain, one of the squadron's originals. Severe thunderstorms grounded most of the RFC the day after his arrival. On July 5, he took his first flight with 24, a 20-minute engine test on the DH 2 he had arrived in. He landed and wrote his first entry in the squadron record book: "Misty @4500. Engine and machine good but vibrating considerably." Then he signed his full name, "A.E. McKay," before squeezing in, apparently as an afterthought, the prefix "Lt."[46] There would be much to get used to, not least of which was the sometimes reckless tomfoolery the pilots got up

40 Jones, *The War in the Air*, 2: 217. The Bristol scout was a prewar, single-seat biplane, originally intended for civilian use, that had been pressed into RFC service. The Morane-Saulnier N was a French-built monoplane, small numbers of which served with the RFC, where it was nicknamed the "Bullet." Both were obsolete by mid-1916.
41 LAC, Air Ministry (UK), MG 40, vol. 35, AIR 2/6/87/4469, Trenchard to War Office, January 20, 1916.
42 Winter, *The First of the Few*, 68.
43 Jones, *The War in the Air*, 2: 217.
44 24 Squadron Record Book, vol. 1, July 1–3, 1916.
45 No. 40 Squadron, Sixth Wing, assessment of A.E. McKay by Major R. Loraine, June 19, 1916. Author's collection via Eugene Kittmer.
46 24 Squadron Record Book, vol. 1, July 6, 1916.

to. McKay's logbook indicates that on July 6 he shot up the "petty bosch." This may be a reference to the "petite boche," a nickname for a target Hawker rigged up on the aerodrome for Lewis gun practice, but it might also refer to one of the squadron's favourite games: staging mock attacks on neighbouring 22 Squadron.[47] Hawker's brother, Tyrell, an artillery officer with a nearby battery, later explained:

> On return to the aerodrome pilots sometimes "shot up" the "Boche" belonging to the other squadron; this was considered an outrage calling for immediate reprisals in the form of an air counter-attack, hangar-zooming, or a land expedition to secure hostages for future good behaviour. The scraps were many and good-natured, the weapons varied and ingenious, and battles often quite well organized. Armoured cars (cane armchairs), bombs (tennis balls), flammenwerfer (soda syphons), chemical warfare (a large size Flit fly-spray) ... these with raids and counter-raids on No. 22 Squadron, became the chief squadron recreation.[48]

With far too few scouts to provide close escort for reconnaissance machines, Trenchard mandated a controversial policy of employing his scouts in "relentless and incessant" offensive patrolling, aimed at keeping the Germans at bay through constant pressure near their own aerodromes.[49] This policy not only subjected RFC scouts to Archie as they crossed the lines but gave the Germans the significant tactical advantage of flying near their own airfields. German pilots, wounded or flying damaged machines, simply had a greater chance of survival than British pilots, who had to fly further and against the prevailing winds. Trenchard was severely criticized for maintaining this policy even when RFC scouts lost their technical edge against their German counterparts in late 1916 and early 1917.[50]

---

47  Logbook, July 5, 1916.
48  Tyrell Hawker, *Hawker, VC: The Biography of the Late Major Lance George Hawker, VC, DSO, Royal Engineers and Royal Flying Corps* (London: Mitre Press, 1965), 157. This, the only biography of Hawker, is a hagiography written by his brother. It is useful nonetheless as a source of primary material.
49  Quoted in Tami Davis Biddle, *Rhetoric and Reality in Air Warfare: The Evolution of British and American Ideas about Strategic Bombing, 1914–1945* (Princeton, NJ: Princeton University Press, 2002), 27.
50  The controversy began with a parliamentary inquiry during the war itself and has continued. Arthur Gould Lee, later air marshal, wrote a highly critical assessment of the offensive policy in *No Parachute*, 224–25, as did Sir Frederick Sykes, who succeeded Trenchard as chief of the Air Staff, in his autobiography *From Many Angles* (London: George G. Harrap, 1942), 220–21. H.A. Jones defended the policy in the official history.

FIGURE 2.3: Painting of Bertangles. *Few good photographs of the Bertangles aerodrome exist. This contemporary watercolour, "The Last Home" by McKay's squadron-mate 2nd Lt. (later Air Marshal) Robert Saundby, is therefore a primary source of great value. Bertangles was the most important RFC aerodrome on the Western Front. (Courtesy Dr. Peter Saundby.)*

Whether an alternative approach would have yielded better results is anyone's guess and a matter for the dubious exercise of counterfactual speculation. What can be said for certain is that Trenchard, with too much sky and too few scouts to patrol it, had few good options. It has been argued that his operational vision was similar to Douglas Haig's for the army as a whole: to wear the enemy down through constant offensive.[51] Trenchard's goal was not aerial bloodletting for its own sake, however: it was to keep German fighters at bay so that his observation and artillery spotting machines could do their crucial work unmolested. In this the policy succeeded for most of the first two months of the Somme offensive. Indeed, during the first phase of the offensive, which ended around July 17 with elements of the bloodied Fourth Army having established themselves on the Bazentin Ridge, just three of Third Wing's machines were lost to enemy air action.[52] By contrast, German reconnaissance machines were almost completely unable to

51  Biddle, *Rhetoric and Reality in Air Warfare*, 27.
52  Henshaw, *The Sky Their Battlefield II*, 44.

reconnoitre over British lines. The Squadron record book for 24 Squadron reveals that, on many days, the greatest difficulty the pilots had, apart from engine trouble, was finding German pilots willing to fight.

The majority of 24 Squadron's offensive patrols in 1916 were flown inside a roughly 30-square-mile triangle whose base ran 8 miles southeast from Pozières on the Albert-Bapaume road to Bouchavesnes-Bergen on the edge of the French flying services' patrol area, and whose apex was Bapaume itself, about 8 miles northwest of Pozières and 25 from Bertangles.[53] On the afternoon of July 6, only three days after arriving, McKay took his first patrol to the lines, flying with Tidmarsh—whom he lost sight of—up the Albert-Bapaume road.[54] Just two days later, he flew his first offensive patrol, with Hughes Chamberlain leading and Manfield alongside.[55] In his first two weeks with 24 Squadron, he weathered almost the full panoply of a scout pilot's flying experiences: defensive patrol, offensive escort, ferrying new machines, being Archied over the line, and a forced landing in a field when his engine quit.[56] On July 20, he had his first combat in the air, and barely survived.

This important battle, considered a milestone in the history of aerial warfare, had its genesis in events that had occurred the week before. On July 14, German squadrons on the Somme began to receive large-scale reinforcements withdrawn from the Verdun sector. This prompted an immediate though ultimately failed attempt to break the RFC's supremacy over the front.[57] On July 19, there were a dozen combats on the Fourth Army's front, with 24 Squadron in the thick of heavy fighting.[58] The next day dawned very hazy, but a break in the weather in the evening brought large numbers of German machines out to fight. McKay and the other members of "B" Flight had spent much of the early evening playing poker, but with the haze diminished, Hawker ordered two flights up.[59] Just before 8 PM, Hughes Chamberlain, Evans, Chapman, and McKay alighted on an offensive patrol with fewer than two hours of daylight remaining. Near Flers, on the Albert-Bapaume road, they met a mixed formation of two-seaters and Fokker monoplanes, 11 strong in all. Hawker's standing order to the squadron, posted a month earlier, had consisted of two words: "attack everything."[60] So they did.

53  Wise, *Canadian Airmen*, 380.
54  24 Squadron Record Book, vol. 1, July 6, 1916. Logbook, July 6, 1916.
55  Logbook, July 10, 1916; 24 Squadron Record Book, vol. 2, July 10, 1916.
56  Logbook, July 8–19, 1916. The forced landing occurred on July 19.
57  Jones, *The War in the Air*, 2: 262.
58  NA (UK), Air Ministry, AHB, RFC Communiqués, AIR 1/2116/207/57, no. 44, July 20, 1916. Henceforth RFC Communiqué, Date or Number.
59  24 Squadron Record Book, vol. 2, July 20, 1916.
60  Hawker, *Hawker VC*, 182.

Hughes Chamberlain led the way, but McKay was far back, struggling with a dud engine again. "In this particular instance McKay had one plug missing," Hughes Chamberlain later remembered, "so he was well down in the formation, but he came along just the same."[61]

While the top formation engaged in a furious combat, dispersing the German machines in all directions and bringing at least one down, McKay fought his first battle in the air, "having fun down below on his own," as Chamberlain put it. Fun might not have been the word. An hour later, McKay wrote the following account in the squadron record book.

> Met 11 H.A.; 3 Type A, 3 Type F & 5 Rowlands East of Flers about 8:20. Had a dud engine & could only get to 8500 ft. A Rowland dived at me. I zoomed & gave him half a drum. I dived & I followed him, giving him the remainder of the drum. He went down steeply in a spin. I changed my drum & saw a Type F diving at me. I fired up at him but he passed over me & got on my tail. I dived steeply to 1000 ft with Type F following me, firing at me.[62]

His engine, already sputtering, was hit several times, and his wings and nacelle were shot through in a number of places.[63] It was a small miracle that McKay himself was not hit—the rear engine probably saved him—and equally fortunate that his main fuel tank was not holed, which would almost certainly have set the plane ablaze. This was the perpetual and primal fear. In Gould Lee's estimation, "[T]here were few flyers with any experience of air fighting who were not obsessed to some degree, though usually secretly, with the thought of being shot down in flames."[64] Some chose to jump rather than burn; others carried pistols to end the matter quickly if it came to that. And it may very well have ended, then and there, with Eddie McKay killed fewer than three weeks after his arrival, as it did for so many other inexperienced pilots. But then Chapman, above, "dove the rescue" (as Hawker described it in his report) and emptied an entire drum—the Lewis gun's distinctive 47- or 97-round, pan-shaped magazine—into the Fokker at close range. The German machine burst into flames and spun

61  Imperial War Museum, audio interview with Robin Hughes Chamberlain (1971), Barrington Gray, interviewer, item number 23153, reel 6.

62  24 Squadron Record Book, vol. 2, July 20, 1916. H.A. was short for "hostile aircraft."

63  The nacelle on the DH 2 refers to the part of the fuselage that held the pilot's cockpit, which jutted out from the front of the plane.

64  Lee, No Parachute, 223.

down into High Wood.[65] The DH 2 had poor rearward visibility, and McKay did not seem to have realized what happened. He finished his account in the squadron record book as follows:

> I turned and started to climb but HA had all gone east so I came home. Engine done in. Machine hit several places. Gun control on joystick unserviceable.[66]

In his frantic effort to escape his pursuer, McKay had driven so low to the ground that a friendly anti-aircraft battery reported seeing a De Havilland go down. "The de Havilland was Lt. McKay," Hawker reported. "But he managed to return low down though his engine was badly shot about."[67]

Hawker was jubilant. In a letter home, he enthused, "4 of my chickens took on 11 Huns and downed no less than 4 or 5 of them!!!"[68] His excitement was not misplaced. The four pilots had performed exceptionally well against a numerically superior force in the biggest aerial engagement yet. At least three German machines were down, and the others dispersed or damaged. Hawker composed a lengthy, two-page combat report, his longest by far while commanding 24. Lt. Col. Hoare, commanding 14th Wing, forwarded it to Trenchard, who dashed off a reply the following day.[69] "Well done No. 24 Squadron in fight last night. Keep it going. We have the Hun cold."[70] It was a significant battle—the first big "dogfight," and a copy of Hawker's report hung for decades in 24 Squadron's mess.[71] For his part, McKay recorded laconically in his logbook, "Scrap with 11 Huns east of Flers. My machine badly damaged by Fokker. Engine very bad. Shot down Roland 2 seater."[72]

So he survived his first combat—though it had been a close scrape indeed—and had brought down his first machine. That is how most pilots reckoned such things. If they kept score at all (and McKay did on his first tour), they usually

65  NA (UK), Air Ministry, AHB, AIR 1/1221/204/5/2634, Combat Reports: 24 Squadron, Combats in the Air, July 20, 1916. All Combats in the Air reports hereafter cited by squadron number, Combats in the Air, date.

66  24 Squadron Record Book, vol. 2, July 20, 1916.

67  24 Squadron, Combats in the Air, July 20, 1916. The report is preceded by a cover letter from Hoare to Trenchard at GHQ.

68  Leeds University, Liddle Collection, Liddle/WW1/Air/152: Hawker, Lanoe George (1890–1916), Letter: Hawker to his sister, July 22, 1916.

69  24 Squadron, Combats in the Air, July 20, 1916.

70  Leeds University, Liddle Collection, Liddle/WW1/Air/152: Hawker, Lanoe George (1890–1916), Trenchard to Hawker, via Captain Baring, 22/7/16.

71  Hawker, Hawker, VC, 195.

72  Logbook, July 20, 1916.

counted machines, not men killed. And what of their own mortality? In their memoirs, many pilots said that it was something they tried not to dwell upon, so paralyzing could the fear become. The physical and mental fatigue imposed by open-cockpit flying, often at high altitudes and freezing temperatures, could by itself wear a man down over time. Combat in the air was torturous for both body and mind. In particular, the hideous sight of men burning or falling—and sometimes suffering the worst of both—could sear itself into a pilot's psyche. "Nobody could stand the strain indefinitely," Cecil Lewis wrote, "ultimately it reduced you to a dithering state, near to imbecility."[73] This was perhaps going too far, as many pilots seem to have come through the war without suffering such extremities of psychological anguish. Some undeniably did suffer psychological breakdown, but at the opposite extreme were others who seem to have relished every moment of their experience. The official history of the medical services includes a lengthy discussion of the unique physical and psychological strain of high-altitude flying and combat in the air. RFC and medical authorities took these problems seriously, instituting a progressively more sophisticated and rigorous screening system for applicants to pilot training in late 1916. For pilots already flying but showing signs of strain, rest was the usually prescribed cure.[74] This could mean leave when circumstances permitted or, for pilots who had been at the front for several months, rotation into the home establishment as an instructor. Fortunately, days of rest were a routine part of the service pilot's experience. Squadron commanders received requests for patrols from their Wing HQ and chose pilots for duty based on a variety of factors—their state of fatigue was one. Except on days of the very highest levels of activity on the ground, 24's squadron record book indicates that Hawker typically kept one of his three flights in reserve. In memoirs and postwar interviews, some of 24's pilots described a gruelling routine of three or more patrols daily, but this schedule is not borne out by an examination of the record. Between bad weather, sickness, leave, and ordinary duty rotation, McKay flew an average of one day in three during his nine months with 24 Squadron. The squadron record book indicates that some of his squadron-mates flew more, but none exceptionally more. Facts such as these are too often neglected in occasionally sensationalist popular literature that assumes that nearly every pilot must always have trembled on the brink of psychological breakdown.[75]

---

73  Lewis, *Sagittarius Rising*, 50.
74  For a lengthy discussion of the medical services' roll in treating and screening pilots, see William Grant Macpherson, *Medical Services: Diseases of the War*, vol. 2 (London: HM Stationery Office, 1922), 161–241.
75  For example, Winter's *The First of the Few* and Mackersey's *No Empty Chairs*.

In their memoirs, pilots almost invariably reflected on the extraordinary contrasts that governed their lives. The disjuncture between their life-or-death patrols at high altitudes and frozen temperatures and the often exuberant and impetuous life on the ground could not have been greater. No. 45 Squadron's Norman Macmillan, who may have trained under McKay at the Central Flying School in March 1917, mused that "the aeroplane produced that most modern psychiatric study, the airman in the air. And the WWI airman in the air was often the Dr. Jekyll of a Mr. Hyde upon the ground."[76] Or perhaps it was the other way around. They were, after all, young men, liberated from home, parents, disapproving schoolmasters, and local vicars, and their choice of military vocation marked them as adventurous, even reckless spirits. At 23, McKay was slightly older than most of the others. Langan-Byrne, the squadron's top ace, was 21. Cowan, in A Flight, was 19. Even Hawker, who did not demur to giddy and even dangerous play, was just 25. At 36, Henry Evans, one of the oldest pilots in the RFC, must have seemed positively ancient to the rest of them. They had not, perhaps, the prolonged adolescence of some future generations, but many were away from parental authority for the first time. They possessed some privileges of rank, decent pay, and lax disciplinary standards by comparison to the rest of the army.

Years later, pilots often remember being moved to pity while overflying or visiting the trenches. On one patrol, Arthur Gould Lee recalled thinking, "Compared with the wretched millions locked in earthly combat, I and my companions are a winged aristocracy among warriors."[77] Driven by the need to liaise with gunners, recover downed enemy machines, or even out of pure curiosity, pilots visited the front line with some regularity. These occasions drew their own experiences into sharp relief compared with those of the men in the trenches. Of an army friend who complained about being stuck in England, McKay, who had just returned from the front, remarked in a letter home, "from what I have seen he is lucky."[78] Lee described a conversation he had with the officers of an artillery battery:

> We talked of the contrast between air and ground, and compared the life of RFC flyers doing highly lethal jobs two or three times a day but with a safe and comfortable home to go to, with the dreary round of the Poor Bloody Infantry—front line, support, reserve, rest in some cheerless village, then front line again, there to be shot at day and night by every kind of missile, with over-the-top massacres to break the monotony, while enduring mud, rats, lice, frost-bite, trench feet and the stench of rotting corpses.

76 Norman Macmillan, *Into the Blue* (New York: Arno Press, 1972), 99,
77 Lee, *Open Cockpit*, 58.
78 McKay's November 5 letter home, published in the *Londoner Advertiser*, November 22, 1916, 1, 3.

Lee told the commander of the battery that he was certain he could not endure such an existence; the commander replied that anything was better than plunging from the sky in flames.[79] What was inarguable was that the everyday conditions in which pilots lived were far better than those experienced by men in the trenches. "When we returned to the aerodrome the war was over," Lewis recalled. "We had a bed, a bath and mess with good food and peace until the next patrol. Though we always lived in the stretch or sag of nerves, we were never under bodily fatigue, never verminous or exposed to the long disgusting drudgery of trench warfare."[80] Bertangles aerodrome, with its huts carved into niches in the woods, was comfortable, though not luxurious. To McKay, who grew up on a farm in southwestern Ontario, where the temperatures in January could plunge to 20 below and six feet of snow might fall over a winter, the slight draft that Hawker complained about in letters home probably did not seem like much of an imposition. At the equivalent of about $6 Canadian per day, he was well paid, making roughly what his professors at Western had and six times what his brothers Sid and Garfield were earning in the infantry.[81] His chosen vocation was prestigious, even exotic. There were moments, to be sure, of sheer, petrifying terror, but when the day's flying was done or when the weather was dud, he and the others were virtually at liberty. Decades later, Cecil Lee recollected not with sadness but with actual fondness summer days spent swimming, "sitting casually in the baking summer sun, smoking, chatting, reading" of "riotous binges" in the mess, and evenings spent "around the piano while bellowing bawdy doggerel."[82]

Like most aerodromes, Bertangles had a piano, and we can imagine these nights of drinking and smoking and pounding out songs in the officer's mess, some popular, others confected for the war itself. The army had "Mademoiselle from Armentières," a bawdy soldiers' song about a prostitute who had seen better days. The RFC's equivalent was "The Young Aviator Lay Dying," sung to the tune of the "Dying Young Lancer," so similar to "My Bonnie Lies Over the Ocean" that they are often mistaken for the same song. As was the case with "Mademoiselle" innumerable and increasingly vulgar variations existed, but one went like this:

*The young aviator lay dying,*
*And as 'neath the wreckage he lay (he lay),*
*To mechanics who 'round him came sighing,*
*These last parting words he did say:*

79  Lee, *Open Cockpit*, 88.
80  Lewis, *Sagittarius Rising*, 101.
81  LAC, RG 24, vol. 4497, 55–1-1, Circular Letter to All Paymasters. Western professors' pay from ARCC, UWO, Braithwaite Papers AFC40 / 41, General Correspondence Series 1, 1914–1915, E–F.
82  Arthur Gould Lee, *Open Cockpit*, 5.

*"Take the cylinder out of my kidneys,*
*The connecting-rod out of my brain (my brain),*
*From the small of my back take the crank-shaft,*
*And assemble the engine again."*[83]

Songs such as these fortified the bonds of camaraderie; that they made light of a real thing may have helped pilots confront the fear of death, if only for a time.[84] And when these did not suffice, there was always the anesthetizing property of alcohol. Victories in the air, a salute to a fallen comrade, the award of a decoration to one yet living—there was always a reason for a good "drunk": birthdays, holidays, promotions, transfers of favourite squadron-mates, the arrival of newcomers in need of a proper initiation. In countless memoirs, pilots return to this subject again and again. Squadron binges could be riotous and frenetic, and frequently ran roughshod over distinctions of rank. In late 1916, one of 24's NCOs described the scene at Boxing Day in a letter home. In the sergeant's mess, he wrote,

> we were once against invaded by the officers (who seem to prefer our own evenings to those in their own mess) ... they turned the place upside down, broke plates and glasses and also the door off the hinges, fell through the floor, bulged the walls, went outside for a walk and came back covered in mud ... some of the officers and two of the sergeants got hopelessly drunk, one officer got his eye kicked by a sergeant whilst dancing.[85]

It might be ill-advised to exaggerate the extent of pilots' drinking and carousing (although it bears repeating that many dwelled upon it their memoirs); after all, they had to fly, and were not suicidal.[86] But if Harry Wood's subsequent recollections were correct, on the night of July 20, after B Flight returned and filed its reports, the pilots hopped in the squadron lorries and took off for Amiens.[87] They had won a great victory, and, besides, "A" Flight's Captain Andrews had turned 20 that day.[88]

---

83  This version is compiled from various renditions but is closest to the one quoted in Alan Bott, *Cavalry of the Clouds* (New York: Doubleday, 1917), 191.
84  I have been influenced by Tim Cook, "Fighting Words: Canadian Solders' Slang and Swearing in the Great War," *War in History* 20, no. 3 (July 2013): 323–44.
85  Imperial War Museum, Private Papers of H.H. Heale, Document 5660.
86  Lewis, *Sagittarius Rising*, 56.
87  Stewart K. Taylor, Letter to the author, April 2007. Taylor based this assertion on correspondence and/or interviews he conducted with Wood in 1958.
88  Oliver's Air Ministry service record is lost. His date of birth is from an interview: "Major John Andrews," in Anna Malinovska and Mauriel Joslyn, eds., *Voices in Flight: Conversations with Air Veterans of the Great War* (Barnsley, UK: Pen and Sword, 2006), 192.

Situated five miles south of Bertangles, the medieval city offered pilots night-time distractions and pleasant diversions on bad-weather days. The capital of the Somme *département* and straddling the river itself, Amiens was a key logistical hub sustaining the BEF throughout 1916. The city's dominating feature was its immense thirteenth-century cathedral, Notre-Dame d'Amiens, bigger even than its counterpart in Paris. Soaring to nearly 400 feet, the cathedral's spire was visible for miles in most types of flying weather, an important landmark for pilots returning to Bertangles from the front.[89] Siegfried Sassoon recounted a rainy evening spent in solitary reflection outside the cathedral. "I felt last night (after a bottle of decent wine) that I would gladly die to guard Amiens Cathedral from destruction," he wrote, though he admitted such thoughts were harder to come by in the light of daytime sobriety.[90] As a precaution against bombing raids or long-range artillery, church authorities had ordered the stained glass removed and placed in storage, along with the holy relics—including the purported head of St. John the Baptist—for the duration of the war. Thousands of sandbags were now stacked like pyramids around the piers of the stupendous, vaulted nave and at the west portal.[91]

Amiens offered temptations earthly as well as sublime, and these were probably the ones that more fully occupied the attention of young officers. The hotels were comfortable, the restaurants good, the shops decently stocked, and there were the additional diversions of motion pictures, live theatre, and legal brothels.[92] The only rule, as Cecil Lewis remembered it, was that "when you went on a 'blind' to Amiens, talk about the job was taboo. You had come in specifically to forget it."[93] In an early postwar memoir, McKay's squadron-mate Selden Long recalled that 24's pilots regularly made their way in to eat in the city's restaurants. One of these would certainly have been the highly regarded Grands Salons Godbert, which had weathered the pall of wartime austerity with alacrity. Long remembered 24's pilots consuming "large quantities of oysters ... without any ill effects."[94] This may not have been entirely true: in November, McKay, renowned at Western for his great appetite despite his small frame, confessed in a letter home, "We don't get much exercise out here and I am getting fat as a hog."[95] There was also the risk of

89  Lewis describes using the cathedral as a landmark, and getting lost nonetheless. Lewis, *Sagittarius Rising*, 47.
90  Siegfried Sassoon, *Diaries 1915–1918*, edited by Rupert Hart-Davis (London: Faber and Faber, 1983), 145–46.
91  These precautions proved prescient. In 1918, the cathedral sustained several direct hits during the Battle of Amiens.
92  W.M. Fry, *Air of Battle* (London: William Kimber, 1974), 64.
93  Lewis, *Sagittarius Rising*, 46.
94  Selden Long, *In the Blue* (London: John Lane, 1920), 93.
95  Letter published in the *London Advertiser*, November 22, 1916, 1.

ill effects from the wine and spirits that flowed so freely in France, and especially in restaurants frequented by officers. Sassoon wrote hazily of a night at Godbert's, drinking Veuve Clicquot with brother officers, as well as three glasses of red wine, two John Collinses, an Oyster cocktail, a sherry and bitters, a "Bénédictine," and a concoction he dubbed a "Japanese ditto."[96] Willie Fry and some pilots of No. 11 Squadron found themselves in a jam at the end of one night in the restaurant. Their driver was dead drunk, but none of the pilots knew how to drive an automobile. They sought the advice of a nearby senior officer, waiting for his own driver outside the restaurant. This turned out to be none other than Lanoe Hawker. With his major's rank and Victoria Cross, Hawker was, Fry remembered, a profoundly imposing figure, "the image of the correct pre-war Regular RE officer." Pushed forward by the others, Fry asked what they should do. Hawker's aloof reply was that one of them should learn to drive. One of them did, and they made it back to their own aerodrome, 30 miles distant, just in time for dawn patrol.[97]

To McKay and many other Canadians, the permissiveness of French culture toward imbibing must have been shocking. Like their counterparts in the United States, influential temperance and prohibition forces in Canada had long argued that alcohol was one of the root causes of social and familial decay. The outbreak of war had afforded the temperance movement a new and persuasive argument— that drunkenness undermined the entire war effort. In April 1916, the month after McKay arrived in England, Ontario went dry with the passage of the Ontario Temperance Act, prohibition legislation that stayed in effect for 11 years.[98] The pastors at McKay's churches and the president of Western had been staunch temperance advocates, but there is no way of knowing what position McKay himself took. He might have been among the rare abstainers from both alcohol and tobacco. One thing is certain: France offered young officers temptations that may have been too great for some of them to resist, even if they had been inclined to try. Nor were these temptations limited to alcohol. At the end of July, McKay was admitted to the New Zealand Hospital in Amiens, with a condition "not yet diagnosed" (but described as "slight"), and subsequently evacuated to No. 39 General Hospital at Le Havre on the Channel coast.[99] Admission and discharge papers for

---

96  "At Amiens," Sassoon Journal, February 15 to June 2, 1917 (MS Add.9852/1/9), 70, https://cudl.lib.cam.ac.uk/view/MS-ADD-09852-00001-00009/70. Digitized version available online from the University of Cambridge Digital Library.

97  Fry, *Air of Battle*, 64–65.

98  On prohibition in Canada, see Craig Heron, *Booze: A Distilled History* (Toronto: Between the Lines, 2003).

99  RAF Museum, Casualty Card Record Series: McKay, A.E., Object ID 0C0208801. Available online at www.rafmuseumstoryvault.org.uk (hereafter referred to as McKay, Casualty Card). Note that daily routine orders for 14 Wing, which might add details to the circumstances of McKay's hospitalization, are lost for July and most of August 1916.

the hospital no longer exist (millions of medical records were subsequently discarded), but based on interviews he conducted with Harry Wood, historian Stewart Taylor concluded that during that raucous night in Amiens, McKay contracted a venereal disease.[100] Hundreds of thousands of Allied soldiers did. At war's end, there were 20 hospitals in the UK alone dedicated solely to the treatment of VD. Canadians at home would have been appalled to know that, in all, 16 per cent of enlisted men in the CEF contracted VD, a rate *six* times higher than the average in the BEF.[101] On leave, the British official history remarked, "The average British soldier proceeded to his home in some village or small country town; the average soldier of the Dominion forces found his way to London," or indeed Paris, where all manner of temptation lurked.[102] As Cecil Lewis, reflecting on his younger self, later wrote, "To him, Paris was not the beautiful city of elegance and gaiety, of palaces, foundations, and boulevards where you sat under chestnuts ... no, Paris in 1916 to him was a sort of gigantic brothel."[103]

Rates for venereal disease among RFC pilots do not exist, but the combination of good pay, an unusual quantity of free time, and the unhappiness and, indeed, the opportunity presented by years of separation from wives and sweethearts might have contributed to higher rates among Canadian pilots. They were, after all, already living in the most morally transgressive world imaginable, where daily they ascended thousands of feet into the air to inflict horrible deaths on other young men like themselves. McKay had been in France for only a month, and he had already killed a man. There were others yet to come. Next to that, the moral opprobrium of puritans and prohibitionists back home must have seemed a trifling matter. McKay was discharged from the hospital around mid-August.[104] He was fortunate not to have been posted back to the pilot pool, which was often the fate of flying officers who were wounded or placed on the sick list. Instead, he returned to Bertangles, probably to endure a good ribbing from his squadron-mates and a dressing down from Hawker. During his absence, the squadron had scored several victories and fortunately no combat fatalities of its own, although Hughes Chamberlain was wounded the day McKay returned.

These were heady days for the RFC, whose squadrons were in a position of aerial supremacy unrivalled even in the closing weeks of the war. That hard-earned

---

100  Stewart K. Taylor, Letter to the author, April 2007. The disease was probably gonorrhoea.
101  Tim Cook, *Shock Troops: Canadians Fighting the Great War 1917–1918* (Toronto: Penguin, 2008), 176.
102  Macpherson, *Medical Services: Diseases of the War*, 2: 120.
103  Lewis, *Sagittarius Rising*, 56.
104  Precise dates are difficult to determine. McKay's casualty card states he was discharged to St. Omer on August 15. Daily routine orders for 14 Wing indicate he was taken back on strength of 24 Squadron on August 14. McKay, Casualty Card; NA, UK, AHB, AIR 1–1572–204–80–32, 14 Wing Daily Routine Orders, August 19, 1916.

supremacy was about to be challenged and then lost. Late August saw the beleaguered German squadrons on the Somme front further reinforced and reorganized to include new Jagdstaffels ("hunting squadrons") equipped with formidable
new scouts whose sudden presence began to be noted in RFC Communiqués late
in the month. Foremost among these were the Albatros DI, a fast biplane and,
in September, the improved Albatros D2, which mounted twin forward machine
guns.[105] The driving force behind the organization of the Jagdstaffels (commonly
abbreviated to "Jastas") was Oswald Boelcke, Germany's leading ace. Already
a national hero in Germany, where officials shared none of the RFC's reticence
about exploiting the propaganda value of its leading airmen, Boelcke was also
feared and respected by British and French pilots. For most of the summer, he
had been on an inspection tour of air units in the Balkans. In August, he returned
to the Western Front with a handpicked group of pilots—Manfred von Richthofen among them—to help organize new squadrons and take command of one,
Jagdstaffel Zwei. Like Hawker, Boelcke was a pioneer of aerial combat and an inspirational leader; unlike Hawker, he was permitted to lead patrols himself.[106]

August 31 saw heavy fighting as the German air services renewed their effort to
tilt the balance over the Somme front. That day, McKay fought a ferocious but in-
conclusive close-range dogfight with a two-seater, emptying an entire drum at it.
Only a malfunction in his gun-site allowed the machine to escape. More notably,
"A" Flight encountered a patrol of new German machines and recognized at once
their superiority in speed and climb over the DH 2.[107] Boelcke personally returned
to the fray on September 2, scoring his twentieth victory that day over Captain
R.E. Wilson of 32 Squadron. Wilson survived his crash, and Boelcke treated his
captive to a meal and a tour of his Jasta's aerodrome before sending him off as a
POW.[108] On the ground, Boelcke could afford these chivalrous gestures. In the
air, he was strictly business. Over the course of the summer he had devised a set
of rules of aerial combat that were widely adopted by German fighter pilots. This
famous eight-point "dicta," often described as the first systematized effort to im-
pose order on the chaos of dogfighting, urged pilots to work in formations and
to take every advantage so as to minimize risk in an engagement. Individual he-
roics were discouraged. Against this, Hawker's famous standing order to "attack
everything" might seem like the kind of reckless bravado that got men killed, but

105   Greg VanWyngarden, *Jagdstaffel 2 "Boelcke"* (Oxford: Osprey, 2007), 10–17.
106   On the Albatros, see James F. Miller, *DH 2 vs Albatros D 1 / D II: Western Front 1916* (Oxford:
        Osprey, 2012).
107   24 Squadron Record Book, vol. 2, August 31, 1916.
108   Boelcke's account is quoted in Johannes Werner, *Knight of Germany: Oswald Boelcke, German
        Ace*, translated by Claude W. Sykes (Philadelphia: Casemate, 2009), 233–35.

Hawker, too, was an innovator in all aspects of combat flying, dedicated to the development of new equipment and training methods. Unlike some squadron commanders, he even encouraged shop talk in the mess, where his pilots considered themselves at liberty to discuss and critique their collective performance.[109] But the experience, morale, and teamwork of 24's pilots could only go so far in compensating for the increasing obsolescence of the DH 2. Re-equipped with superior machines, reorganized, and re-energized by dynamic leaders like Boelcke, the German air service gradually tilted the balance over the Somme in its favour.

Preparatory work for the third phase of the Somme offensive, planned for September 15, kept 24 Squadron very busy in the first two weeks of the month. It was hot work indeed, with heavy fighting on several days. The squadron gave nearly as much as it took, but the casualties were wearing nonetheless. Between September 3 and 14, Hawker's squadron lost four pilots, including "B" Flight's Evans, killed by Archie on the 3rd; Glew, killed on the 8th when his engine threw a cylinder and severed his tail boom; and Manfield and Bowring on the 9th and 14th, respectively, brought down by Boelcke himself, the former in flames.[110] September 15 saw the heaviest action in the air since the beginning of July. Among the squadron's numerous combats that day was McKay's sharp, indecisive clash with a type of scout he had not encountered before.[111] This was probably one of the new Albatros machines that had just been received by Boelcke's Jasta 2. The fame and infamy of Boelcke's squadron grew proportionally with every victory its pilots earned. Boelcke personally claimed 20 victories in September and October, 4 of them over 24 Squadron. Among those who fell was Hawker's favourite, Lieutenant Patrick Langan-Byrne, a recipient of the DSO and the squadron's highest scoring ace, demonstrating once again that even the best RFC pilots were at a severe disadvantage in obsolete aircraft.[112] The DH 2 at its best was a stolid performer, and its ascendancy, if it can be called that, had been very brief. "These machines were not very popular with the average pilot," wrote 29 Squadron's James McCudden in his wartime autobiography, and if other anecdotal literature is anything to go

109  Hawker's role as an inspirational leader to the pilots of 24 Squadron is confirmed in numerous letters, memoirs (published and otherwise), and postwar interviews. On how Hawker encouraged discussion of tactics and other matters in the mess, see Hawker, *Hawker VC*, 180. On Boelcke's dicta, see VanWyngarden, *Jagdstaffel 2*, 12.

110  Imperial War Museum, Private Papers of Major V.A.H. Robeson, MC and A.M. Wilkinson, "The Somme Battle," IWM Location Ref 99/14/2. For Evans, Manfield, and Bowring, see Henshaw, *The Sky Their Battlefield II*, 50–52.

111  24 Squadron Record Book, vol. 3, September 15, 1916.

112  Patrick Langan-Byrne was killed in action October 16, 1916: see A.E. Illingworth and V.A.H. Robeson, *A History of 24 Squadron, Sometime of the Royal Flying Corps and Later of the Royal Air Force* (London: Printed for private circulation, 1920), 69.

by, he understated the case considerably.[113] In 1917 and 1918, McCudden, flying the vastly superior SE 5A, earned the Victoria Cross and became one of the war's most prodigious aces, with an astonishing 57 victories to his name. In 1916 and early 1917, on the DH 2, his record barely surpassed McKay's. Armed only with a single Lewis gun in a wobbly mount, the DH 2 could not hope to match the rate of fire or ammunition capacity of German scouts that increasingly were equipped with twin machine guns fed by belts of 500 rounds each. It turned tightly but could not match the aerodynamic performance of the new German machines. In an unpublished postwar memoir, "C" Flight leader Captain Alan Wilkinson recalled, "owing to the superior diving power of the Hun at this time they could nearly always keep out of range if they wished. There were a large number of in-decisive combats as the Hun could put his nose down and with his heavy engine could easily outpace us."[114] Above all, the DH 2's underpowered and mechanically unreliable rotary engine continuously undermined the hapless pilots. Wilkinson described mechanics working nonstop through the night to keep the machines flying. That autumn, he recalled, "we suffered very badly from an epidemic of engine trouble," an opinion supported by entries in the squadron record book and McKay's own logbook, which recounts no fewer than 40 patrols during which he suffered engine problems. Some of these were so serious as to be life threaten-ing. On several occasions, he was forced to land at neighbouring aerodromes and once in a field. For one period, as Wilkinson remembered, "there was as great a danger from one's machine as from enemy action," adding that this would have been crushing for the squadron's morale but for the "exceptional leadership" of Lanoe Hawker.[115] All this may have the appearance of casting about for excuses for lacklustre performance in the air, but Wilkinson was a highly decorated pilot and knew of what he spoke. He served a remarkable nine months flying DH 2s with No. 24 Squadron, a record rivalled only by McKay and one or two others. With ten "victories" in DH 2s, he was tied with Langan-Byrne for the title of ace of aces on that particular machine.[116]

Nonetheless, the RFC did not surrender its air superiority easily nor all at once. October saw McKay and his squadron-mates fight a number of fierce dog-fights, bigger even than the July 20 action, with its most experienced pilots giving

---

113  James McCudden, *Flying Fury: Five Years in the Royal Flying Corps* (1918; repr., Havertown: Case-mate, 2009), 107.

114  IWM, A.M. Wilkinson, "The Somme Battle," IWM Location Ref 99/14/2.

115  IWM, A.M. Wilkinson, "The Somme Battle," IWM Location Ref 99/14/2.

116  Entry for A.M. Wilkinson in Christopher Shores, Norman Franks, and Russell Guest, *Above the Trenches: A Complete Record of the Fighter Aces and Units of the British Empire Air Forces, 1915–1920* (Stoney Creek, ON: Fortress Publications, 1990).

the best account they could for themselves under the circumstances. One such instance occurred very late in the month. Saturday, October 28, was the second consecutive day of high winds, rain, and heavy cloud, dreadful weather that grounded much of the RFC on the Somme.[117] Undaunted, 24 attempted two patrols that day. Returning from an offensive patrol that morning, Saundby, whose engine was giving him trouble, fought a west wind so strong he could barely make headway against it. Low on fuel, he landed at 9 Squadron's aerodrome at Morlancourt. After refuelling and repairs, he clawed his way the remaining 20 miles west to Bertangles, arriving late but intact, no doubt much to the relief of his squadronmates.[118] The weather had hardly improved by 3 PM when McKay and Knight alighted in the rain on patrol.[119] High winds, dense cloud cover, and what Knight described as intermittent "gales and storms" led one of their German adversaries to think them "impertinent" for flying at all.[120] Worse still, McKay's engine was acting up, and he had already returned to the aerodrome once with a dud to switch machines.[121] Buffeted by wind, rain, and sleet, he had what must have been a horrid flight through frigid grey skies over a devastated grey landscape, nursing his engine, sputtering along at 7,000 feet, trailing Knight but 1,500 feet below him, and unable to climb higher. Beneath them, for miles in every direction, the armies hunkered down in their waterlogged trenches, wearily and grimly bracing themselves for the denouement of the Somme.

By 3:40 PM, McKay and Knight reached what remained of Pozières. In July and August, 23,000 Australians had been killed or wounded wresting the town and its adjacent ridge from the Germans in a series of violently contest assaults.[122] Now, it lay in shell-pocked ruins, like so many towns that dotted the length of the Western Front. On the two Canadians pressed, flying through cloud and rain. Then, peering into the distance, McKay spotted a single German machine, well below them to the north. It was a tempting target, but experienced pilots knew that this sort

---

117  Weather reports in RFC Communiqué, no. 60. See also Gerald Gliddon, *When the Barrage Lifts: A Topographical History and Commentary on the Battle of the Somme 1916* (Norwich: Gliddon Books, 1987), 421–23.

118  24 Squadron Record Book, vol. 3, October 28, 1916.

119  McKay reported taking off in the rain in his letter home, November 5, 1916, published in the *London Advertiser*, November 22, 1916, 1. In his log he recorded, "weather very bad." Logbook, October 28, 1916.

120  Knight's description of the weather is in the 24 Squadron Record Book, vol. 3, October 28, 1916. "Impertinent" was Manfred von Richthofen's later description: see his *The Red Baron* (Barnsley, UK: Pen and Sword Military, 2009), 96. This heavily propagandized "autobiography" of von Richthofen was first published in Germany in 1917. An English translation, *The Red Air Fighter*, appeared the following year.

121  24 Squadron Record Book, vol. 3, October 28, 1916. Logbook, October 28, 1916.

122  For arrival over Pozières, see 24 Squadron Record Book and 24 Squadron, Combats in the Air, October 28, 1916.

of thing was often a trap, designed to lure reckless newcomers into formations of scouts lurking at high altitudes.[123] Scanning the sky above, McKay saw them between the clouds: nearly an entire squadron at 10,000 feet. "Halberstadter and brown scouts," he called them in the squadron record book, but they were in fact the new Albatros fighters, much faster than the DH 2 and mounting twice its firepower.[124] Knight had seen them, too. Probably both men had guessed their identity. This was Jagdstaffel Zwei, and after five minutes of pursuit, half a dozen of them, led by Oswald Boelcke himself, slipped to the side and came screaming down upon them.[125]

## Triangulation and Reading Against the Grain

Two weeks later, on November 9, 1916 (coincidentally the same day McKay got credit for downing his second German machine), a curious article about him appeared in the sports section of the *London Advertiser*:

### Eddie McKay Takes Part in Big Air Raid

Local Athlete Gaining Fame in France as British Aviator—Friends Worry at Four Days' Absence, But Eddie Pops up Smiling

Eddie McKay, one of the best-known of local athletes who have gone overseas to play the game against the Huns, is having some exciting experiences and narrow escapes in his career as a British aviator in France. Eddie makes trips over the German lines frequently, and rushes the enemy in the same thorough manner as he did his opponents on the football field in seasons past. From advices received here, the famous Eddie is in the midst of the present excitement. He took part in a big air raid made the middle of last month, and was away for four days. His friends were beginning to worry about him, when he popped up serenely, stating that he had been away on a little trip.[126]

---

123  On German "traps," see J.J. Breen, "War Experiences," in *A Selection of Lectures and Essays from the Work of Officers Attending the Fifth Course at the Royal Air Force Staff College, 1926–1927* (London: Air Ministry, 1928) in the collection of the RAF Museum. Breen, later air marshal, served with 24 Squadron from March to December 1916.

124  24 Squadron Record Book, vol. 2, October 28, 1916. "Halberstadters and Small Aviatics" is the term used in Hawker's Combats in the Air report, October 28, 1916.

125  24 Squadron Record Book, vol. 2, October 28, 1916; 24 Squadron, Combats in the Air, October 28, 1916.

126  "Eddie McKay Takes Part in Big Air Raid," *London Advertiser*, November 9, 1916, 8.

We have already discussed the centrality of source criticism to the historian's craft. Sources, once located, have to be subjected to rigorous critical interrogation. This source differs from others we have examined because its central claim almost certainly cannot be true. The idea that McKay vanished for four days and then "popped up serenely" with no more explanation than a glib quip should arouse our skepticism immediately. Obviously, pilots could not simply disappear with their planes without serious consequences. And where would McKay have disappeared to? Like most aircraft of the era, the DH 2 had a short range, with just over two hours' worth of fuel. It was for this reason that pilots who failed to return from patrol were reported missing. Moreover, neither McKay's logbook nor 24 Squadron's record book recount any sort of four-day adventure, no occasion when, for example, he was brought down behind enemy lines, evaded capture, repaired his machine, and then returned to Bertangles.

So is the entire article false, the result of sloppy reporting or wartime hyperbole? Or might there be a kernel of truth here? Can we authenticate certain facts in an effort to triangulate others? The article makes one plausible claim when it states that McKay "took part in a big air raid made the middle of last month." During the war, the term "air raid" came to refer specifically to aerial bombing. While the DH 2 was not equipped to carry bombs, 24 Squadron sometimes escorted machines that were. McKay formed part of such an escort on October 21, shepherding FE 2s from 22 Squadron on a raid over German lines.[127] Is this the "big air raid" or was the author of the article, unfamiliar with the terminology of this new form of warfare, simply referring to a major air battle? This interpretation, too, is plausible. McKay and his squadron-mates clashed with a dozen or more hostile aircraft on October 17, 23, 26, and 28.[128] So the claim that he took part in a "big raid" could be a reference to one of these engagements, although only one of them can reasonably be said to have occurred in the middle of the month. That still leaves us with the article's central claim, that McKay disappeared for four days. His logbook reveals two periods around mid-October when he did not fly for at least two consecutive days: October 11 to 13 and again on October 18 and 19.[129] What was he doing? Had he indeed gone missing? He was never reported missing, so a more likely explanation is a simpler one. The weather was bad on all of those days, grounding most of the RFC.[130] It is also possible that from October 11 to 13 he was ill. On the 14th, he returned early from patrol, reporting

127    Logbook, October 21, 1916.
128    24 Squadron Record Book, vol. 3, October 17–28, 1916.
129    Logbook, October 11–13, 1916 and October 18–19, 1916.
130    RFC Communiqués, October 11–19, 1916.

being sick to his stomach.[131] This is the only time he noted an illness in his log-book, and a pilot would have to be quite ill indeed to justify turning back from patrol. Moreover, apart from periods of intense activity on the ground, such as the opening of the Somme offensive, pilots in 1916 rarely flew every day regardless of the circumstances. Between ordinary duty rotation—Hawker usually kept one of his three flights in reserve—leave, illness, and bad weather, McKay averaged only about one day of flying out of every three during his first tour in France. Is there anything at all, then, that might account for the report of his disappearance? One possibility is this: McKay and four other members of 24 Squadron fought a violent and protracted action early in the morning of October 26 against three formations of German planes. Having battled their way back to the British side of the lines, the flight returned to Bertangles, except for McKay, whose engine prob-lems forced him to land at No. 3 Squadron's aerodrome at Lahoussoye. Refuelled and repaired, he returned to Bertangles in the afternoon.[132] Perhaps, as the story passed from mouth to mouth, this delay of four hours was stretched into four days. It is impossible to know for certain, and we might be giving the article more credence than it deserves.

So far, we have assessed this source in terms of the reliability of its claims. Another important part of assessing a source is to inquire about the authority, competence, reliability, and intention of its creator. As E.H. Carr reminds us, sources never come to us "pure" but "are always refracted through the mind of the recorder."[133]

In this case, however, the article is anonymously written, which makes it more difficult to gauge authorial competence and intent. The article refers to "advices" received but it does not say what these actually are.[134] A letter from the front? Word of mouth from a returned veteran? We do not know, but the claim is so improbable, so contrary to what we know about First World War aviation, that we can assume the source was not another pilot. By way of contrast, we can compare the story above with another published two weeks later in the *London Free Press.*

A letter from Pte. Ritchie, who went overseas with No. 10 (Western Uni-versity) Stationary Hospital, writing home recently, said that Lieut. McKay,

---

131   Logbook, October 14, 1916, notes his feeling ill; 24 Squadron Record Book, vol. 3, October 14, 1916, notes specifically that he was sick to the stomach.
132   Logbook, October 26, 1916; 24 Squadron Record Book, vol. 3, October 26, 1916; 24 Squadron, Combats in the Air, October 26, 1916.
133   Carr, *What Is History?* 22.
134   The *Oxford English Dictionary* says that the word "advices" was once used to mean "news." A *good* dictionary, like the *OED,* is an indispensable tool for any writer, especially when it comes to fixing the precise meaning of a word.

having learned of the coming of his old friends, flew from France to England to meet them. A plane appeared over the hospital camp and, after circling for a time, descended. Lieut. McKay alighted and greeted his old companions. He had obtained permission to take his machine on a flight from France across the channel.[135]

This story, too, might strike us as rather fanciful. Could McKay, during a period of intense fighting on the Somme, get permission to fly across the English Channel to drop in on friends? Here, however, we have a source for the story whose identity we can confirm. Joseph "Rico" Ritchie had been a classmate of McKay's at Western and an alternate on the 1914 rugby team. In 1916, he signed up with Western's No. 10 Stationary Hospital, arriving in England in August.[136] We might be justified in simply taking Private Ritchie at his word, on the basis that people can be considered truthful (though not necessarily accurate) when they have no motive for being otherwise. On the other hand, there are grounds for thinking that Ritchie might not have been accurately reported, because McKay's logbook contains no reference to such a flight.

In this case, however, we can use the principle of triangulation to establish that the story is probably true, if not entirely accurate. Let's begin, once again, with what we know: we have Ritchie's statement that McKay visited the "hospital camp" by plane. On November 5, McKay wrote a letter home in which he said, "I saw a number of London boys while on leave, including Mel Brock, Reid and Alfie Gatecliffe." The letter does not mention Ritchie, but Mel Brock had been McKay's professor at Western and a coach to the rugby team. Like Ritchie, he joined the Canadian Army Medical Corps in 1916.[137] Roy Leonard Gatecliffe, a Londoner, also served with the stationary hospital in question.[138] They had all arrived in England at the end of August, so McKay must have visited them sometime in September or October. His logbook can help us determine when. He recorded no flights between September 26 and October 6, by several days the longest stretch in either of those months, much longer than could be accounted for by weather and the like.[139] Using the RFC Communiqués, we can even check the weather for that period: most days were good for flying. So from his letter, we know McKay

---

135    "No Official Word but M'Kay Could Do Business," *London Free Press*, November 20, 1916, 1.
136    According to Western's *Arts Calendar, 1914*, Ritchie was a third-year arts student in 1914–15. Numerous articles in the *Advertiser* identify him as an alternate on the 1914 rugby team. His military service record is recorded in LAC, RG 150, accession 1992–93/166, Private Joseph Stewart Ritchie.
137    LAC, RG 150, accession 1992–93/166, box 1087–92, George Melbourne Brock.
138    LAC, RG 150, accession 1992–93/166, box 3437–24, Roy Leonard Gatecliffe.
139    Logbook, September 27 to October 5, 1916.

was granted leave, and from his logbook, we have a good idea of when.[140] We also know what he did on one of his days in England. Finally, we have another list of names we may wish to investigate further. Could we find their diaries or correspondence? What about the most interesting part of the story, however: that, when visiting his friends, McKay made a grand entrance from the air? Having established the veracity of some of Ritchie's claims, we may wish to take this one at face value. How do we account for the fact that this flight is not entered in McKay's logbook, however? The most obvious answer is that he did not take it with him on leave. Perhaps he had not expected to fly. He certainly would not have flown in one of 24 Squadron's DH scouts. Instead, he might have hitched a ride in a two-seater crossing the Channel for England from one the air depots, or borrowed a machine while in England. (There are records, partially intact, that document the movement of aircraft from one base to another. I checked them, also to no avail.) There is also a very interesting discrepancy in McKay's logbook. On each page, McKay meticulously carried forward his total hours in the air from the previous page, recorded his subsequent flights and time in the air, and wrote his new total at the bottom. On the page for the week in question, and *on that page only*, the hours do not add up. The total at the bottom of the page is 3.2 hours greater than the recorded flight times should be. So maybe he flew after all, entering his additional hours but not, for whatever reason, logging the flight itself.

There are several lessons to be learned here. The first is that establishing barebones facts can be difficult. As we know, history is much more than a bill of facts about the past, but establishing facts is nevertheless an important part of our job. We need theories, too, in order to explain facts, but we cannot theorize over a void. As these examples demonstrate, deciding what happened can pose major challenges even before we pose the question of why things happened or think about what those things mean in the broader context. The second lesson underscores the importance of using multiple, independent sources, whenever possible, to establish the validity of claims in our sources. This is especially true in cases where the claim is an unusual or particularly important one. Although we might let certain commonplace claims pass without independent confirmation, claims such as the one that McKay disappeared for four days are extraordinary and demand a higher standard of evidence. The same can be said for one rather sensitive possibility that I raised in the preceding chapter. McKay's service record and

---

140   After the first draft of this manuscript was written, I learned the precise dates of McKay's leave in the daily routine orders of 14 Wing: September 26 to October 5. NA, UK, AHB, AIR 1–1572–204–80–32, 14 Wing Daily Routine Orders, August 1916–October 1916, which confirms the guess I made based on his logbook entries.

RFC casualty cards confirm that he was hospitalized for two weeks in late July and early August 1916; his logbook and the squadron record book provide further confirmation because he did not fly during that period. I have only one source, however, that purports to tell me *why* he was hospitalized: a letter I received from the historian Stewart Taylor, who interviewed some of McKay's squadron-mates in the 1950s and 60s as part of his research into Canadians who served in the RFC. It is entirely plausible, as I suggested, that McKay contracted a venereal disease; thousands of Canadians who went overseas did. Given the sensitive nature of the claim and the paucity of direct, primary evidence, however, I made the decision to be noncommittal about it. Admitting to uncertainty is often taken for weakness. In historical scholarship, it is frequently the strongest position we can take.

The third lesson is that, generally speaking, historians prefer first-hand accounts on the grounds that facts can be distorted in the retelling. As intermediaries compound, so too does the possibility of error, or of important details being omitted. There are therefore gradations in the value of primary sources. For example, pilots' combat reports were written down in the squadron record book, sometimes by the pilots themselves but more often by a recording officer, whose job it was to record pilots' oral accounts almost immediately after they had landed.[141] Those handwritten records, in turn, formed the basis for the typewritten Combats in the Air reports, usually prepared by the squadron's commanding officer in cases where a combat resulted in a victory claim. Those were passed on to higher headquarters, where a précis of them was recorded in the war diaries. The war diaries, in turn, formed the basis for the RFC Communiqués, a bulletin of flying news that went out to all squadrons for posting. All of these are primary sources. Forced to choose between them, historians prefer those most immediate to the event: the squadron record book. Having said that, discrepancies between primary sources are often of interest, and we should not automatically assume that they are mistakes. Combats in the Air reports, for instance, sometimes reconciled differences between accounts in the squadron record book, noted any subsequent independent confirmation (from other pilots, soldiers on the ground who had witnessed the battle, and so forth), and, as we shall see, occasionally were based on follow-up interviews with pilots. Of course, it is often the case that historians have no choice but to make do with what is available. We have already discussed how a large percentage of the official records of the RFC have been lost. The significant point is that historians prize first-hand accounts, or whatever source is nearest to our subject, while not neglecting to take note of others.

---

141   24 Squadron pilots usually wrote their own accounts until December 1916, when a recording officer was assigned to the squadron for the first time.

It seems very likely, then, that the story of McKay's disappearance is entirely untrue. Common sense calls it into question and no evidence corroborates it. At this point, we might be tempted to discard the source altogether, but that would be a serious mistake. Though this source is authentic (it really did appear in the newspaper at the time), it is not a reliable source about McKay's military career. Many scholars would argue, however, that the apparent or intended meaning of a text is not necessarily the most important thing about it. Recall once again Carr's axiom that sources do not come to us "pure." What if the impurities themselves are of interest precisely because they reveal something about the "mind of the recorder" or the circumstances of their creation? Whatever else it might be, the article about McKay's alleged disappearance is still a historical primary document. The language it uses, the errors it contains, and the distortions they generate can shed light on the past in unexpected ways, and we should be mindful of them. In literary criticism, assessing sources in this fashion is sometimes called "reading against the grain" and can send us down many fruitful avenues of investigation. For example, this article might tell us something about propaganda and the evidentiary standards of wartime journalism. It suggests how people on the home front were keen to read about the exploits of pilots overseas, even if they barely comprehended what pilots actually did. Consider, too, the many possible implications of the article's use of sport metaphors to describe battle overseas, or the sense of high adventure and derring-do conveyed in such phrases as "exciting experiences" and "narrow escapes." A certain generation of readers would call this "*Boy's Own* stuff," after a popular magazine of the time, aimed at British boys, that recounted tales of adventure in grandiloquent and moralizing language.[142] The article also conveys something further about the ongoing societal construction of a myth—the myth of the Knights of the Air: lionhearted, dashing, skillful and cunning, dutiful but also audacious, qualities that future generations would ascribe to the first astronauts. The Eddie McKay described here goes about his deadly business with a reckless, youthful abandon, indifferent to fear, rushing German fliers as if they were no more than opposing players on the rugby pitch. This Eddie may very well be a fiction, but a society's fictions have a reality of their own, worthy of historians' full attention. In a future discussion, we will chase these ideas a little further down their intellectual rabbit hole, but not as far as they can go, as they go very far indeed. In the meantime, we left Eddie McKay in very precarious position. He was about to become famous, and for something he did not even do.

---

142   Kelly Boyd, *Manliness and the Boys' Story Paper in Britain: A Cultural History, 1855–1940* (New York: Palgrave Macmillan, 2003).

# CHAPTER THREE

# The Battle: October 28,
# 1916–March 14, 1917

*The sequel of to-day unsolders all*
*The goodliest fellowship of famous knights*
*Whereof this world holds record. Such a sleep*
*They sleep—the men I loved. I think that we*
*Shall never more, at any future time,*
*Delight our souls with talk of knightly deeds,*
*Walking about the gardens and the halls*
*Of Camelot, as in the days that were.*

—Tennyson, *Morte d'Arthur*

Luck, blind and cruel, was perhaps the defining difference between pilots who lived to be legends and those who died unheralded. Every pilot who lived long enough had a story about a close call or a near miss: the bullet that tore a hole in his collar as it whizzed by, the enemy machine that had him dead to rights but inexplicably broke off, the miraculous landing in a plane shot to pieces. Arthur Gould Lee survived, among other things, three crashes, an engine that quit at 17,000 feet, and an anti-aircraft shell that lodged directly under his seat, unexploded. He escaped fate, as he later recollected, "again and again, by the most unholy luck."[1] Billy Bishop returned from one scrap to find a grouping of bullet holes only inches from where he sat.[2] Vivian Ross had a remarkable stroke of good fortune when his two-seater, flying unescorted, somehow passed unseen beneath a flight of

---

1   Arthur Gould Lee, *Open Cockpit*, 6. Lee describes his various brushes with death throughout *Open Cockpit* and its companion, *No Parachute*.
2   Billy Bishop, *Winged Warfare: Hunting Huns in the Air* (Toronto: Hodder and Stoughton, 1918), 135.

20 German triplanes.[3] Norman MacMillan recounted the story of a squadron-mate (a Canadian coincidentally named MacKay) whose cap was ripped off by a passing bullet, leaving him badly shaken but otherwise unharmed.[4] There were countless variations. An inch here, a second there, an eye-blink at the wrong moment— this was often the difference between living another day or dying then and there. Theirs was an unforgiving profession, practiced in perilous times. The fatality rate among pilots could be fully the equal to that of front-line infantry. In all, McKay served nine months with No. 24 Squadron. During that period, the squadron suffered eight pilots killed in action, four killed in flying accidents, five wounded, and four shot down and taken prisoner.[5] Based on its establishment strength of 19 pilots (including the squadron major, who only occasionally flew) this represents a fatality rate of just under 70 per cent and a casualty rate of 120 per cent. Of the roughly 68 pilots who flew with No. 24 at some point in that period, 29, or 44 per cent, were killed either with the squadron or in subsequent service.[6] Even among the war's most decorated pilots, the butcher's bill was appalling. Of their respective country's top ten aces, Germany suffered the loss of four, the United Kingdom four, and France five. Of the war's 30 highest scoring aces, 10 were killed during the war; two others, both Germans, were killed in revolutionary violence just after; five more perished in flying accidents in the 1920s.[7] These were the deadliest of the deadly; decorated by their leaders; revered by their nations; pilots that other pilots admired, envied, and feared. If their victory claims are to be believed, they brought down over 1,500 aircraft between them. Yet for all their "deadly talent" and accumulated experience, they too were subject to the cruel turn of the wheel of fate: an inch here, a second there, an eye-blink at the wrong moment. The cause of Manfred von Richthofen's death is debated, but one dominant theory has it that he was brought down by a lucky shot from the ground.[8] Lucky ground fire was the certain cause of the death of Mick Mannock, the UK's top-scoring pilot.[9] Erich

---

3  Ross, *Flying Minnows*, 140.

4  MacMillan, *Into the Blue*, 100–101.

5  This includes Eric Clowes Pashley, who was killed three days after McKay departed 24 Squadron. See Illingworth and Robeson, *A History of 24 Squadron*, 69–70.

6  Figures compiled by correlating several sources, including an (incomplete) list of squadron casualties in Illingworth and Robeson, *A History of No. 24 Squadron*, 69–70; the Commonwealth War Graves Commission database at www.cwgc.org, and various NA Air Ministry service files.

7  On the British aces, their victories, and their fates, see Shores, Franks, and Guest, *Above the Trenches* and Norman Franks, Frank W. Bailey, and Russell Guest, *Above the Lines: The Aces and Fighter Units of the German Air Service* (London: Grub Street, 1993). For others, see the database on www.the-aerodrome.com.

8  Kilduff, *The Red Baron*, 202–3.

9  On Mannock, see Norman Franks and Andy Saunders, *Mannock: The Life and Death of Major Edward Mannock, VC* (London: Grub Street, 2008).

Löwenhardt and Fritz Rumey, two of Germany's leading aces, were killed late in the war when their parachutes, an experimental device not issued to British pilots, failed to open.[10] James McCudden, one of England's most decorated airmen, perished accidentally in a routine take-off.[11] Oswald Boelcke, a pioneer of aerial warfare, father of the German fighter force, mentor to von Richthofen, hero to the nation, a prodigious assassin—ranked tenth among Germany's aces—was killed in a fluke collision with another German machine while pursuing two RFC pilots over the Somme. One of them was Eddie McKay.

Just after 4 PM on October 28, 1916, under a low, grey sky, Eddie McKay and Arthur Knight landed at Bertangles, wet, cold, rattled, and lucky to be alive.[12] They did not know it yet, but they had just fought one of the most consequential dogfights of the war. Without downing an enemy aircraft, they had secured themselves a place in the history books. When they are remembered at all, it is because of what happened in the 20 minutes they spent fighting for their lives that day in the sky between Pozières and Bapaume.

The dreadful weather had not deterred Jasta 2 from flying several patrols on October 28. According to his personal servant, Boelcke himself had been aloft five times.[13] Given the weather, this seems improbable, but there is no doubt that Boelcke maintained a gruelling patrol schedule. In the past two months, he had claimed 20 victories—no fewer than 3 of them against McKay's squadron-mates—bringing his total to the incredible number of 40.[14] No pilot in 24 had accounted for more than ten. The nonstop flying and fighting wore heavily upon him, and he bore all the signs of mental and physical exhaustion. "My captain kept on growing thinner and more serious," recalled his servant. "The superhuman burden of seven take-offs a day for fights and worries about his Staffel weighed him down."[15] Around the same time that McKay and Knight departed Bertangles for their defensive patrol, Boelcke and his favourite subordinate, Erwin Böhme, were settling in for a game of chess. At 37, Böhme was very old for a scout pilot, but exceedingly capable. Like his other protégé, young von Richthofen, Böhme was then a six-victory ace, handpicked for inclusion in the squadron. Two days later, in a letter to his fiancée,

---

10 See Norman Franks et. al., *Above the Lines: The Aces and Fighter Units of the German Air Service* (London: Grub Street, 1993).

11 Barker, *The Royal Flying Corps in World War One*, 474.

12 Time of flight and weather conditions recorded in 24 Squadron Record Book; 24 Squadron, Combats in the Air, October 28, 1916. Also Logbook, October 28, 1916.

13 Werner, *Knight of Germany*, 257. Boelcke's servant seems given to hyperbole at times.

14 VanWyngarden, *Jagdstaffel 2*, 6–24 details Boelcke's career over the Somme. Historian Fred Hitchins compiled a list of Boelcke's victories over the Somme that can be found in University of Western Ontario, Archives and Regional Collection Centre, the Beatrice Hitchins Memorial Collection of Aviation History.

15 Quoted in Werner, *Knight of Germany*, 256.

he recalled, "We were called to the front because there was an infantry attack going on. We soon attacked some English machines we found flying over Flers."[16] These were flown by Knight and McKay. The following year, in his propagandistic "auto-biography," von Richthofen wrote, "From a long distance we saw two impertinent Englishmen in the air who actually seemed to enjoy the terrible weather. We were six and they were two. If they had been twenty and if Boelcke had given us the signal to attack we should not have been at all surprised."[17] This was bravado: Boelcke was highly cautious and taught his pilots to avoid combat when at a disadvantage. And yet in the subsequent engagement they violated one of his eight dictums: that it was dangerous for too many pilots to attack a single enemy simultaneously. The battle drove that lesson home in the most emphatic way possible.

It was almost certainly Boelcke who led the attack, slipping under Knight so as to draw him into a dive that would leave him exposed to the others. Knight would have none of it. The others came down on him nonetheless.[18] So the battle was on, a whirling, swirling, frenzied engagement. "Spiralled and attempted to retaliate," Knight recorded in the squadron record book, "but the other six joined in."[19] That made 12 machines in all, according to McKay and Knight's report. One group, probably led by von Richthofen, dove to attack McKay. With customary glibness, McKay later wrote, "Had a good scrap until about 4 PM, from Pozier to east of Bapaume."[20] He had been in good scraps before and lived to tell, including a three-to-one engagement two days earlier and the famous duel on July 20, but he had never had Manfred von Richthofen on his tail before. A month later, Hawker would, and would not survive; a month after that, Knight fell to him also. With no chance of outrunning their adversaries, McKay and Knight pressed to the fullest the DH 2's sole advantage: its ability to turn more tightly than the Albatros. "It would have been fatal to concentrate on any one machine as four or five were ready to close in," Knight wrote, "so I merely spiralled and fired when a HA came across my sights."[21] A minute of this passed. Two. Five. Turning and firing.[22] Böhme described a battle of "wild turns" in which he could only squeeze off a few brief bursts. "The English pilots defended themselves well," he wrote.[23] Years later, the ordinarily dour British official history called Knight and McKay's flying "brilliant."[24] It may even

---

16  Quoted in Werner, *Knight of Germany*, 258.
17  von Richthofen, *The Red Baron*, 96.
18  24 Squadron, Combats in the Air, October 28, 1916.
19  24 Squadron Record Book, vol. 4, October 28, 1916.
20  24 Squadron Record Book, vol. 4, October 28, 1916.
21  24 Squadron Record Book, vol. 4, October 28, 1916.
22  24 Squadron, Combats in the Air, October 28, 1916.
23  Quoted in Werner, *Knight of Germany*, 258.
24  Jones, *The War in the Air*, 2: 312.

have been true. They were not the equal of Boelcke, perhaps, but they were not without resources, either. They were experienced combat pilots, but their experience must also have driven home a resounding, inescapable conclusion. They were dead men. Outnumbered six to one, outgunned by twice that, swarmed by superior machines flown by expert pilots, drifting further from their own lines on the prevailing winds, and with McKay suffering engine trouble, the odds were heavily in their enemies' favour. They did what they could: turning and turning, never flying straight or level for more than a few moments, firing in short bursts at their foes, who crowded the sky and one another, but the eventual outcome could hardly have been in doubt. And then the wheel of fire turned. An inch here, a second there, an eye-blink at the wrong moment. Every pilot who lived long enough had a story, and this one would belong to McKay and Knight forever.

There are four extant accounts of the battle written by its participants: McKay and Knight's respective entries in the 24's squadron record book; von Richthofen's recollections in his autobiography; and Böhme's letter to his fiancée, reprinted in a 1932 hagiography of Boelcke called *Knight of Germany*. In addition, Hawker's Combats in the Air report includes additional details not found in the squadron record book, suggesting he conducted follow-up interviews with McKay and Knight. Each source has a slightly discrepant account of what occurred next, as might be expected, given the speed and confusion of aerial combat. Böhme's account is the most detailed:

> [W]e tried to force the English down, by one after another of us barring their way, a manoeuvre we had often practiced successfully. Boelcke and I had just got one Englishman between us when another opponent, chased by friend Richthofen, cut across us. Quick as lightning, Boelcke and I both dodged him, but for a moment our wings prevented us from seeing anything of one another—and that was the cause of it.
>
> How am I to describe my sensations from the moment when Boelcke suddenly loomed up a few metres away on my right! He put his machine down and I pulled mine up, but we touched as we passed, and we both fell earthwards.[25]

Böhme recovered rapidly; Boelcke did not. McKay and Knight later reported that the machine that fell was apparently under control, so light had been the collision, even though parts of it broke off in the air.[26] Richthofen had initially thought the

25  Quoted in Werner, *Knight of Germany*, 258.
26  24 Squadron Record Book, vol. 4, October 28, 1916. The claim that parts were seen to come off of Boelcke's machine appears in the 24 Squadron, Combats in the Air, October 28, 1916.

same, writing later: "Boelcke drew away from his victim and descended in large curves. I had not the feeling that he was falling, but when I saw him descending below me I noticed that part of his plane had broken off."[27] Böhme and some of the others followed Boelcke down, but he crashed near an artillery position where it was impossible for them to land. Frantic, Böhme returned to their aerodrome, flipped over on landing, clambered out and into a car, and, with others, raced to the site of the crash. Boelcke was dead.[28] Meanwhile, the battle had gone on, drifting east, with McKay and Knight still severely disadvantaged. But deterred, perhaps, by the ferocity of the two "English" pilots, weakened numerically, and no doubt shocked by the still uncertain fate of their squadron leader, the Germans broke off after about 15 minutes.[29] McKay and Knight returned to Bertangles with a story to tell of another close scrape. Within an hour, they learned it was to be much more than that. The new spread rapidly by wireless throughout the German side: Oswald Boelcke, dean of the German fighter force, legend on both sides, was dead. The British found out shortly thereafter. In his logbook entry, McKay noted laconically, "D.P. Scrap with 12 H.A. Scouts with 1 other. Boelcke done in by colliding with another H.A. Weather very bad. Poor machine."[30]

Boelcke's loss was a severe blow for the German air service and keenly felt throughout Germany as a whole. He had been built up by Germany's wartime propaganda machine into a national hero. His funeral, held at occupied Cambrai's cathedral (over strong objections of the local French archbishop) was attended by royalty and high-ranking generals.[31] As for McKay and Knight, their victory—if it can be called that—apparently earned them a presentation with Douglas Haig. This was probably no more than a handshake and pat on the back, but it provided McKay with a story for later. In the first week of November, Boelcke's death was widely reported in the United Kingdom, Canada, and the United States, often in brief front-page articles. That the press would devote attention to the death of a single enemy officer is a reminder of the immense interest that the air war generated on the home front. Then something McKay could never have anticipated happened. On Saturday, November 18, people in London, Ontario, found an extraordinary headline in the evening edition of the *Advertiser*: "London Boy Sends Great German Flier to Death." A large reproduction of the portrait photo of McKay in uniform looked out at them. "Eddie McKay, London's Master Aviator" read the

27  von Richthofen, *The Red Baron*, 97.
28  Quoted in Werner, *Knight of Germany*, 259.
29  24 Squadron, Combats in the Air, October 28, 1916.
30  Logbook, October 28, 1916. D.P. is "defensive patrol," although McKay and Knight were decidedly on the German side of the lines when the battle occurred.
31  Werner, *Knight of Germany*, 262–63.

caption. The accompanying story, which took up a third of the front page and carried onto another page, began with the boldfaced header, "Aviator Eddie McKay of this city was heroic airman who caused death of 'King of German Fliers' Capt. Boelke."[32] A letter from an anonymous "London officer at the front" followed.

> Eddie McKay is getting more fame here every day. He and another airman are responsible for the death of Captain Boelcke, known as the "King of the Boche Fliers" and another enemy airman. It seems that McKay and his friend went up to beat off an attack of twelve German planes, and they did the work handsomely. The Huns were out-manoeuvred beautifully, and were forced to retire, the last two machines to turn tail were cornered and collided, going to the ground with a crash.[33]

The *Advertiser* quoted alleged German sources about how "their king-pin aviator fell before the London boy and his comrade, after he had been jockeyed into such a position that he collided with one of his squadron mates." On Monday, the *London Free Press* carried the story as well,[34] while on its front page, the *Advertiser* offered an affectionate piece of doggerel as tribute to London's most favoured son, advising readers to "give McKay the Scottish pronunciation" to facilitate the rhymes:

> *'tis but two short years since Eddie McKay*
> Lived here in our city, a broth of a bye;
> And the papers today recount his air fight
> In which he put Germany's finest to flight.
>
> Was ever a tale so wonderful heard?
> Sure Eddie's no birdman—he's just a real bird—
> And he's risen to heights in our people's esteem
> That no airship could reach—except in a dream
>
> Words fail what we think of his feat to express,
> We are lost in amaze at his courage—no less—
> We just throw up our caps and with one accord cry
> Three cheers and a tiger for "the real McKay." [35]

---

32  Note that Boelcke's name is misspelled in the headline.
33  "Aviator Eddie McKay," *London Advertiser*, November 18, 1916, 1. The author of the letter is unknown.
34  "No Official Word but McKay Could Do the Business," *London Free Press*, November 20, 1916, 3.
35  "To Eddie McKay," *London Advertiser*, November 20, 1916, 1.

The story of McKay's supposed victory over Boelcke was carried across the country, in newspapers including Canada's leading daily, Toronto's *Globe*, in the *Toronto Daily Star*, in Alberta's *Lethbridge Daily Herald*, and in the *Daily Nugget* in Cobalt, Ontario, where the editors added with pride that McKay's brother Joe was a well-known local insurance broker.[36] Even the *New York Times*, which had interviewed Boelcke on the day he died, carried the story, with its punctilious though not always accurate editors giving McKay's first name as "Edward" and describing him as a "British athlete," which at least was technically correct.[37]

So McKay became Canada's first famous military pilot, months before Billy Bishop scored his first victory in the air. But fame is fleeting, and although the local papers continued to carry news of his exploits, McKay never attained recognition on this scale again. His brief moment in the spotlight, however, serves as a reminder of the symbolic importance that Canadians on the home front attached to the figure of the aviator. If the misery, mass casualties, and apparently endless stalemate of trench warfare represented all that was worst about modernity, the aviator represented the hope that knightliness and chivalry might yet be preserved in the technological age. As the papers described it, McKay's victory over Boelcke extended naturally, almost predictably, from the "manly qualities" he had cultivated as "hockeyist and footballer." On the rink and rugby pitch, McKay was "lithe as a cat, cool and hard as steel." In defeating Boelcke, he had "made one of his sensational runs for a touchdown" and become "one of the big scorers in Haig's machine." Like his achievements in sports, McKay's victory was as much a moral victory as a physical and technical one. On the playing field, McKay had been "a heady, fair, and clean sportsman."[38] Thus, the *Advertiser* predicted, he would "brand on the forehead, so to speak, of many an aviating Hun" Western's motto, "*Veritas et Utilitas*" ("truth and service").[39] Indeed, unlike the savage "Hun," McKay, in his "conquest" of Germany's "kingpin airman" (as the *London Free Press* put it), had not merely applied brute force but had shrewdly outwitted him, bringing about his demise by "jockeying him into such a position he collided with one of his squadron mates."[40] Such tactics, the *Advertiser* informed readers, are "considered a greater feat in the flying profession than to kill an aviator by machine gun fire in the air."[41] However briefly, Eddie McKay became the very

---

36  "Cobalter's Brother Responsible for Death of Aviator," *Daily Nugget*, November 20, 1916, 2.
37  "Caused Boelcke's Death," *New York Times*, November 19, 1916, 3. The paper published the interview with Boelcke in January 1917. "A Talk with Boelcke on the Day of His Death," *New York Times*, January 28, 1917, 21.
38  "McKay of Western," *London Advertiser*, November 20, 1916, 6.
39  "McKay of Western," 6.
40  "No Official Word," *London Free Press*, November 20, 1916, 3.
41  "Aviator Eddie McKay," *London Advertiser*, November 18, 1916, 1.

symbol of what many Canadians longed for. The aviator may have been a product of modernity, but he was also the antidote to its alienation, materialism, and the emasculating influences of the soft life. As the papers described it, McKay embodied all that was best about the civilization he defended. He was the very exemplar of self-sacrificing manhood: patriotic, dauntless, virtuous, wily, skillful, and even modest. Of course, much of this was myth making, at odds with the truth of what happened, but in those dark days of late 1916 that probably mattered very little. Great deeds in the air performed by "conspicuous aeronauts" like McKay offered Canadians something that the trenches seldom could: identifiable heroes, clear and decisive outcomes, and the promise that chivalry had not perished in the mud and blood. On November 5, two weeks before the news broke at home, McKay had written a letter to a friend in London, briefly describing the engagement in a decidedly cursory fashion.

> I suppose you have read that Boelcke, the best Hun airman, has been killed. I was in the scrap in which he was "done in." Two of us had a scrap with twelve very fast Huns, in which two of them collided. One of the machines went down. From our "perch" it looked funny to see the bits of aeroplane floating about in the air. The chap that went down was Boelcke.[42]

McKay then pressed on to other important matters: "How is football in London? I would certainly like a game now. We don't get much exercise out here." On November 22, the letter was published in the *Advertiser* and subsequently picked up by other papers. That McKay claimed no credit for the victory over the "kingpin" of "Hun" airmen only confirmed his knightly virtues. Even though he belonged to the foremost ranks of British airmen, the *Advertiser* opined, "he is out to fight, not gain personal glory."[43]

The *London Free Press*, always less effusive in its editorial style than the *Advertiser*, had contacted McKay's family for comment when the news broke. They seemed as surprised as anyone. His sister Lillian's husband, William, told the *Free Press*, "We hear from him regularly and though he says he had been in many flights, he did not say that he had personally brought down any enemy machines."[44] He had, of course. So there may have been something to the *Advertiser's* observations

---

42  The letter was reprinted in the *London Advertiser* under the title "Eddie McKay's Own Story of Fight in Which Capt. Boelcke was Slain," November 22, 1916, 1, 3.

43  "Eddie McKay's Own Story," *London Advertiser*, November 22, 1916, 3.

44  "No Official Word but McKay Could Do the Business," *London Free Press*, November 20, 1916, 3. The word "flights" appears in the *Free Press* but the word "fights" would seem more proper given the context. Lillian McKay died in 1945.

about his modesty, or perhaps he did not like to share the grisly facts with his family. Did he ever learn how widely the inflated claims about his duel with Boelcke were circulated back home? It would be surprising if his many siblings did not mention it in letters. The false claims may even have embarrassed him, as would the fact that his friend Arthur Knight received no comparable credit. Given how widely the story spread, it would be surprising if it did not reach the ear of RFC authorities, who would have recognized its falsity and perhaps been suspicious of where it came from. Probably it did him no good.

Neither Eddie McKay nor Gerald Knight had killed the German ace of aces by any deliberate means, but there is one inescapable fact. They had met, and Oswald Boelcke was dead, and they were alive. For now.

November came and the weather began to turn, but when conditions permitted, the RFC still had serious work to do in support of ongoing operations on the Somme. This included reconnaissance and artillery cooperation in preparation for a major attack by the Fourth Army up the Ancre River valley, planned for mid-month. On November 3, 24 Squadron's neighbour at Bertangles, 22 Squadron, suffered the loss of three of its FE 2Bs and their aircrews on a single photographic reconnaissance of new German defences in the intended battle zone. It was the heaviest blow suffered by either squadron in 1916.[45] Recognizing the damage to morale, Lt. Col. Cuthbert Hoare, commanding the 14th Air Wing, invited the officers of both squadrons to join him and Lt. Colonel Ludlow-Hewitt, commanding Third Wing, for dinner at the nearby Chateau de Bertangles.[46] Senior officers from other local squadrons attended as well. After dinner, McKay was entreated to tell the story of the duel with Boelcke. This he did, much to the delight of all assembled. Then the "very amusing" Canadian apparently went too far. He recounted the story of his and Knight's audience with Douglas Haig, but could not resist what historian Stewart Taylor called an "irreverently humorous" impersonation of the general. The joke went over poorly with the senior officers, and Taylor believes that this incautious gag may have cost McKay a decoration. Knight received the Military Cross by the end of month. McKay, who shared another victory over a German machine on November 9, never did, even when his total number of victories surpassed Knight's in 1917.[47]

---

45  See Jones, *The War in the Air*, 2: 314; Henshaw, *The Sky Their Battlefield II*, 60.

46  Cuthbert Hoare (1883–1969) subsequently commanded the Royal Flying Corps training establishment in Canada.

47  Stewart Taylor recounts the events of the evening in "Eyes on the Storm, Part III," *Over the Front* 8, no. 2 (Summer 1993): 147–80, see page 164. McKay's victory on November 9 has been the source of some confusion, as he flew more than one patrol that day and made more than one claim. His logbook indicates that he received credit for a machine, confirmed by British AA batteries, destroyed on an afternoon patrol with Harry Wood of "C" Flight, with whom he often flew.

Though he had just two confirmed victories until January, McKay fought frequently throughout the entire Somme campaign. The squadron record books reveal a pilot who seems to have grown in confidence over the course of the summer and into the early autumn, attacking more boldly and more often as time went on. Like most of his squadron-mates, however, he was at pains to score decisive victories. A large part of the problem was the DH 2, with its middling speed and service ceiling, troublesome engine, and single Lewis gun. An analysis of the squadron's record books reveals just how badly outclassed the DH 2 became after the arrival of reorganized German squadrons flying superior machines in September. No. 24 Squadron fought approximately 186 combats in July and August, the period in which the RFC was most ascendant over the Somme. Of those, roughly 26, or 14 per cent, subsequently were counted as "decisive," with an enemy machine probably destroyed or captured. In September, October, and November, the squadron fought roughly 425 combats, with 18 recorded as decisive, a rate of just under four per cent. The casualty figures illustrate the point as well. In July and August, when German pilots were as likely to flee for their lines as stand and fight, the squadron had no pilots killed in aerial combat, although 2nd Lt. Kerr was shot down and taken prisoner in mid-July and Hughes Chamberlain was seriously wounded a month later. By contrast, in the three months beginning in September, facing a more aggressive and better equipped enemy, the squadron suffered five pilots killed in aerial combat and three taken prisoner.[48] Seen in this light, McKay's seemingly mediocre tally of two victories appears far more creditable, as very few of the squadron's pilots accounted for more than three or four enemy machines decisively destroyed or captured in the same period.[49]

"B" Flight's morning patrol on November 16 illustrates the difficulties faced by the squadron's pilots late in the year. Shortly after 10 AM, the five-man patrol engaged a mixed flight of German machines near Bapaume and then fought almost unceasingly for over an hour. McKay personally fought in half a dozen combats on that single patrol. He drove enemy machines off and down, one of them trailing smoke, and probably killed the observer in a two-seater. For once, his engine was running well, but twice he had to break off to clear a stoppage in his Lewis gun. Near Raincourt he dove to the rescue of an FE 2B under attack by three German

---

48  NA (UK), Air Ministry, AHB, AIR 1/168/15/160/1, No. 24 Squadron History, Summary of Decisive Fighting (Table). For a month-to-month breakdown, see the summary notations in 24 Squadron Record Book, vols. 1–5. These handwritten notations were probably added postwar. See also tables derived from the Squadron Record Book in Illingworth and Robeson, *A History of 24 Squadron*, 73–75. List of squadron casualties from same, pages 69–70.

49  Judging from his logbook, McKay apparently believed he had accounted for three, two of them on November 9. The Squadron Record Book and 24's Combats in the Air reports for the day yield confusing results.

scouts. "The FE plane at once shut down engine and dived straight home," McKay wrote in the squadron record book. "H.A. tried to get on my tail without much success. I spiralled firing when possible. Drove H.A. away. Chased one and saw tracer bursting in fuselage." The faster machine made off to the east, surviving to fight another day. In six engagements against a total of over a dozen enemy machines, McKay scored no decisive "kills."[50] The number of combats in a single patrol was unusual, but the outcome was not. Decisive combats were the exception, not the rule. Well handled by experienced pilots, the DH 2 was still capable of frustrating even superior numbers of German machines, but air supremacy had been lost. No longer could the RFC's machines reconnoitre with the near impunity they had enjoyed earlier in the summer; no longer did the Germans turn tail at the sight of 24's pushers.

That the balance had shifted was illustrated emphatically a week later. Several days of cloud, rain, and mist followed the end of the Somme offensive, but November 23 dawned clear, with several artillery shoots against the feeble German line planned. In all, RFC machines registered 128 targets that day.[51] No. 24 had several scraps near Bapaume, with McKay diving on and driving off a number of hostile aircraft. That morning, "C" Flight's 2nd Lt. Henry "Bernie" Begg, who had arrived fresh from 10 Reserve Squadron in the third week of October, was killed in a clash with Jasta 2. Did the death of one of his "chickens" provoke Hawker to join an offensive patrol up the Bapaume Road that afternoon? Despite what has sometimes been claimed, Hawker largely abided by Trenchard's prohibition on squadron majors flying patrols. Since September, he had been up only seven times, and J.O. Andrews, commanding "A" Flight, later opined that Hawker did not know the lay of the land well.[52] Late that afternoon, Hawker, Andrews, and Saundby found themselves in a hard scrap near Bapaume. Separated from the others, who lost sight of him, Hawker engaged in a whirling duel with an Albatros DII, piloted, as fate would have it, by Manfred von Richthofen. Their battle has been speculated about to the finest detail, but we are almost entirely reliant on von Richthofen's own account for a description of what happened. After several minutes of turning, Hawker, diving down to nearly tree-top height and at a serious disadvantage against the faster, more heavily armed Albatros, made a straight-line dash for British lines. A single round to the back of the head killed him instantly.

---

50   24 Squadron Record Book, vol. 4, November 16, 1916.
51   RFC Communiqué, no. 63.
52   Hawker's flights compiled from an inspection of the 24 Squadron Record Book, vols. 2–4. Andrews, later air marshal, gave his opinion in a lecture at the RAF Staff College in the 1920s: NA (HK), Air Ministry, AHB, Papers (Series 1) RAF Staff College, AIR 1/2388/228/11/91, J.O. Andrews, "Service Experiences."

Hawker became the eleventh and most famous victim of the future "Red Baron," who had fired 900 rounds to score the single shot that won the battle.[53] For the pilots and men of No. 24 Squadron, the news was shattering. "Everyone liked him, and had absolute confidence in him as commanding officer," J.O. Andrews recalled years later.[54] "Irreparable," was Alan Wilkinson's description of Hawker's loss. "One could not know him without loving him."[55] But they would have to go on without him nonetheless.

The Somme offensive ended in the third week of November, but the debate about it never has. The five-month attritional slogging match had seen the Anglo-French armies gain seven miles at the deepest point of penetration, which seemed a meagre return for the appalling cost of well over half a million casualties. But the German Army had suffered grievously too.[56] The end of the year saw the Germans on the Somme depleted, demoralized, and holding a defensive line that stood in very poor condition. With their army badly bloodied, the German High Command planned a deliberate withdrawal to a shorter, well-prepared defensive position, dubbed the Hindenburg Line by the British, once conditions permitted in the spring.[57] The outcome of the battle in the air is equally difficult to assess. Determining losses to aircraft is imprecise, as about a third of damaged or worn-out machines recorded as "struck off charge" were completely rebuilt to fly again, but even by its own reckoning, the RFC lost more than the Germans. Some 190 RFC machines were definitively "missing" (presumably destroyed or captured) versus the roughly 164 German aircraft accounted for in RFC squadron reports—a figure that almost certainly exceeded the real one by a significant margin. Casualties among pilots and observers of the RFC are equally difficult to compute, in part because of the challenge of distinguishing losses in the Somme battle as opposed to those in flying operations in France generally. The RFC estimated 308 pilots killed, wounded, or missing in the Somme battle, including those suffered in flying accidents. There were a further 191 casualties among observers. This, too, probably exceeded casualties to German pilots and observers by a considerable margin.[58]

---

53  von Richthofen, *The Red Baron*, 100–2. A German officer observed part of the battle from the ground, as well, confirming at least part of von Richthofen's account. See Hawker, *Hawker VC*, 252–53.

54  In Malinovska and Joslyn, eds., *Voices in Flight*, 197.

55  IWM, Private Papers of V.A.H. Robeson, VAR 2/3, A.M. Wilkinson, "Major Hawker."

56  John Keegan, *The First World War* (Toronto: Random House, 1998), 298–99.

57  Keegan, *The First World War*, 323.

58  Figures above: NA, Air Ministry, AIR 2/124/B11000, Royal Flying Corps Technical Statistics Regarding the Battle of the Somme, July 1–November 17, 1916.

That the balance in terms of planes and pilots lost favoured the Germans should not be taken as an indication that the RFC had been defeated, however. Trenchard's strategic priority had never been to destroy the German air service through attritional combat, only to keep it at bay through aggressive patrolling. The RFC's *raison d'être* was cooperation with the army. The 260 tons of bombs dropped from RFC machines during the battle may have been pinpricks in the overall scheme of things, but the nearly 9,000 artillery targets they registered from the air, and the importance of the 19,000 reconnaissance photographs they took ought not to be underestimated. That Trenchard's machines were, on the whole, qualitatively inferior to those fielded by the Germans was a serious deficiency that would not be rectified until well into the following spring. Moreover, despite suffering just over 70 per cent casualties (based on strength at the beginning of the battle) the RFC in France expanded by more than a third in terms of both pilots and planes over the course of the battle.[59] Future historians might debate the efficacy of air operations, but the senior political and military commanders at the time needed no persuading. As the Battle of the Somme came to a close in November, Haig proposed expanding the RFC in France to 86 squadrons, over three times the number available when the battle began.[60]

The end of the offensive and the onset of a very harsh winter gave both sides a much needed respite and time for consolidation and reorganization. For Eddie McKay and the remaining "old hands" in 24 Squadron, the single heaviest loss they had suffered during the battle was Hawker's. Perhaps only another legend could replace a man like Hawker, and, in some respects, the new squadron major, Euan Cuthbert Rabagliati, known to his friends as "Ragbags," came close. One of the RFC's old guard, Rabagliati had arrived in France with 5 Squadron on August 14, 1914, just ten days after Britain declared war. He had flown some of the RFC's first reconnaissance missions over the Western Front in the earliest battles of the war.[61] His claim to fame stemmed from an incident on the 25th of that month. Flying in the observer seat of an Avro 504 and armed with only a rifle, he forced down a German machine. The pilot and observer were captured. This may very well have been the RFC's first victory in the air, though there are

---

59  Ibid.
60  Jones, *The War in the Air*, 6: 90–91. Even before the Somme offensive had begun, Haig had proposed an expansion to 56 squadrons. The number proposed in November 1916 took nearly two years to achieve.
61  The story of No. 5 Squadron's arrival in France is told in Barker, *A Brief History*, 22–28. See also "The Departure of the Royal Flying Corps Expeditionary Force" on Andrew Pentland's website, *The Royal Flying Corps*, http://www.airhistory.org.uk/rfc/EF3.html.

plausible rivals.[62] Whatever the case, Rabagliati was a pioneer and of some renown. He arrived at Bertangles at the end of November, just as the weather was beginning a severe turn for the worse. There is reason to think, however, that his rather brief, four-month association with 24 Squadron was an unhappy one. He declined to speak of it in a 1971 interview and, significantly, the rather quixotic 1920 souvenir *A History of 24 Squadron* does not discuss him at all.[63] He was a tauter disciplinarian than Hawker, and, finding that squadron members had little to do given the weather, imposed a drill regimen upon them, something his predecessor had never done.[64]

At least it kept them occupied. One of the worst winters in a century now descended on the Western Front. In December, McKay flew just four patrols, for a meagre six-and-a-half hours in the air.[65] On December 17, the entire squadron transferred from Bertangles, the only home in France it had known, to a new aerodrome on a muddy field near Chipilly, 15 miles east of Amiens and closer to the new front line.[66] Apart from this ten-minute hop, the squadron as a whole had only one flying day between December 4 and 20. There were just 9 days of decent flying weather in the 30 that followed. McKay flew on the 20th and, granted two weeks' leave just after Christmas, did not fly again for another month.[67] It was probably just as well. A trickle of new machines, such as the agile Sopwith "Pup," had begun to appear in RFC squadrons, but, on the whole, the RFC in France at year's end was burdened with obsolete planes, and its numerical advantage in scouts had evaporated.[68] Good new machines were in the offing, but it would take several months before they were available in significant numbers. No. 24 Squadron's pilots had been eagerly awaiting a replacement for

62 Several slightly discrepant versions of the story exist. See the interview with Cuthbert E.C. Rabagliati by Barrington Gray, audio recording, Imperial War Museum, http://www.iwm.org.uk/collections/item/object/80021542; John Xoyall, "No. 5 Squadron: A History of the Fighting Fight, Part I," *Flight* 72, October 18, 1957, 618–23, see pp. 621–22, http://www.flightglobal.com/pdfarchive/view/1957/1957%20-%201532.html. See also Barker, *A Brief History of the Royal Flying Corps*, 39. In addition, there are rival claimants. One historian who apparently does not accept the legitimacy of Rabagliati's claim is Trevor Henshaw. See Henshaw, *The Sky Their Battlefield II*, 4.

63 Imperial War Museum, audio recording of interview with Cuthbert E.C. Rabagliati by Barrington Gray, 1971, catalogue no. 23151. Gray states that Rabagliati's association with 24 Squadron was unhappy, based in part on his sterner approach to discipline. Email to the author, March 2015.

64 Edmund Lewis writes about the unwelcomed drill regimen in several letters reprinted in Lewis, *Wings Over the Somme*.

65 Logbook, entries for December 1916.

66 Logbook, December 17, 1916; Jefford, *RAF Squadrons*, 32.

67 24 Squadron Record Book, vol. 5, entries for December 1916 and January 1917; Logbook, entries for same. Dates of McKay's leave from NA (UK), Air Ministry, AHB, AIR 1–1562–204–80–34, 14th Wing Daily Routine Orders, December 27, 1916.

68 Henshaw, *The Sky Their Battlefield II*, 65.

the DH 2 for months. "The DH is no longer attacking but is fighting for its life against these fast Huns," Edmund Lewis complained to his father as early as October.[69] His letters returned to the machine's inferiority again and again, and also to his high hopes for the promised replacement. For his part, McKay wrote in a letter home,

We are getting new machines in a short time now. They are specifically designed for our squadron. The Huns have a surprise in store for them in the very new future. I would like to tell you more about these, but I think it would not be a good policy. Suffice it to say that they are very fast and have features not seen in fighting scouts before.[70]

As matters would have it, their enthusiasm for the DH 2's replacement was misplaced. The DH 5, a single-seat scout in a tractor configuration, turned out to be badly designed and already obsolete by the time the squadron finally received it in May 1917, by which time McKay was gone and Lewis was dead.

Despite his reputation for sternness, Rabagliati did permit a riotous two-day Christmas celebration at Chipilly, some of which has already been described. One of the squadron's NCOs enthused to his daughters about the Christmas meal of "roast pork, turkey, Brussel sprouts, potatoes, Xmas pudding and custard ... washed down with copious draughts of beer and lemonade." Later in the evening, for the entertainment of all, the officers mounted a vaudeville revue of songs, dance, magic, and "comical and pitiable sights"—the comedy fuelled perhaps by "plentiful supplies of ... lemonade, beer, whiskey, champagne, etc."[71] The revelry went on very late, and one wonders if the former social convenor of the freshman class at Western University had a hand in organizing it all. Here again, we find the extreme contrast between the pilots' lives on the ground and in the air brought into sharp relief. On Boxing Day, the weather was fair for flying. Edmund Lewis, who for so long had yearned for the arrival of new machines, was shot down in flames.[72] The revelry continued that night without him.

Although temperatures remained well below freezing, and positively hypothermic at high altitudes, a spell of clear weather at the end of January and early February permitted 24 to fly. Freezing temperatures had solidified the muddy

69  Gwilym Lewis, "Appendix II: Edmund Lewis to His Father, October 18, 1916," in *Wings Over the Somme*, 191.
70  Extracted from McKay's letter published in the *London Advertiser*, November 22, 1916, 1–2.
71  IWM, Private Papers of H.H. Heale, Document 5660.
72  Air Ministry Service Records, 2nd Lt., E.L. Lewis, AIR 76/298/11; Air Ministry and Royal Air Force Records, AIR 1/967/204/5/1098, Pilot and Observer Casualties: R.F.C. France.

terrain, enabling the Fifth Army to mount a series of relatively small but notably successful attacks up the Ancre Valley. Compared to the attacks the previous year, these saw light casualties and a substantial number of prisoners taken. The assault also forced the German High Command to order a withdrawal to the Hindenburg Line sooner than it had anticipated.[73] Between weather and leave, McKay was one of the squadron's old hands. He had been transferred to "A" Flight in December, and flew most often with his friend Harry Wood, who had become its flight leader around the same time with the departure of Andrews for the home establishment. Wood outranked McKay but regarded himself as "a step or two behind" McKay as a pilot.[74] At some point, McKay had also earned the rather telling nickname "Lucifer," a fact noted in one entry in the personal diary of the squadron's first recording officer, Lt. William Jaffray, who had arrived in early December.[75] The moniker seems to have been affectionately applied: McKay was known to be funny and friendly although, according to Stewart Taylor, considered "too outspoken and reckless a 'colonial' to command."[76] On January 23 and 24, he scored a remarkable two victories in two days. In both cases, the machines were brought down on the British side of the lines, indicative of the newfound boldness of the re-equipped German squadrons.[77] He shared the first victory with Harry Wood. The second was his own and particularly notable, as it resulted in the capture of a new Albatros DIII, the first to fall into British hands.[78] Occasional victories such as these proved that, in experienced hands, the DH 2 still had teeth, but they were few and far between. The weather worsened in early February but McKay managed 15 hours of patrol nonetheless. Apart from a sharp "scrap" on the 10th and another on the 11th, he reported few sightings of the enemy. He did not fly at all for the next two weeks, and then flew half a dozen desultory patrols in bad weather in early March. On March 11, in rain and snowstorms, he put in a frigid hour and 40 minutes over the front and returned to Chipilly without a single sighting of any German impertinent enough to fly in such weather. It was his last patrol with 24 Squadron.[79]

---

73  David Stevenson, *Cataclysm: The First World War as Political Tragedy* (New York: Basic Books, 2004), 140.

74  Quoted in Taylor, "Eyes on the Storm, Part III," 174.

75  The relevant passage in the diary of William Jaffray is quoted in Illingworth and Robeson, *A History of 24 Squadron*, 24. The authors do not name Jaffray but his identity as its author is confirmed by a letter in Robeson's personal papers. IWM, Personal Papers of VAH Robeson, VAR/2/3, Letter: W.E. Jaffray to Robeson, January 7 (1919?).

76  Taylor, "Eyes on the Storm, Part III," 174.

77  24 Squadron Record Book, vol. 5, January 23 and 24, 1917; 24 Squadron, Combats in the Air, January 23 and 24, 1917; Logbook, entries for the same.

78  VanWyngarden, *Jagdstaffel 2*, 28.

79  Logbook, February–March 1917.

At some point in the preceding week or two, it is likely that 24 received an important visitor: Lieutenant-Colonel Archibald MacLean, commandant of the RFC's first and most prestigious training centre, the Central Flying School. In the words of its later assistant commandant, John Slessor, "the Commandant was privileged to hand-pick his fighting instructors from officers nearing the end of their operational tours, for which purpose he used to make periodic raids on the squadrons in France."[80] McKay and Harry Wood were among those he claimed in his raid. On March 14, 1917, they departed 24 Squadron for the last time.[81] The squadron's aerodromes had been their home and its pilots their family for nine months. Now they were the last of that fellowship of famous knights who had seized the skies above the Somme when the great battle had begun in July. Wood had been promoted to captain, but McKay still languished as 2nd lieutenant, undecorated, with a creditable but undistinguished four victories to his name and the Boelcke story probably becoming a bit threadbare in the mess. But he was alive. "Little" Eddie McKay, "cool headed" Eddie McKay, "lithe" and "dogged" Eddie McKay, who liked to bore on in with his heart on the line against bigger men and bring them down. He was alive. Gray, Wigglesworth, Evans, Manfield, Gooderich, Langan-Byrne, Crawford, Begg, Glew, Wilson, Holtom, Knight, and Lewis were not.[82] And Hawker was not. McKay left. England and the home establishment beckoned.

The next day, 19-year-old 2nd Lieutenant James Kenneth Ross of Crouch End, a comfortable middle-class suburb in the north of London, arrived fresh from No. 6 Training Squadron to fill McKay's empty chair. He was dead in 20 days.[83]

## Mentalité and the Military Past

The fate suffered by James Kenneth Ross, who died so young and for so little apparent purpose, was suffered by so many millions of young men in the First World War that some in that generation, and a great many in the generations that followed,

---

80  John Sleesor, *The Central Blue: Recollections and Reflections* (London: Cassel and Company, 1956), 26.

81  McKay, Air Ministry service record; NA (UK) AIR 1–1563–204–80–35, 14th Wing Daily Routine Orders, March 14, 1917. An incomplete copy of Harry Wood's logbook (now apparently lost) is located in the University of Texas at Dallas, Eugene McDermott Library, George H. Williams Jr., World War One Aviation Library, Ola A. Slater Collection, box 11.

82  See respective entries in the CWGC database at the Commonwealth War Graves Commission website, www.cwgc.org. List includes pilots posted or attached to 24 Squadron who subsequently were killed serving with other squadrons.

83  Air Ministry Service Records, James Kenneth Ross, AIR 76/436/460 or 154. Ross's file is interfiled with that of another J.K. Ross, a common record-keeping error at the time. Eddie McKay's is interfiled with one for A.E. MacKay, who joined the RAF in late 1918.

ascribed the era's apparent enthusiasm for war to patriotic naiveté, simple-minded jingoism, and even mass delusion. We must be cautious, however, not to assume that our own attitudes about the First World War were shared by those who fought it. In the past generation, historians of war, drawing inspiration from developments in other fields of history, have elaborated new methods for trying to understand the way people thought about war and conflict in their own time.

War is one of the defining aspects of human existence, possibly even predating civilization itself.[84] The consequences of wars are often seismic, transforming societies in revolutionary ways and sometimes destroying them altogether. Even the outcome of a single battle has, at times, determined the fate of whole peoples for generations. It is no exaggeration to say that the geopolitical world we inhabit has, in large measure, been forged through war; given the lethality of our weapons, war might yet bring that world to an end. Not surprisingly, then, war has always been one of the core subjects of historical inquiry. The very first works of history in the Western tradition, Herodotus's *Histories* and Thucydides's *History of the Peloponnesian Wars*, written in the fifth century BCE, are studies of war, its causes and consequences. The interest in war has continued unabated down to the present. Tens of thousands of books have been written about the world wars alone, a staggering output vastly exceeding the capacity of any historian to read in a lifetime. Admittedly, many of these are popular histories that repackage old scholarship or are picture books about such things as tanks and planes, but there is enough new scholarship to make it difficult even for specialists to keep up within fairly narrow subfields.[85]

Today, historians of war often distinguish between "operational" military history and "war and society" studies, which was sometimes called the "new" military history in the 1980s and 90s. Operational military historians study campaigns, battles, and the decision making involved in their planning and execution. By contrast, war and society historians situate war in the broader social and cultural context, sometimes with very little reference to battle at all. They consider the impact of war on society and, indeed, how different societies wage war in different ways. In many respects, the emergence of war and society studies can be viewed

---

84 The "war before civilization" hypothesis has been the subject of intensive debate, in part because it seems to relate to larger questions of "human nature," such as whether or not war is in our genes. Read Lawrence Keeley, *War Before Civilization* (Oxford: Oxford University Press, 1996) and R. Brian Ferguson, "War Before History" in *The Ancient World at War*, edited by Philip de Souza (London: Thames and Hudson, 2008), 15–28, for different views on the subject.

85 According to the firm R.R. Bowker, which compiles statistics on publishing, over 55,000 books on the world wars were published in English between 1960 and 2013 alone. Anna Russell, "Publishing's Battle to Win the Great War," *Wall Street Journal*, January 13, 2014, http://www.wsj.com/articles/SB10001424052702303433304579306733788183534.

as part of the larger transformation that occurred in the historical profession after the Second World War, as part of the growing interest in social history and what French historians call the *"mentalité,"* or worldview, of different eras. Social history—often described as "history from below"—had its roots in approaches pioneered by French historians in the interwar period, but it subsequently received a powerful impetus from the social movements of the 1950s and 60s. Social historians of the influential "Annales" school, named after the journal *Annales d'histoire economique et sociale,* broke sharply with the historical profession's emphasis on the study of great men, power politics, and diplomacy. The French founders of this school, Lucien Febvre and Marc Bloch (who was executed by the Nazis in 1944), wrote sweeping histories of the medieval and early modern periods that emphasized the lived experience of ordinary people rather than elites. The new social history of 1960s and 70s went a step further, making women, racial minorities, the working class, and others often excluded from traditional historiography the focus of their inquiries. Doing history of this kind required social historians to seek out new sources and to develop new skills to evaluate these sources. To that end, they began to incorporate the methodology of economists, sociologists, anthropologists, geographers, and others in the social sciences. Quantitative methodology, such as the use of statistical analysis, became a key component of their toolbox. The members of the "Annales" school were especially interested in *mentalité*. Like many influential ideas in the philosophy of history, *mentalité* is the subject of a large body of highly sophisticated literature, and there is no consensus about what successive generations of Annales school historians have meant by the term.[86] In general, we might say that the concept stems from the belief that people in the past often possessed dramatically different ways of understanding the world than we do because the world they inhabited was often dramatically different from our own. It is therefore an urgent task for historians to understand not simply what people did, but how they thought about things. Understanding the *mentalité* of a bygone era requires immersion in the primary sources of the period and, it bears repeating, can involve the incorporation of theoretical and methodological perspectives from other fields such as anthropology and sociology, which have developed specialized techniques for studying societies.

---

86  There is an extensive literature on the Annales school. Both Febvre and Bloch wrote about the historical theory and method. Bloch's unfinished reflection on his profession, *The Historian's Craft,* translated by Peter Putnam (New York: Vintage Books, 1953) is a vital read. Febvre's mediations on craft are compiled in *A New Kind of History,* edited by Peter Burke (London: Routledge and Kegan Paul, 1973).

The "new" military historians reflected the unease with traditional history that social historians felt. They came to regard military history as inordinately focused on military operations at the expense of the broader picture. The result, the critics charged, was an actual distortion of the past because this sort of history tended to overlook the complex interplay between armies and the civilian societies from which they were drawn, the impact that wars had on the character of those societies, and even the lived experience of rank-and-file soldiers themselves.[87] The development of the new military history was also reflective of changing societal attitudes toward war and conflict in the 1960s. Its emergence at the height of Cold War tensions and anti-war protests over the Vietnam War was not coincidental. In part, the academic reputation of military history declined because, to many scholars disillusioned with the global nuclear standoff and the war in Southeast Asia, it often seemed patently jingoistic. The more nuanced approach of "war and society" studies, which incorporated the insights of such subfields as social, cultural, economic, and gender history, helped to renew the academic respectability of a field that seemed to some scholars at risk of becoming moribund.

The microhistory movement of the 1970s also had an influence on the writing of the new military history, especially when the experience of ordinary soldiers was involved. You will recall that, though they were often social historians themselves, the microhistorians believed that social history was so focused on the "big picture" that it effectively silenced the distinct individual voices of the ordinary people it claimed to champion. Microhistorians advocated focused examinations of smaller topics, believing that such investigations could help reveal the whole as well as exceptions to general trends.[88] In a seminal mid-1970s work, *The Face of Battle*, historian John Keegan attempted to recreate, at an intimate level of detail, the experience of ordinary soldiers in three important battles in British history: Agincourt, Waterloo, and the Somme.[89] Similarly, Denis Winter's 1982 work *The First of the Few* deftly wove together insights drawn from a vast body of memoir literature in an attempt to convey the visceral experiences of pilots in the British flying services.[90] From what pilots ate, drank, and wore to the routine aspects of take-offs and landings and the physically gruelling and mentally exhausting

---

87  For discussions on the "war and society" studies or the "new" military history, see Stephen Morillo, *What Is Military History?* (Cambridge: Polity, 2006); Robert M. Citino, "Military Histories Old and New: A Reintroduction," *American Historical Review* 112 (October 2007): 1070–90; Peter Paret, "The New Military History," *Parameters* 21, no. 3 (Autumn 1991): 10–18.

88  Carlo Ginzburg, "Microhistory: Two or Three Things I Know about It," translated by John and Anne C. Tedeschi, *Critical Inquiry* 20, no. 1 (Autumn 1993): 10–35.

89  John Keegan, *The Face of Battle: A Study of Agincourt, Waterloo and the Somme* (London: Jonathan Cape, 1976).

90  Denis Winter, *The First of the Few: Fighter Pilots of the First World War* (London: Penguin, 1982.)

experience of open-cockpit flying, few of the everyday aspects of the pilots' lives escaped Winter's razor-sharp scrutiny. In looking so closely and carefully, Winter captured what Keegan has called the "thrill and horror of combat."[91] Thrill? It may seem disrespectful to refer to something so grisly as warfare as "thrilling," but there is every reason to think that people find accounts of violence and war highly entertaining. From the *Iliad* to Shakespeare's *Henry V* to cinematic blockbusters such as *Saving Private Ryan* and video games such as *Call of Duty* in the modern period, audiences have been captivated by depictions of warfare.

History differs from most other academic disciplines in having a large non-specialist following. One seldom meets sociology, demography, or epidemiology "buffs," for example. By contrast, the general public seems to possess a vast appetite for history, and especially military history in its various forms. It is also a rare occasion to meet labour, gender, or farm history "buffs" (which is unfortunate, as there is a great deal to learn and enjoy about labour, gender, and farm history.) By contrast, visit any bookstore and you will find that the shelves positively creak under the weight of new hardcovers about old wars, famous generals, and the like, in addition to picture books about things such as tanks, planes, ships, and small arms. On television, history networks seem at times devoted almost entirely to documentaries about battles and military hardware, while popular movies, video games, and novels use military history as a source of inspiration. Even academic history departments often subsidize highly specialized seminars in less popular topics with surveys about war and conflict.

A moment ago, I referred to one ubiquitous genre of military history: books that focus not so much on soldiers but on their equipment. An avalanche of lavishly illustrated new titles about military hardware is released every year. There are successful publishing houses devoted entirely to producing books of this kind. Aficionados of such things—the material stuff of the past—are often referred to as "antiquarians." Militaria, or the collectable historical artefacts of the military (uniforms, helmets, medals, weapons, and all manner of ephemera), is a particular fascination for many antiquarians. There are even societies that restore original or build working replicas of military vehicles, including, as dangerous as it may seem, First World War aircraft. Antiquarians are sometimes dismissed by professional historians as obsessively and inordinately concerned with minutiae, but, in many respects, what they do does not seem much different from historians of material culture. The difference may lie in the fact that antiquarians tend to be *object centred* in their approach, meaning that they are focused on the properties of the thing itself. By contrast, material culture historians tend to be *object driven*, or

---

91  John Keegan, *The Battle for History: Refighting World War II* (Toronto: Vintage, 1995), 37.

concerned primarily with what the thing tells us about the world it came from.[92] Historians would be unwise to ignore the accumulated knowledge of antiquarians and other hobbyists, including historical re-enactors. One of the sources I used for my discussions of the DH 2 is Barrington Gray's glossy, magazine-style book *The AMC DH2*.[93] It was published as part of a series called "Windsock Datafiles," which offer detailed accounts of the development and design of various airplanes. The target audience for the series is airplane enthusiasts and especially the community of modellers who want to get details right. The book is focused, laser like, on the DH 2 and its design variants and is less concerned with the "big picture." Professional historians, quite frankly, sometimes look down their noses at this kind of work, even though they themselves often produce highly specialized studies. But a careful examination reveals that, in writing this "datafile," Gray has undertaken careful and thorough primary source research of a calibre that no academic historian would be ashamed of. Over the decades, along with other members of his "DH-2 Research Group," Gray scoured archives; acquired logbooks, letters, and rare photographs from families of pilots; and, in the early 1970s, conducted interviews with a number of surviving DH 2 pilots. Although the interviews focus on what it was like to fly the DH 2, they are at times surprisingly broad ranging and constitute an invaluable resource documenting many different aspects of the wartime experiences of RFC pilots. They were, moreover, produced at a time when academic historians were not very interested in what aging veterans had to say about war. Gray's work and other works like it propelled my research in unexpected directions. For example, I discovered that detailed records concerning many of the individual aeroplanes of the British flying services are intact. Various records tell us when machines were manufactured, repaired, and refurbished, where they were deployed, and what their eventual fate was. Using these sources, I learned things about McKay I would never have otherwise known, such as the fact that he survived a bad crash three weeks before his death while flying SPAD B6734. This is not recorded in his logbook (inexplicably, he did not keep accurate logbook records in the last two months of his life), but because an aeroplane was wrecked, his squadron commander had to file a report, which still exists, explaining the loss.[94] If at times antiquarians seem inordinately interested

92  For a discussion of material culture studies in its various forms, see Karen Harvey, ed., *History and Material Culture: A Student's Guide to Approaching Alternative Sources* (New York: Routledge, 2009).

93  B.J. Gray, *The AMC DH2*, Windsock Datafile #48 (Berkhamsted, UK: Albatros Productions Ltd., 1982).

94  NA (UK), Air Ministry, AHB, AIR 1/866/204/5/519, Report on Casualties to Personnel and Machines (When Flying), December 8, 1917, SPAD B3530. I discuss the crash in the following chapter.

in military hardware, in their defence it must be remembered that pilots were also very concerned with the minutiae of their aeroplanes, engines, and guns—how they worked and how they were maintained—because their lives depended on this knowledge. Future historians might shrug their shoulders at future antiquarians who collect iPhones and make them run again, but those antiquarians will know something very valuable about how millions of people at the beginning of the twenty-first century interacted with the world around them. Understanding such things is not trivial: recreating the *mentalité* of an age, to the best of our ability, can help us avoid anachronistic biases.

As we discussed earlier, sources can sometimes help us to understand the *mentalité* of the past in ways that their authors never intended. One source I used on many occasions while researching McKay's life is a curious book called *A History of 24 Squadron*. Co-authored by A.E. Illingworth and V.A.H. Robeson, who was the squadron's last commander during the war, the book was published in small numbers in 1920. It is brief, brisk, and chatty, filled with in-jokes and amusing asides, more of a souvenir for squadron personnel than a serious attempt to produce an actual work of history.[95] The book also includes some very useful, albeit occasionally inaccurate, reference information, such as a squadron roster and a day-by-day record of combats in the air. From the perspective of a "war and society" historian, however, the work's real value lies in its anecdotes about the social lives of 24's pilots. These are the kinds of personal observations that such historians relish, not merely because they add colour to historical narratives but because they help us reconstruct the *mentalité* of an age long gone. For example, the book includes an appendix called "A Chronological Inquisitor: Being a Brief Reminder to Those Directly Concerned in Many Quaint Events," which consists entirely of a series of questions such as,

Who shot Lt. Morgan's pet hedgehog?
Who's "Armstrong" got blown up by a "Primus stove"?
Which Squadron won the snowball fight?
Which Officer won the wager as to how many tins of "Bully" "Dan" could eat,
    and what was the expression used when No. 9 was reached?
Who was the driver who did *not* win the motor race with the Frenchman on the
    Villers-Bretonneux-Amiens road?

---

95  The authors even concluded the book with a list of addresses of surviving officers and men so that squadron personnel could keep in touch. Neither author served with McKay, and they do not seem to have known that he had been killed in action, as they included his contact information as well.

Who won the wager the night the Russian pilots came to dinner with the reputation of having defeated every Squadron (French and English) in France?
Why [was] their car still resting only 2 ¹/₂ miles away at 6 a.m. the next morning?[96]

Questions, but no answers! I, for one, would very much like to know what happened the night the Russians came to dinner—presumably, some sort of drinking
game was involved. Incidentally, I think I can answer one of these questions. A
November 1916 article in the *London Free Press* mentioned that McKay had lost a
number of personal effects when the stove in his hut caught fire.[97] An "Armstrong"
was a type of military hut that pilots lived in, so it seems likely that McKay was the
officer whose Armstrong "got blown up by a Primus stove." As much as we might
like to know the answers to the rest of these questions, it may be more fruitful to
think instead of the tantalizing suggestions they make about the social lives of
the officers and men of 24. The "Chronological Inquisitor" was compiled by one
of the squadron's NCOs, Sergeant J.W. Welch. In the preface, Robeson remarked
that Welch's contribution was "provided as a means of recording the many trifling
incidents which did so much to form the happy associations which all members
retain for No. 24."[98] Once again, it may seem astonishing to us that men could
retain "happy associations" with something so terrible as the First World War, but
this only underscores the importance of coming to grips with how people thought
at the time. In the years that followed, many who served preferred not to reflect
on the suffering and misery of the conflict. Instead, they remembered their service
with pride, recalling the friendships forged and the profundity of life when it was
lived with clear purpose and at an often feverish pitch.

*A History of 24 Squadron* covers the long winter of 1916–17 by quoting very lib-
erally from an unnamed officer's diary from that period. Like the "Chronological
Inquisitor," these diary entries are amusing and intriguing, providing the kind of
personal details that are absent from official reports.

January 13th. Dud day—horribly cold. Russian Officers coming to dinner.
Unfortunately, I am not present am dining with the General, with "R." and
"U.P." One of the Russians has escaped from Germany twice and has a price
of something over 20,000 marks on his head. He is a good pilot. *Later.*
Had a good dinner with the General and came back to find the orgy in full
swing.[99]

96  Illingworth and Robeson, *A History of 24 Squadron*, 57–58.
97  "No Official Word, But McKay Could Do the Business," *London Free Press*, November 20, 1916, 3.
98  Illingworth and Robeson, *A History of 24 Squadron*, 6.
99  Illingworth and Robeson, *A History of 24 Squadron*, 23.

At this point, I wish to reiterate that I really want to know what happened when the Russians came to dinner.

> January 17th. Dud day—more snow. After lunch, 22 Squadron invades us with snowballs. We turn out and give them hell with food and syphons of soda as well as snowballs. One of them falls in a gun pit. They depart.[100]

Who wrote this diary? Can we find out? Is there more to it than the excerpts in *A History of 24 Squadron*? By starting with what we know and by paying close attention to the language of the entries, we can begin to answer that question. First, the diarist was an officer with the squadron in the winter of 1916–17. This narrows the list to about 20 or so possibilities. In addition, the diary is not quoted prior to January 1917, which *might* suggest that the diarist arrived around that time. If so, this narrows the list to about half a dozen or so candidates. Now notice the kinds of things he writes about. Here is another entry from the diary:

> January 7th. Patrol of six scouts with "L." They all came home by mistake, leaving "L" by himself. No H.A. seen. "L" returns in a furious temper at 2 p.m. and, added to that, he got a cold lunch which made matters worse.[101]

"L" is clearly the flight leader, so that would probably make him Captain Selden Long, who was "C" Flight leader from October 1916 to March 1917. We can confirm he returned around 2 PM using the squadron's record book. He can therefore be ruled out as the author. Here is another entry:

> January 23rd. Twelve degrees, frost. Clear day, not a cloud in the sky. One patrol under "P" goes up at 9 AM and returns at 10.50. It was supposed to escort two F.E.'s for photography, but no F.E. appeared. No H.A. seen. A.A. inactive. Second patrol goes up at 10.50 under "W" for escort of two corps machines for photography. One B.E. goes home with engine trouble. They escort the other B.E. home with engine trouble. "S" in this patrol has forced landing at F8d, a place S. of Fricourt. Return home in the afternoon. Third patrol under "L" goes up at 11.10 AM for OP (Offensive Patrol.) "P" from high of 12,000ft sees a Hun on tail of B.E. firing at him at a height of 4,000ft. "P" dives with engine full on, on to tail of H.A. unobserved.

---

100  Illingworth and Robeson, *A History of 24 Squadron*, 23–24.
101  Illingworth and Robeson, *A History of 24 Squadron*, 23.

Fires 15 rounds at 25 yards range. H.A. nose-dives vertically and "P" sees pilot of H.A. fall out of his machine. He claims Hun. Not yet confirmed. This happened between Grandcourt and Thiepval. Fourth patrol consists of two pilots going out in the afternoon to strafe H.A. unsuccessful. An R.E. 8 crashes just in front of our aerodrome when landing. It was a brand new machine out for its first flight![102]

Using the squadron record book, we can determine who all the people in this entry are. ("P" who leads the first patrol would be von Poelnitz, "B" Flight commander; "W" is McKay's friend Harry Wood, "A" Flight commander; "P" in the third patrol under Long is 2nd Lt. Eric Pashley, who was credited with a victory that day.) So all three flights in the squadron went up that day, and a fourth patrol was even flown, but the diary author stays on the ground. In fact, he never mentions flying himself in any of the entries that appear in *A History of 24 Squadron*. This suggests that he is not a pilot and reduces the list of potential candidates to only a handful of officers: the recording officer, the equipment officer, the armament officer, and possibly even the squadron's commanding officer, who seldom flew. Now consider the following entry:

Jan. 28th. Sunday. At least a few hours rest, but I didn't go to church, as I don't quite know where they keep the church round here. The whole day was "dud," and so I read and smoked.[103]

What else is evident, apart from the fact that this officer is not an avid churchgoer? On "dud" days, when the pilots are not flying, he has no apparent duties. He can spend those days reading and smoking. The commanding officer always had other duties to attend to, and the work of the equipment and armament officers went on regardless of the weather. This strongly suggests that the diarist is the recording officer for the squadron, whose main duty was to keep records of flight operations. This supposition fits with another we made, that this officer may not have arrived much before January 1917. Checking squadron rosters, we find that 24 Squadron got its first full-time recording officer at the end of December 1916. His name was 2nd Lieutenant Sir W.E. Jaffray, Bart.—Bart. being short for "Baronet," a hereditary title in the UK.[104]

---

102  Illingworth and Robeson, *A History of 24 Squadron*, 24.
103  Illingworth and Robeson, *A History of 24 Squadron*, 24.
104  Illingworth and Robeson, *A History of 24 Squadron*, 85. Air Ministry Service File, W.E. Jaffray, AIR 76/252/168.

I searched for Jaffray's personal papers to no avail, but then something remarkable happened. Two independent lines of inquiry came crashing together. While reading a book about the RFC in the Battle of the Somme, I encountered a lengthy quotation from Captain Alan Wilkinson of 24 Squadron's "A" Flight. Always alert to the possibility of finding letters or memoirs by McKay's squadron-mates, I checked the citation. The source for this passage was cited as Wilkinson, "The Somme Battle," a file in the Imperial War Museum.[105] Investigating further, I discovered that Wilkinson's memoir was part of a larger collection, not catalogued online: the private papers of none other than Major V.A.H. Robeson. It had simply never occurred to me to look for Robeson's papers, as he never served with McKay. Why would Wilkinson's unpublished memoir be part of Robeson's papers? My guess: Robeson kept the source material for his book. I ordered Robeson's papers, and, sure enough, they included some of the primary sources he and Illingworth used to write *A History of 24 Squadron*. Unfortunately, Jaffray's diary was not among them, but there was a letter from Jaffray to Robeson asking for his diary's return when Robeson was done with it, so this at least confirmed the diarist's identity.[106] "It's mostly piffle but a few facts can be got from it," Jaffray forewarned Robeson in the letter, once again illustrating that historians, reading against the grain, can often find value in sources in ways that their creators never intended.

Our sources have sources, and those can sometimes be located. Just as physicists have peered more deeply into the structure of reality and have been surprised to discover that what they once believed to be fundamental is not, so too can historians sometimes find sources nearer to the past through diligent research. No amount of effort can completely bridge the divide between history and the past, but we can narrow it. *A History of 24 Squadron* was written immediately after the war and by people who were present for some of the events it describes. It can, in some respects, be considered a primary source, but a historian can often go deeper still. The passages in the book concerning mechanical problems with the DH 2, to give one example, are very good sources. Alan Wilkinson's brief unpublished memoir, which Robeson derived them from, is better. It gives a fuller account of the machine's defects and the frustrations pilots felt with it, and it offers the reader an unmediated encounter with a voice from the past. Finding it was, in part, pure luck, but historians, like scout pilots, need that, too.

---

105   Peter Hart, *Somme Success: The Royal Flying Corps and the Battle of the Somme, 1916* (Barnsley, UK: Pen and Sword, 2012), 130.
106   Imperial War Museum, VAR/2, The Private Papers of Major V.A.H. Robeson, 99/14/2 VAR 2/3, Letter: Jaffray to Robeson, January 7 (1920?).

CHAPTER FOUR

# The Choice: March 15 to December 28, 1917

... twofold fates are bearing me toward the doom of death: if I abide here and play my part in the siege of Troy, then lost is my home-return, but my renown shall be imperishable; but if I return home to my dear native land, lost then is my glorious renown, yet shall my life long endure, neither shall the doom of death come soon upon me.

—Homer, *Iliad*, 9.410.

On March 27, 1917, just over a year after his own first flight in the RFC, Eddie McKay began teaching basic flight in "D" Squadron at the Central Flying School (CFS).[1] He was fortunate to spend that April on the windy hilltop outside Upavon, near Stonehenge, where the school had established itself in 1912: "Bloody April," they called it later, when 319 pilots and observers of the RFC were killed in a valiant struggle to gain supremacy over the Arras front.[2] This was the low point of the war for the RFC, the heaviest monthly casualties its airmen suffered until March 1918 and the highest, in proportional terms, of the entire war.[3] McKay's former comrades in 24 Squadron, attached to the Fourth Army and not directly involved in the spring offensive, were spared the worst of it, but even they suffered three killed that month.[4]

---

1 Logbook, March 27, 1917. On the establishment of the CFS, see John Taylor, *Central Flying School: Birthplace of Airpower* (London: Jane's Publishing, 1958), chap. 1.
2 See Peter Hart, *Bloody April: Slaughter in the Skies Over Arras, 1917* (London: Weidenfeld and Nicolson, 2009).
3 Casualty figures for April from Henshaw, *The Sky Their Battlefield II*, 85. Comparison to other months from Hobson, *Airmen Died*, 414.
4 Illingworth and Robeson, *A History of 24 Squadron*, 69; Henshaw, *The Sky Their Battlefield II*, entries for April 1917.

While infantry regiments struggled to fill their ranks, recruiting volunteers was never a problem for the RFC. The bottleneck was the inability of the training system to keep pace with the growth of the flying services and their insatiable need for replacements. Rationalizing the training system under such circumstances proved exceedingly difficult. Losses on the scale suffered in April, nearly as great as in the entire Somme battle, coupled with the continued expansion of the RFC—there were now twice as many squadrons in France as there had been a year earlier—imposed tremendous burdens on the already ramshackle structure of the training system.[5] By the spring of 1917, dozens of training squadrons were turning out new pilots at a frenetic pace, with correspondingly uneven results. Though instructors continued to be drawn almost entirely from the ranks of service pilots sent home for rest, Gwilym Lewis, posted to the CFS three months after McKay, thought he detected a marked improvement in the overall quality of training over the previous year.[6] Medical standards for prospective pilots were higher.[7] All cadets (as they were now called) were required to complete an expanded ground school course at Reading or Oxford. There were more and more stringent examination requirements for pilots. They spent more hours in training—the proscribed minimum was about 28 hours solo now—and had the benefit of a series of new manuals and pamphlets based on lessons learned the year before.[8]

At this point, McKay's story must necessarily recede for a time into the background. His service record indicates the dates of his postings in England: to the CFS until the first week of June; then to 81 Squadron at Scampton in the northeast, until mid-July; and finally to the newly formed 74 Training Squadron at London Colney, where a portion of his three-month posting was spent retraining for the front.[9] Very few records of the training establishment have survived, regrettably, and details about his service during this period are few and far between. His logbook, which hitherto had been thorough and precise, with laconic but revealing remarks about his patrols, now descended into a dull routine that may have reflected the comparative tedium of his new position. Memoirs by McKay's

5  Casualties in the Battle of the Somme from H.A. Jones, "Appendix XXXVII: Comparison, by Months, of British Flying Casualties (killed and missing) and Hours Flown on the Western Front, July 1916 to July 1918," in *The War in the Air*, 6 vols. (1992–1937; repr., Uckfield Naval and Military Press and the Imperial War Museum, 2002), Vol. 6: Appendices. Size of the RFC in France from Jones, *The War in the Air*, 2: 285.
6  Gwilym Lewis, " Letter, 7 June 1917," in *Wings Over the Somme*, 89.
7  Macpherson, *Medical Services: Diseases of the War*, 2: 176–213.
8  See the discussion in Jones, *The War in the Air*, 3: 297–301. The volume reprints several manuals, produced in late 1916, in its appendices. Other manuals included "Notes on Flying" and "Hints for Officers on Joining a Training Squadron": see LAC, Air Ministry (UK), MG 40 D1, vol. 5, AIR 1/134/15/40/272.
9  McKay, Air Ministry service record.

contemporaries reveal that, just as few cadets enjoyed their training, few instructors looked back fondly on their time spent teaching. The hours were long, the work ungratifying, and the flying repetitious and unexciting. In his 5 months as an instructor, McKay accumulated more flying hours than in the previous 12, but most of it in 20- or 25-minute jaunts within sight of the aerodrome—tepid stuff compared to the fear and excitement of combat patrols over the Western Front. "I am really living a most awful life here," Gwilym Lewis groused in a letter to his parents after he was posted to the CFS in July. "I must start by pointing out that I had to get up at 4:30 *am* every morning (the weather always being fine) and finishing by 9 *pm* in the evening."[10] This seems to have been a fairly typical sentiment. When time permitted, there were dances, movies, and markets in the bigger towns of Devizes, Andover, and Salisbury, all of which were within 20 miles. London, where McKay had a membership in the Overseas Officers' Club, was only two hours away by train when leave permitted.[11] Perhaps with justification, the CFS itself had a reputation for being the dullest of places ("Ten times worse than France," complained one cadet, "because there is not a single thing to do except an occasional game of billiards"[12]) although the school's newspaper, *Speedy*, suggests that they tried to make the best of it. Written for the most part in the breezy tone that was a hallmark of British unit newspapers, *Speedy* included humour, doggerel verse, melodramatic short fiction, and coverage of the school's remarkably well-organized sports league. Given the chance, McKay surely would have played, especially rugby, although that league's final standings indicate that the instructional staff received a very rough treatment indeed from the mechanics and other members of the ground crew.[13]

There were other consolations to be had, not the least of which was promotion. At the beginning of April, McKay finally made lieutenant and then, barely a month later, temporary captain while employed as a flight leader.[14] He also had the company of friends he had made in France, including Harry Wood. And if any posting in the home establishment could lessen the occasional ignominy of serving as an instructor, it would be one at the CFS, which had retained its cachet as an elite centre of handpicked instructors, dedicated to producing scout pilots and testing new aeroplanes. Very occasionally, McKay's logbook erupts with a

10  Gwilym Lewis, "Letter, 7 June 1917," in *Wings Over the Somme*, 89–90.
11  McKay's Overseas Officers' Club membership card is in the author's collection via Robert Mackay.
12  Imperial War Museum, Letters of Miss Hilda Gosling, 2nd Lt. J.L. Booth to Hilda Gosling, October 10, 1917.
13  *Speedy* commenced publication the month McKay left the CFS, but it reported sports scores from the previous months. Very few issues have survived. IWM, *Speedy*, June 1917.
14  McKay, Air Ministry service record.

remark when something exciting happens: a long cross-country jaunt, a mock dogfight, or "joy riding a Hun"—which probably involved subjecting terrified and airsick cadets to death-defying stunts.[15] McKay also had numerous opportunities to test different types of machines, and his logbook indicates that he delighted in their particulars and eccentricities. In mid-May, he took his first flight in a plane he identifies as a "Sopwith Scout." This was probably the "Pup," adored by pilots for its nimble flying, but it may also have been the new Sopwith Camel, a superb fighter that would help to tilt the technological balance back in the RFC's favour. For 30 minutes, he hurled it around the sky near Upavon—no doubt with nearby Stonehenge in sight—performing loops, stalls, spins, fast and level flying, and gliding with the engine off.[16]

McKay had been a proficient scout pilot, but what kind of instructor was he? We have no way of knowing for certain. In their memoirs, very few pilots recalled their instructors fondly. The shock of service flying seems to have left them jaded about how badly they had been trained. Years later, Ira "Taffy" Jones, one of Britain's leading First World War aces, was positively excoriating in his assessment of his instructors. Pupils in his newly formed squadron, he wrote,

could honestly claim that they had learned to fly in spite of their instructors, who came and went almost as often as their students crashed. During eight and a half hours' flying instruction, I had no less than twelve instructors. To this circumstance, coupled with the poor quality of the teaching, I always attributed the weakness of my aerodrome flying. Many of the instructors were pilots who had been sent home because they were afraid of fighting. It was a great pity that they were not transferred to the infantry in France instead of being dealt with this way. Frequently, they were given promotion and then given jobs in which they were worse than useless.[17]

This may have been an overgeneralization and an unkind one at that, especially given the emotional anguish suffered by Jones's friend, mentor, and idol, Mick Mannock, about whom he wrote an admiring biography. Nevertheless, the sentiment is a commonplace one in pilots' memoirs. Cecil Lewis, who served as an instructor himself, was unusual in offering a balanced assessment in *Sagittarius Rising*:

---

15  Logbook, June 18, 1917. The derogatory term for Germans, "Hun," was also applied to cadets.
16  Logbook, March 11, 1917.
17  Ira Jones, *Tiger Squadron: The Story of 74 Squadron, R.A.F., in Two World Wars* (London: W.H. Allen, 1954), 56. This is a reference to 74 Squadron, but after McKay had left. Jones joined the squadron in 1918. Major Edward Corringham "Mick" Mannock, VC (1887–1918) was one of the war's leading aces.

I always regarded instruction as a come-down, a confession that the pilot was finished, no use at the Front, and condemned to flip young aspirants round and round the aerodrome day after day on obsolete types of machines. Of course it was unreasonable, for competent instructors were most valuable to the rapidly expanding Force. Although their qualities were not necessarily those of successful active service pilots, they were equally important. A good instructor was, and still is, a pretty rare bird. It needs some guts to turn a machine over to a half-fledged pupil in the air and let him get into difficulties and find his way out of them ... add to this, great patience, the quality of inspiring confidence, and an extremely steady flying ability in the man himself, and it will be obvious that nobody need look down his nose at an instructor.[18]

*two block quotes right in a row*

It may be tempting to see McKay's rapid promotion from lieutenant to captain as a reflection of his ability as an instructor, but, as Jones observes, more than a fair share of incompetent men were promoted quickly to fill vacancies. There is, however, one interesting and unsolicited anecdote about McKay from this period. In August 1917, the *Toronto Daily Star* published a letter from Doug Addison, a well-known Toronto hockey player then training with the RFC. While discussing Canadians he had met at Scampton, he remarked offhandedly,

> The best flyer at that station was a chap from London, Ontario. His name is *three!* Capt. Mackay, and he was my instructor. He played hockey with the London intermediate O.H.A. team before coming over. He is the most wonderful aviator I have ever seen, and it would be quite easy for him to write his own name with a bus.[19]

This was high praise indeed, but some caution may be warranted, *shade* as novices are sometimes too easily impressed. This is, moreover, a comment on McKay's ability as a pilot, rather than as an instructor. About that, we know almost nothing.

We do know that he grew tired of it. In June, McKay and Harry Wood had been posted to new training squadrons forming at Scampton: McKay to 81 and Wood to 60. Late July brought McKay a further posting to the newly formed 74 Training Squadron at London Colney under the command of Arthur Holroyd

---

18  Lewis, *Sagittarius Rising*, 139.
19  "London Hockey Player Best Aviator in English Station," *Toronto Daily Star*, August 17, 1917, 14 and "Toronto Athletes in the Big Fight," *Globe*, August 18, 1917, 18.

O'Hara Wood, a medical doctor and tennis star from a prominent Melbourne family.[20] Stewart Taylor remarks that McKay "became the driving force" behind the organization of the squadron, but virtually no squadron records survive from this period.[21] According to Taylor, McKay subsequently received "an offer to become senior resident instructor" back at Scampton. He declined the offer and pressed instead to return to France, where the summer offensive in Flanders was underway.[22] Why did he make this choice? He was safely established in England, having done more than his share already, poised, perhaps, for another promotion and even command of a training squadron. Many pilots who rotated into the home establishment, including Harry Wood, remained there for the duration of the war.[23] Certainly his choice cannot be ascribed to naiveté: having narrowly survived one tour in France, he knew exactly what he was getting into. He would also have known and probably resented the reputation that instructors had for being burn-outs, broken men no longer fit for "real" flying, and he may very well have wanted to test his mettle. Since his departure from France, the air war had changed dramatically. There were more and more powerful machines, and the age of the great aces had dawned. Over the Somme in 1916, an RFC pilot who downed four or five machines had really accomplished something—Albert Ball with his extraordinary two-digit victory total being a stratospheric exception to the norm. By October 1917, however, there were British aces with over 30 victories to their name. Billy Bishop of Owen Sound, Ontario, had claimed an astonishing (some would say literally unbelievable) 47 since March.[24] As the fame of the great aces grew, McKay may have yearned to join their ranks and to achieve the long-denied Military Cross, if not greater accolades. He might not have looked unfavourably on his chances, either. He had, after all, survived nine months over the Somme in the plodding, troublesome, and under-armed DH 2. He had accumulated the remarkable total of over 400 hours flying time—eight times what he'd had when he departed for France the previous June, ten times what many German newcomers would have in late 1917. Moreover, the RFC was now equipped with several excellent scouts that were fully the equal of their German counterparts. And he

20  Douglas Tidy, *I Fear No Man: The Story of No. 74 (Fighter) Squadron Royal Flying Corps and Royal Air Force (The Tigers)* (London: Macdonald, 1972), 1–2.
21  Under the leadership of Mick Mannock, No. 74 went operational the following year (albeit with an entirely different roster of pilots) and emerged as one of the RAF's premier fighter squadrons.
22  Taylor, "Eyes on the Storm, Part III," 174. Wood was promoted to major and assumed command of a training squadron.
23  NA, Air Ministry Service Records, Harry Allison Wood, AIR 76/558/124. After the war, Wood never flew again.
24  Shores, Franks, and Guest, *Above the Trenches*, 77–78.

had met Oswald Boelcke in battle and flown away, and Boelcke had not. That must have counted for something.

The popular literature on the air war stresses its terrors and the immense psychological and physical burden it imposed on pilots.[25] To the modern mind, it seems incredible that McKay would volunteer to subject himself to such horrors once more. In their letters, diaries, memoirs, and postwar interviews, however, pilots revealed something else about themselves, common among many British soldiers of the Great War. Undeniably, the war had been dreadful. It had broken many men in both mind and body, and few could withstand the strain of combat indefinitely. But pilots also recalled with great affection the unbreakable bonds of friendship forged above the trenches and on the ground; the carefree, even reckless, fun of off-duty hours; and the immense pride that came with honours earned in a cause most of them believed to be just. On Armistice Day, 1918, Frank Mathers, a Canadian in the RAF, wrote to his mother: "If so many good fellows hadn't been killed and maimed, I can't say that I haven't enjoyed the war. It has been a wonderful experience and full of excitement. I am very sorry for anyone who hasn't been in to it because it is an experience that comes once in a very few lifetimes."[26] This was a generation that possessed a profound sense of patriotism and duty, that clung to Victorian conceptions of the virtues of courage and manliness, believed in God and eternal reward for those who did good works, and considered such things worth dying for. Most of them no more doubted the justice of their cause than the next generation would in its own struggle against the Axis. An editorial in the CFS's newspaper, *Speedy*, waxed rhetorical about a near future where those who had fought could unburden themselves and take up the rich rewards of victory.

> Take comfort in the thought that hour must inevitably come, sooner or later, when our ordeal will end, when we shall repeat all the benefits, Heavenly in their richness, and beauty, for which we are suffering so much now ... nothing so fashions a man, a real man as adverse conditions ... these times are the finest lesson in life a man can have. He who does not benefit by them will never attain any measure of success, whatever, in business, socially, or in any other sphere.[27]

Indeed, those who had not fought—including those born too late or died too soon—were to be pitied, for they had been "denied the most truly marvellous trial

25  For instance, Winter's beautifully written but relentlessly pessimistic *The First of the Few*, 159–73; Mackersey, *No Empty Chairs*, 4, 67–78.

26  LAC, MG 30 A2, vol. 7, Lloyd Rochester Fonds, Mathers to His Mother, November 11, 1918.

27  "August 14–17," *Speedy: The CFS Magazine* 1, no. 2 (August 1917): 30.

of endurance, the most powerful test a man could have in patience, forbearance, courage, and all the other virtues that mould the shining hour of triumph."[28]

Subsequent generations have been far more cynical about such ideals, in part because so many who had believed so fervently in them had died to so little apparent purpose in the trenches or the skies above them. The cynicism runs so deep that, at times, it has been easier to conclude that the generation that fought the Great War could not possibly have sincerely held such values, that these ideals existed, if they existed at all, as a figment conjured up in wartime propaganda and jingoistic commemoration. Yet Eddie McKay went back to France nonetheless, willingly and knowing full well what awaited him. On September 3, he took his last flight in a trainer. Over the next six weeks, he accumulated 31 hours on the RFC's new service scouts, the Sopwith Camel, the SE 5A, and the French-designed SPAD VII, superb machines that had helped restore the balance over the Western Front.[29] On October 20, he took his last flight in England. A week later, he withdrew £11.7.6d from his account at Cox and Co. and departed for France.[30] He had eight weeks to live.

McKay's new squadron was No. 23, based at La Lovie, Belgium, a tiny town six miles northwest of Ypres.[31] No. 23 was one of only two squadrons in the RFC equipped entirely with the SPAD VII, the ruggedly built scout that had been the backbone of the French flying service for much of the past year.[32] Although still dependable, the SPAD was losing its edge against the best German machines, in particular for having only one machine gun when most German scouts had two. The French were in the process of replacing the aircraft with the faster and more heavily armed SPAD XIII, which 23 Squadron would also begin to receive in December. The other squadron based at La Lovie was No. 21, flying the RE 8, a stolid two-seater used for reconnaissance, artillery spotting, and light bombing. The nearby Château Lovie served as headquarters to Lt. General Michael Gough's Fifth Army, and the adjacent road pulsed with a ceaseless stream of traffic coming from the HQ.[33] It was Gough's army that had delivered the opening blow in the BEF's summer offensive in Flanders, the nightmarish bloodletting known to

28  IWM, "August 1914–1917," 30–31.
29  Logbook, September 3, 1917 to October 20, 1917.
30  NA (UK), War Office: Officers' Services, First World War, Long Service Papers, WO 339/62435, Captain Alfred Edwin McKay, Royal Flying Corps, Cox and Co. statement of account, June 17, 1918. Hereafter, McKay, WO Service File, item description.
31  Less than a week after McKay's arrival, 23 Squadron transferred from the authority of 22 (Army) Wing, V Brigade, RFC, to 11 (Army) Wing, II Brigade, while remaining on station at La Lovie.
32  SPAD is an acronym for the French manufacturer Société pour l'aviation et ses dérivés.
33  Fry, Air of Battle, 150–51.

history as the Battle of Passchendaele.[34] Horrendous casualties and disappointing results in the struggle for the ridges east of Ypres had led Haig to transfer command of the offensive to Second Army under Lt. General Herbert Plumer at the end of August. Millions of artillery shells combined with almost unremitting rain had transformed the battle zone into a muddy quagmire, an apocalyptic landscape upon which the opposing armies fought two months of bitter, annihilating combat.[35] McKay arrived just after the culminating battle began. On October 26, the Canadian Corps spearheaded the attack against the German positions in and around the Belgian town of Passchendaele. McKay had missed the Canadian Corp's great victory at Vimy Ridge in April. No doubt it cheered him now to be supporting Canadian soldiers as they fought their way into Passchendaele. By November 10, they had taken the town and the adjacent ridge, but at the appalling cost of nearly 16,000 casualties in two weeks.[36] No battle fought by the BEF in the First World War, not even the Somme, has been the subject of such acrimonious debate as Passchendaele. The controversy began during the war and has continued unabated ever since. For some, the battle, with its quarter-million British casualties exchanged for about five miles of ground, has become the very symbol of the misery and futility of the war. It is equally true, however, that the campaign again delivered a heavy blow to the Germans. Despite the German Army's tenacious resistance in Flanders and great victories on other fronts against Russia and Italy, its resources were strained to the breaking point by the end of 1917, and what was true on the ground was also true in the air.[37]

A paucity of sources makes the story of these, the last eight weeks of Eddie McKay's life, difficult to tell. Wing- and brigade-level operations orders give a general sense of 23 Squadron's duties, but specific details were lost with the squadron's record books in a postwar fire at Farnborough.[38] Inexplicably, McKay's conscientious logbook keeping ended with his return to France, and he summarized his 65 hours of patrol with 23 Squadron in just four lines and five curt words of description: "Ypres front patrols, service flying." He left no entries at all for the ten days prior to his death.[39] Only one of the pilots McKay served with in 23 produced a memoir: "B" Flight leader Willie Fry, who had a long and distinguished career with the RAF. In 1974, Fry published his brisk and unassuming memoir, *Air of Battle*. Written

---

34 Some sources prefer the name "3rd Battle of Ypres."
35 Stevenson, *Cataclysm*, 274–75.
36 On the Canadians at Passchendaele, see Cook, *Shock Troops*, 329–66.
37 On the Battle of Passchendaele generally, see Robin Prior and Trevor Wilson, *Passchendaele: The Untold Story* (New Haven, CT: Yale University Press, 1996.) For the German side, see Jack Sheldon, *The German Army at Passchendaele* (Barnsley, UK: Pen and Sword, 2005.)
38 Stewart Taylor, letter to the author, December 2007.
39 Logbook, October 28, 1917 to December 20, 1917.

half a century after the fact, it is occasionally inexact. He discusses only a handful of his squadron-mates and McKay is not one of them. McKay does receive a very brief mention in the unpublished personal diary of Captain J.M. McAlery (a "splendid Ulsterman" in Fry's estimation), with whom he served for just two days in 23 Squadron.[40] McAlery described McKay as a "friendly" officer who had "come out to take over 'A' Flight."[41] Apart from these sources, we have a handful of Combats in the Air reports and a few other official documents that refer glancingly to McKay's service in these weeks. The rest must be pieced together through plausible inference.

McKay arrived at Lovie on October 27, the day before the new squadron major, 33-year-old Charles Bryant. Bryant had received the Distinguished Service Order after heroic service on horseback with the 12th Royal Lancers during the Battle of Mons in August 1914. No one questioned Byrant's personal courage or fitness for command, but he was a mediocre pilot. He had been appointed flying officer only a year earlier and, like most squadron majors, seldom flew.[42] Willie Fry later recalled one near disaster on a rare occasion when Bryant took to the air:

Major Bryant, although not in full flying practice and a little old for SPADs, announced one day that he was coming on patrol with us the next morning. True to his character he did not say that he would lead us but was quite happy to be in the formation. On taking off, his machine somehow failed to gain height quickly and flew straight into the telegraph and telephone wires along the side of the road leading to 5th Army Headquarters in the chateau. He did a circuit of the aerodrome with telephone wires festooned over his machine and hanging from his undercarriage and luckily managed to land safely.[43]

He was highly respected nonetheless, in large part for his even-tempered approach to command. He was "a perfect gentle knight, *sans peur et sans repoche*," as Fry recollected.[44] On the day Bryant arrived, coincidentally the one-year anniversary of the great duel with Oswald Boelcke, McKay flew his first patrol with

40  Fry, *Air of Battle*, 146. McKay and McAlery had served together before, at Gosport while in training, although it is possible neither remembered. See NA (UK), Air Ministry, AHB, AIR 1/1273/204/9/149, Daily Routine Orders, RFC Station Gosport.
41  Imperial War Museum, Doc 14405, Private Papers of Lieutenant J.M. McAlery, October 27, 1917. This item, described in the IWM catalogue as a logbook, is in fact McAlery's personal diary. There is some slight confusion here as it has been claimed that McKay replaced McAlery as "A" Flight leader *after* McAlery was wounded on the 30th (Taylor in *Over the Front*, op. cit.). McAlery's diary makes it clear that McKay arrived with the intention of being "A" Flight leader, while McAlery was "C" Flight leader.
42  Air Ministry Service Records, Charles Edgar Bryant, AIR 76/63/73.
43  Fry, *Air of Battle*, 148–49.
44  Fry, *Air of Battle*, 148.

23 Squadron, accompanying McAlery, who led, 2nd Lt. Herbert Drewitt, and probably four others. McKay had about nine hours on SPADs but was unfamiliar with the countryside around the Ypres salient. Learning the local geography and its landmarks was critical for a flight leader, but on this first patrol the weather was so overcast that even McAlery was unsure where they were. They did, however, find the enemy: a dozen Albatros scouts at 7 to 10,000 feet. For McKay, this was being thrown into the fire indeed. Though he had accumulated an additional 200 hours flying time in the home establishment, he had not been in a scrap since February, and the evolving air war had changed significantly in his absence. The planes were more powerful, the patrols bigger, combats in the air more frequent, and formation flying a matter of routine, even if battles still tended to devolve into disorganized brawls, as this one apparently did. After nearly 25 minutes of fighting, McAlery gave one German machine a long burst as it got on Drewitt's tail. The Albatros turned over and spiralled, apparently out of control, into the heavy cloud below. A few minutes later, a patrol of SE 5s arrived to reinforce 23. The Germans put their noses down and roared off to the east.[45]

As McKay was to discover, a further revolution in the utilization of airpower was underway. Almost from the very beginning of the war, pilots had experimented with attacking troops from the air, and McKay himself had from time to time strafed German positions on the Somme. By the late summer of 1917, however, both sides were bombing and strafing enemy positions comprehensively. As the autumn weather worsened and heavy rain and cloud made offensive patrolling more difficult, scout pilots increasingly found themselves put to work performing low-level reconnaissance and ground attack. Flying over the battlefield at treetop height, they were aghast at what they saw beneath them. No. 45 Squadron's Norman MacMillan described the view from above:

> We flew at 50 feet above the duckboards of the swamps of Passchendaele, and looking down upon that sodden mess of filthy, shell-pocked mud I felt a sudden thankfulness that I was flying and no longer engulfed in the miserable conditions of ground warfare on the Flanders Front.... Every now and again, when we rocketed past above their heads, we saw the mud-stained British troops stand still and look up for a moment, many of them doubtless envying our swift passage over their slough of mud.[46]

---

45  NA, Air Ministry: AHB Papers, AIR 1/1221/204/5/2634, Combat Reports: 23 Squadron, Combats in the Air, October 28, 1917. Hereafter 23 Squadron, Combats in the Air, date. McAlery's report describes the flight as dividing into two echelons—upper and lower. His report concerns the lower echelon of three pilots: himself, McKay, and Drewitt.

46  Norman MacMillan, *Into the Blue*, revised edition (London: Jarrold's Publishers, 1969), 178.

Fast flying at 100 or 200 feet was dangerous work, offering pilots no margin of error. Arthur Gould Lee recounted a gun run his patrol made in November 1917:

> Splinters suddenly splash my face—a bullet through a centre-section strut. This makes me go hot, and I dive at another group of guns, giving them 100 rounds, see a machine-gun blazing up at me, swing on to that, one short burst and he stops firing.
>
> As I climb up, a Camel whizzes past me out of the mist, missing me by a yard. It makes me sweat with fright. This is too dangerous, and I lift into the cloud to 300 feet, stay there half a minute, come down.... There isn't much room below, I nearly hit a high tree, swerve violently, skim through tree-tops with the mist clinging to the branches, then suddenly no trees, an open road. I flying along it, trying to get my breath....
>
> A long column of artillery limbers.... I zoom, then switchback along the column, spraying short bursts in each little dive. I glance back—it is a shambles, half of them in the ditches. I'm sorry for the horses, though.[47]

On the day McKay arrived, scouts from the two air brigades fired 6,000 rounds at enemy infantry. On November 6, as the fighting for Passchendaele reached its crescendo, they fired 11,000 in support of the Canadian advance.[48] These were pinpricks compared to the immense weight of explosive shell that the artillery could deliver, of course, but aeroplanes had the advantage of reaching where artillery could not, causing havoc in rear areas.

The Germans reciprocated with regular night-time bombing raids. Crude bomb sites, together with the comparatively light loads that the aeroplanes of the day could carry, meant that the effect of such raids was very limited, even if they were terrifying to live through. On October 30, McKay got his first taste of being on the receiving end. That night, General Gough and some of his HQ staff dined with the squadron, no doubt to greet the new squadron major. The weather had been uncharacteristically fair all day, and 23 had flown several patrols and fought a number of sharp actions, once again alongside SE 5s from nearby squadrons. After sunset, German bombers took advantage of the full moon and "brilliantly clear night" to attack Lovie, probably aiming at Gough's headquarters rather than the aerodrome. "Gave us the worst raid of the year so far," McAlery wrote in his diary. "Got all around but did not get us."[49] The next day, he complained that

---

47  Lee, *No Parachute*, 169–70.
48  Jones, *The War in the Air*, 4: 210, 212.
49  IWM, McAlery Diary, October 29, 1917.

bombing had kept him up for much of the night, but otherwise no serious damage had been done. The same could not be said for the bullet that passed through his thigh when his patrol was attacked that morning. He barely made it back to Lovie alive. He was evacuated to a hospital in England, where he convalesced for the remainder of the year.[50]

McAlery's loss left Bryant without an experienced flight commander—Fry having only held the position for ten days—and may have forced McKay, who had not yet had time to learn the local geography nor the squadron's routines, to take up the duty in full before he was ready. The next day, October 31, two years to the day after he entered the United States to begin his flight training at the Wright School, McKay led his first patrol as leader in 23 Squadron. Around 7:45 AM, the eight-member flight, flying in two formations of four, was jumped in heavy mist by fast and powerful Fokker triplanes from Jasta 36. Two of McKay's pilots—2nd lieutenants Norman Kemp and Russell Smith, a Canadian from Ottawa—were shot down, though miraculously both survived to become prisoners of war. It was the kind of debacle that could happen to any flight leader, especially when up against a skillful foe flying superior machines. Stewart Taylor has speculated that McKay's unfamiliarity with the use of Verey lights—flares used as signals in the air—may have been "directly responsible" for the loss.[51] But Smith's own highly detailed account of the action, recorded in a diary he kept while prisoner of war, makes no such claim. Nor does a letter written to Smith's family by his squadron-mate, Ronald Cross, who was not there but pieced together his account of the battle from those of pilots who were.[52] Whatever the case, the loss of two pilots on his first patrol as leader was no doubt a heavy, perhaps even morale-shattering blow for McKay.[53] It was a very bad start. In short order, however, he established himself as 23 Squadron's most aggressive flight leader and pilot. Weather was a constant nemesis, but he flew over three times as many hours in November and December 1917 as in the same months a year earlier. In part, this was because the SPAD was simply a more robust flier than the underpowered and mercurial DH 2, but McKay also seems to have returned to France more driven and determined than before. If, over the Somme, the less experienced McKay had seemed

---

50  IWM, McAlery Diary, October 30, 1917. McAlery returned to 23 Squadron and was wounded again in January. He was killed in a postwar flying accident.

51  Taylor, "Eyes on the Storm, Part III," 176.

52  LAC, Russell M. Smith Fonds, POW Diary; see also Letter: Ronald Cross to Mrs. Smith, December 14, 1917.

53  NA, Air Ministry, Air Historical Section, AIR 1/852/204/5/397 Report on Casualties to Personnel and Machines (When Flying), December 28, 1917. See also Henshaw, *The Sky Their Battlefield II*, 128–29; Taylor, *Eyes on the Storm*, 174.

at times tentative or even timid, especially in his first weeks at the front, over the Ypres salient a year later he seemed a different man altogether. His combats were short, sharp, and fought at point-blank range—as close as ten feet in one case—and once he nearly collided with his prey. One of the pilots in his flight later remembered him being "on a mission," a man who seemed as though he "wanted to win the war all by himself."[54] Fry wrote that the squadron had no "stars" during this time, but McKay was credited with twice as many victories in those two months as any other pilot in the squadron.[55] Of the 14 decisive victory claims 23 Squadron amassed in November and December, McKay accounted for six (a seventh claim was ruled indecisive), more than in his nine months with 24. When weather curtailed combat in the air, he made it his habit to empty his machine gun on the German lines, despite the poor downward visibility in the SPAD. In mid-November on a low patrol, he reportedly knocked out a German machine-gun post.[56] When Bryant later referred to McKay as the "best man I had, by far," he may not have been exaggerating.[57] Bryant put him in for a Military Cross, but McKay did not live to receive it.

The Flanders offensive ended in the second week of November, although sporadic minor operations continued into the following month. On November 20, the British Third Army launched a surprise attack on German positions west of Cambrai, 100 kilometres to the south. The attack, aimed at threatening the German line to the north by severing the logistical hub at Cambrai, was notable for involving the first large-scale employment of tanks in warfare, with nearly 500 of the lumbering behemoths committed to the initial assault. Despite remarkable successes on the first day—church bells rang out in the UK at the news—the offensive soon faltered in the face of skillfully conducted German counterattacks. By December 7, nearly all ground gained had been lost.[58] Although 23 Squadron was nominally assigned to II Brigade, in support of the Second Army, it remained on station at Lovie. When weather permitted, there was work enough to do on the Ypres Salient, particularly in the form of wireless interruption patrols—attacking German artillery spotters that were directing fire onto the British forces consolidating their new positions. Over the coming weeks, 23 Squadron endured a steady toll of casualties, losing one pilot on November 18 and three more between December 5 and 7. When these are added to the two lost on October 31, the squadron suffered one-third casualties in just

54  Stewart Taylor, letter to the author, December 2007.
55  See the discussion of confirming victory claims in the appendix.
56  RFC Communiqué, November 17, 1917.
57  Arthur Bryant, Letter to Joe McKay, December 29, 1917. Author's collection via Robert Mackay.
58  Hew Strachan, *The First World War* (London: Penguin, 2003), 313–14.

over a month. Some newcomers lasted only a short while. Second Lieutenant Murray Gunn of Toronto, shot down northwest of Passchendaele on December 7, had been with the squadron for a considerable five weeks when he was killed, but William Whitaker, killed a day earlier, had served for just two. Sidney Kendall, bounced east of Ypres on December 5 by an entire flight of enemy aircraft, lasted one. He, at least, survived as a prisoner of war.[59] McKay himself was lucky to survive a dreadful crash on the December 8, when his engine failed on take off. He managed to put the SPAD down hard in a nearby clearing, smashing the longerons, wing struts, and undercarriage and wrecking the engine. Incredibly, he walked away unharmed.[60] By some remarkable trick of fortune—or perhaps a skillfully performed crash landing—he had bought himself three weeks. At some point in these wearing days of hot fighting and cold flying, one of 23's Canadians, Lt. George Trudeau of Longueuil, Quebec, who owned a camera, got his captain to pose for a picture. In this, his last photograph, McKay is smiling, though rather wanly, hands clasped in front of him, leaning on sandbags near "A" Flight's quarters, looking like he has aged ten years in the past two.[61]

On December 27, McKay celebrated his twenty-fifth birthday. Bryant was not averse to throwing birthday celebrations, with nearby squadrons invited. In mid-November, Fry had been fêted at a considerable birthday bash, attended by French pilots from the famous "Stork" squadron. With Christmas only just over and the weather bad, there would have been little incentive not to have another.[62] The following day, however, the snow and high winds ended at last, and the Germans were out in force. McKay took a patrol of "A" Flight up. He alighted around 11:45, taking the lead in a new SPAD XIII, the fastest and most heavily armed machine he had ever flown, with its powerful 200 horsepower Hispano-Suiza engine and twin synchronized machine guns. It was very cold over the Ypres salient and cloudy. Up and up they went, Archie pounding away at them as they crossed the lines. How far he had come from the student who had crossed the border at Detroit on Halloween 1915 with $290 dollars and dreams of flight, how farther still

59  For No. 23 Squadron casualties, see Henshaw, *The Sky Their Battlefield II*, 129–38. See also Air Ministry Service Records for 2nd Lt. Murray G. Gunn, AIR 76/199/172; 2nd Lt. William Whitaker, AIR 76/541/140; and 2nd Lt. Sidney Kendall, AIR 76/271/130.

60  NA, Air Ministry, AHB, AIR 1/866/204/5/519, Report on Casualties to Personnel and Machines (When Flying), December 8, 1917, SPAD B3530.

61  The photograph is in the author's possession via Stewart K. Taylor. Taylor believed that the photo was taken on the last day of McKay's life, but Trudeau's diary, held by the Directorate of History and Heritage of Canada's Department of National Defence, indicates that Trudeau was on leave at that time. Trudeau, seconded from the CEF, returned to the Canadian Army postwar and rose to the rank of brigadier general.

62  Fry recounts his birthday celebration with 23 Squadron in *Air of Battle*, 151.

FIGURE 4.1: Captain McKay. *Captain Eddie McKay, 23 Squadron, looking older than his 25 years. This photo, snapped by his squadron-mate Georges Trudeau, a fellow Canadian, was taken very near the end of McKay's life. (Photo Courtesy Stewart K. Taylor.)*

from his boyhood in that tiny cosmos of farm life in West Zorra Township. He had met the first man to fly in an aeroplane, crossed the Atlantic, visited the capital of the British Empire, looped the loop in a Sopwith scout near Stonehenge, and soared over the great Gothic cathedral at Amiens—such stupendous things. And he had seen terrible things, and done terrible things. He had witnessed friends go hurtling from the sky trailing smoke and flames, and he had dealt the same hand to at least half a dozen young men on the other side. He had flown with legends and fought with legends—and, briefly, had been poised to become one himself. Now, two years from home and 10,000 feet from the earth, in the cockpit of the newest, deadliest machine on either side, with 500 flying hours and dozens of combats behind him, with 11 months at the front when many pilots were lucky to survive that many days, what did he feel? Exhilaration? Exhaustion? Fear? A sense of power in his new machine? Little Eddie McKay; lithe, cool-headed, and careful Eddie McKay. What did he think or feel on this, the day after his twenty-fifth and final birthday? And what did he think when, just after noon, in an expanse of sky rent with bursting flak between Gheluvelt and Dadizeele, he spotted a German two-seater? We cannot know, but he attacked.[63]

## Thinking about Thoughts: The Past as a Foreign Country

In previous chapters, we discussed sources, facts derived from them, and ways of assessing the reliability of both. To begin this discussion, let's establish what occurred during the defensive patrol by 24 Squadron's "A" Flight on January 25, 1917. Here is the report McKay made in the squadron record book.

> About 10:35 saw 1 HA coming from E. just S. of Bapaume at my height, about 6,500 ft. He came across lines. I flew to attack and when about 30 yards away the HA dived to get on tail of another DeH below me. I followed him down driving him off DeH's tail following him down firing at him to about 500 or 600 ft., when he crashed at T26A. The machine was a single-seater Albatros with a Nieuport's struts and planes. It had a large K on side of fuselage.[64]

Notice once again that historians have to develop special competencies for reading documents. In this case, we have to know military jargon (that "HA" is short for "hostile aircraft," for example), names of planes, places in France, and maybe even something about British map coordinates. McKay received credit for this victory, but his friend Captain Harry Wood was in on the action, too. Wood wrote:

> HA appeared at various times well E. One high HA came and went as he pleased over our lines. At 10:30 I saw one HA which came right towards me, apparently without seeing me. When he got alongside of me, I swung onto his tail. He got his nose down and all the DH's and one Sop Pup went down to the ground on him, where he landed, partly crashed, near Maricourt.

Note that the two accounts have slightly discrepant details. McKay describes how he dove on the German machine, driving it away from one of his squadron-mates, while Wood adds the interesting fact that a number of British machines, including a Sopwith Pup—an agile British scout not flown by 24 Squadron—were part of

---

63 The only official account of McKay's last patrol is NA, Air Ministry, AHB, AIR 1/852/204/5/397, Report on Casualties to Personnel and Machines (When Flying), December 28, 1917. Weather reports from RFC Communiqué, December 28, 1917.
64 This and all subsequent entries relating to this combat from 24 Squadron Record Book, vol. 5, January 25, 1917.

the pursuit. McKay describes the German pilot as crashing at a map coordinate; Wood describes him as *landing* (though very hard) at a town in that vicinity.

Another account of this action is the Combats in the Air report filed by Major Rabagliati, which largely restates McKay's version, specifying that McKay was in the lead in driving the German pilot down, but also adds the names of the other 24 Squadron pilots who were there: Lts. Sedgwick and Woollett. Henry Woollett, who went on to become one of Britain's leading aces, wrote this brief account in the squadron record book:

One HA low down over our lines. I dived with the rest of the patrol but being higher than the rest, I did not fire. He finally landed near Maricourt.

Lieutenant Sedgwick witnessed the engagement as well, albeit from a very different vantage point: he was the one who fled with the German machine in pursuit, as McKay described. His account reads:

10:30 one HA dived on my tail—I turned and he lost height and got 2 D.H.'s on his tail. We followed him down—tried to cut him off, but he landed.

What of the Sopwith Pup that Wood described as being part of the scrap? Checking two reference sources, one on British aeroplanes and one on squadrons, we find that Sopwith Pups, equipped several British squadrons, including No. 54, which had just relocated to Chipilly, the same aerodrome as 24 Squadron.[65] This would make 54 Squadron's records the most likely place to find the Pup pilot's account of the action. Unfortunately, 54 Squadron's record book has not survived from that period, but some of its Combats in the Air reports have. Searching them, however, we find that they are prefaced with an ominous note inserted by an archivist:

54 Squadron, RFC. Combat Reports 25 January 1917 to 9 November 1918: Papers from this class and six other classes of public records relating to air operations ... were discovered in 1989 and 1990 to be missing. Investigations led to the conviction of a PRO (Public Records Office) reader on charges of theft and criminal damage, and many of the papers were subsequently recovered.

---

65  J.M. Bruce, *The Aeroplanes of the Royal Flying Corps (Military Wing)* (London: Putnam, 1982) and C.G. Jefford, *RAF Squadrons: A Comprehensive Record of the Movement and Equipment of All RAF Squadrons and Their Antecedents Since 1912*, 2nd edition (London: Airlife Publishing Ltd., 2002).

The note goes on to say that some of the stolen files were never recovered. Historians are accustomed to records that were poorly kept, misplaced, destroyed by accident, and even disposed of because someone believed them to be unimportant, but here is yet another obstacle, and one that we might not have anticipated—the intentional theft of archival documents.

Fortunately, the report we are looking for is among those that were recovered. If it had not been, it still might have been possible to find it if some other researcher had made a copy of it prior to its theft. In addition, the great redundancy of the military's reporting structure might have worked in our favour, as we might have found a synopsis of the report in the brigade war diaries or RFC Communiqués. In any case, the pilot of the Sopwith Pup in question was one Captain Alan Lees. His squadron commander, Major Horn, filed the following report:

> H.A. approached 4 de Havillands, and Captain Lees, and did a steep downward spiral. Captain Lees followed from 8000 to 3000 firing about 120 rounds when gun jammed. 2 de Havs and Captain Lees followed H.A. down to the ground when it was surrounded by soldiers.[66]

This adds an entirely plausible and important detail not found elsewhere: that the German machine, driven to the ground by McKay and the others, was immediately captured by British infantry. It is also worth noting one of the peculiarities of the British claim system here: McKay and Lees have both been "credited" with bringing down a German machine—the *same* German machine.

There is one other primary source pertaining to this action, an entry in the personal diary of Squadron Recording Officer Lt. William Jaffray, presumably made later that day based on what the pilots told him.

> Jan. 25. Fine; 20° frost. "A" flight at 10:30 go up on patrol. "Lucifer" engages another Hun with rest of patrol behind him. H.A. gets "wind up" and spirals down, and eventually lands at Guillemont. Machine intact except for broken compass. Two-seater Albatros, brought back to aerodrome.[67]

---

66  NA, Air Ministry, AHB, AIR 1/1223/204/5/2634/70, Air Combat Reports: 54 Squadron, RFC, January 1917.

67  Jaffray's diary is quoted in Illingworth and Robeson, *A History of 24 Squadron*, 24. The report from 54 Squadron also calls the German machine a two-seater, but this would seem to be a mix-up as well. Ten minutes earlier, Lees and another pilot for 24 Squadron, Seldon Long, engaged a German two-seater.

Jaffray's account adds some interesting details: it was a "fine" (clear) day, but very cold; the machine that McKay brought down was not destroyed but captured intact near Guillemont, a very short distance from Maricourt. There is a curious discrepancy here, however: Jaffray calls it a two-seater, but McKay described the German plane as a single-seater. This might be a simple mistake, or Jaffray might be confusing the machine with the two-seater McKay and Wood had forced down the day before.[68] Finally, we learn that McKay had a nickname—and a highly revealing one at that: "Lucifer"—because we know it was McKay who pursued the German machine with the rest of the patrol behind him.

Using these seven accounts, we could, with confidence, write a factually accurate description of this brief combat. With sufficient time, ambition, and the requisite language skills, we might buttress our description by searching surviving German records for additional details, discovering, among other things, who the German pilot was and what happened to him.[69] Even without these additional records, however, we have met the criteria for factual accuracy described in previous chapters. Around 10:30 AM on January 25, 1917, a clear but cold day, a German Albatros scout, flying west at about 6,500 feet, crossed British lines near Maricourt and engaged Lt. Sedgwick from behind. McKay, seeing this, dove to the rescue and drove the German machine down, firing all the way, with Captain Lees, who was in a Sopwith Pup from 54 Squadron, and Wood, Woollett, and Sedgwick bringing up the rear. The German machine crash landed between Maricourt and Guillemont, where it was captured by nearby British troops. It was brought back, largely undamaged, to the squadron's aerodrome as a prize.

So there we have it: a brief narrative account of an aerial combat. Contemporary historians are usually interested in much more than that, however. In fact, many military historians would probably not be very interested in a single combat at all. Operational military historians would want to understand how this engagement related to some larger picture, such as the history of 24 Squadron or RFC operations as a whole on the Fourth Army's front. War and society historians might be more interested in how combats such as these were reported at home or subsequently recollected in the popular imagination, while other proponents of the "new" military history have been fascinated by the visceral aspects of combat and might seek to reconstruct what the battle was actually like from the perspective of the people in it. This last approach poses one of the chief difficulties facing contemporary historians: understanding the subjective experiences of people in

---

68  24 Squadron, Combats in the Air, January 24, 1917.

69  Historians of the German side have, in fact, identified the pilot. He survived the forced landing to become a POW. His name was Gustav Kinkel, a German naval aviator now serving with the army. See VanWyngarden, *Jagdstaffel 2*, 28.

the past. What was it actually like to be in the cockpit of Eddie McKay's DH 2 at that moment; to feel the frigid air searing the skin in a 100-mile-per-hour dive; to hear the deafening roar of wind, engine, and pounding Lewis gun; to feel the vibrations of all three in the flimsy fuselage; and to experience the changing g-forces while diving and turning in pursuit of an enemy? These physical sensations would have been common to many pilots and can, to a degree, be comprehended through reading memoir literature and perhaps even through experiential learning (one could take a ride in a replica First World War aeroplane, for example.) But what was McKay himself thinking at that moment? Was he afraid? Exhilarated? If he killed the German pilot, did he feel remorse? Or was he glad to exact revenge for dead friends? Is it even possible to "get inside the head" of historical figures, to try to see the world as they saw it? With good enough source material, can we capture the *mentalité* of bygone eras?

I concluded the chapter above by saying that we cannot know what Eddie McKay was thinking in those last minutes of his life. Or can we? In some respects the concept of *mentalité* was echoed in the work of the British archaeologist, philosopher, and historian R.G. Collingwood, whose influential writings on the philosophy of history were compiled in *The Idea of History*, posthumously published in 1946. Collingwood believed that history, more than any other discipline, was the key to understanding the human condition. To him, the bare-bones facts of the past were not very interesting, and he denounced scholars who focused on such matters as "scissors-and-paste" historians.[70] What mattered, in his view, was the internal world of an historical event, the thought processes that led to it or resulted from it. Indeed, Collingwood insisted that human thought is the *only* valid subject of historical study. "The history of thought," he contended in a famous passage, "and therefore all history, is the re-enactment of past thought in the historian's own mind."[71] The facts of history were of interest to the historian only "in so far as these reveal to him the thoughts of which he is in search."[72] Collingwood might ask, then, what thought processes led Trenchard to insist on offensive patrolling over the German line? Why did Eddie McKay, safe in the training establishment in England, decide to request reassignment to a service squadron in France? Perhaps surprisingly, Collingwood probably would not have advocated the approach of some of the "new" military historians who have tried to reimagine the visceral aspects of combat: the sounds, smells, and sensations such as fear, anger, and pain. To him, these were mere biological impulses, the stuff of

---

70  R.G. Collingwood, *The Idea of History* (Oxford: Clarendon Press, 1946), 257.
71  Collingwood, *The Idea of History*, 215.
72  Collingwood, *The Idea of History*, 217.

the physical sciences, not history. History was the record of our "reflective acts," those informed by our fundamental rationality.[73] Through rigorous questioning of the evidence and by understanding historical evidence in its context, historians, Collingwood believed, could *rethink* past thoughts in the present. In this way, the choices made by history's decision makers could become comprehensible.

Collingwood has been criticized for being too dogmatic in his insistence that thought alone is the proper subject of history. Moreover, his belief that a historian in the present can recreate or even rethink past thoughts might seem altogether naïve about the complex ways in which our thought processes are socially conditioned and informed. Many scholars in the social sciences would contend that our thoughts are inextricably bound by or even determined by our social circumstances. If so, any effort to "rethink" past thoughts might be a forlorn one. We can never fully understand why McKay thought he had to go to war in 1915 because we are not ourselves a young man in the summer of 1915. On the other hand, this statement only acknowledges what we already have claimed: that our knowledge of the past is always imperfect and subject to revision. Whatever the case, Collingwood's *The Idea of History* retains its appeal among many historians today for two main reasons. One is that he reminds us that asking intelligent questions, and most particularly questions about what people were thinking, is a vital part of the historian's craft. These questions guide and inform our investigations and, in turn, give rise to new questions as we answer them. The second reason is that, in his insistence on recreating past thoughts, Collingwood admonishes us to understand decision making in its historical context. At times, historians have been too quick to criticize and condemn decision makers in the past, judging them by contemporary standards and ignoring one of the greatest perils of historiography: that, in one crucial respect, we know more about the past than the people who lived through it. We know what happened next. Consider, for example, the well-known fact that British pilots in the First World War were not equipped with parachutes. Parachutes were still an experimental device at the time, but by mid-war, the British began to issue them to the crews of tethered observation balloons. German pilots began to receive them late in the war as well. Why were they not issued to British pilots? Some writers have seen this as another example of the alleged indifference on the part of senior British officers to the suffering of their men, just as Haig and other generals are accused of having remorselessly used up the lives of infantry in one pointless trench battle after another.

Today, it may seem unthinkable that military pilots were not issued parachutes. To us, it seems to compound the manifold horrors we associate with flying

---

73  Collingwood, *The Idea of History*, 309.

in flimsy, unreliable, open-cockpit aeroplanes at high altitudes. But consider the following, by way of analogy: today, most people automatically put on their seatbelt the very moment they get into an automobile. Only a generation ago, this was often not the case. Seatbelts were not standard equipment in automobiles until the late 1960s. It was not merely automobile manufacturers who had to be persuaded to incorporate seatbelts into their automobiles; car owners and passengers had to be persuaded to use them, often through the compulsion of fines. In the United States, it was not until the 1990s that the majority of people began to wear seatbelts, in spite of overwhelming evidence that they reduce the risk of injury and death in most kinds of accident. I use this analogy to illustrate the point that what seems obvious to us in retrospect might not be to people in the moment. For many pilots, particularly early in the war, it simply never occurred to them to ask for parachutes for the same reason it did not occur to drivers for many decades to ask for seatbelts and other safety features in automobiles. In addition, the members of Britain's "parachute committee" had an array of quite legitimate technical concerns with the parachutes of the day. They had serious concerns about the reliability of parachutes, especially if they were deployed at high speeds, and they did not wish to issue unreliable equipment to pilots. Other authorities doubted that there would be many circumstances under which they could be used in the first place and wondered if they were worth the effort of development. Furthermore, the cockpits of some aeroplanes could not accommodate the bulky and heavy parachutes of the time. Nonetheless, the RAF *did*, in fact, make the decision to start issuing parachutes in late 1918, but the war ended before these became generally available.[74] We might criticize the RAF leadership for making this decision so late in the war, but this censure would be a careless judgement that fails to account for the fact that no one in the summer of 1918 knew for certain that the war would end that year. If the war had gone on, and many of Britain's senior military commanders thought that it might, we could today be praising them for their foresight in issuing parachutes early enough to save the lives of many pilots who otherwise would have died in 1919. Understanding the context in which people made the choices they did is not the same as approving of those choices, but it is a necessary part of the historian's craft.

Historians have long acknowledged the difficulties involved in comprehending the worldview of people who lived before us. As the novelist L.P. Hartley famously put it, "The past is a foreign country: they do things differently there."[75]

---

74  NA, Air Ministry, AHB, AIR 1/1071/204/5/1637, Parachute Process and Minutes of Meetings: Parachute Committee.

75  This famous quotation is the opening sentence of Hartley's 1953 novel *The Go-Between*.

This statement is particularly true in cases utterly unlike our own lived experience. It may not require a huge leap of imagination to picture Eddie McKay playing rugby or studying for a French exam because these are things many of us have done. By contrast, imaging aerial combat, with machine-gun bullets rending the sky and planes bursting into flames thousands of feet from Earth is another matter entirely. This is something so far outside the experience of most living people that historians who want to write about it must imagine the experience through the most diligent and exacting examination of primary sources. Even then, of course, we can never be certain that we are recreating accurately the internal world of the pilot. Pilots' recollections, whether recorded in a diary that day or in a memoir decades later, will always be imperfect and influenced by a whole variety of social factors. History will never come to us pure, as E.H. Carr warned.

Consequently, we must reject one of the most common criticisms made about historians. Anyone who has taught history or written about controversial historical topics has probably heard this dismissive objection: "You weren't there, so you can't know for sure." Historians of the more recent past sometimes encounter a mirror-image argument from older people who say they *were* there, so they *do* know for sure. One immediate response is that historians rarely claim to know things for certain—only certain things with an acceptable margin of error. Leaving aside for a moment the caveat that how people perceived reality can be just as important to historians as reality itself, most historians would also argue that "being there" is no guarantee of historical accuracy. Seeing is not necessarily believing. Our senses are highly imperfect. People do not always understand what happened to them, let alone why. They make mistakes and can deliberately lie—to themselves, even. Moreover, although it is certainly not true that "hindsight is 20/20" (if it were, we would have no need for historians), it is, once again, often the case that historians know more about the broader circumstances of the past than the people who lived it. I do not know much about the visceral experience of aerial combat over the Somme in 1916, but I know more than Eddie McKay did about the political and military context of the battle as a whole because I have a century of scholarship to drawn upon.

It is for all these reasons that triangulation is so important when our goal is factual accuracy. These cautionary points are particularly relevant to historians conducting oral history, which is usually done through conducting interviews. Although it is true that some societies cultivate oral historical traditions, enabling members to retell stories with remarkable stability even across generations, this talent has not been widely cultivated or practiced in the Western world in modern times.[76] Living memory is a valuable thing, and it is a great pity that more was not done to record the recollections of those who fought the First World War before they passed into history. It is also true, however, that we forget most of what we experience in short order, and we remember imperfectly what remains. Memory is frail and by itself seldom a reliable guide to the past. Oral testimonies are tremendously valuable, but they do not trump all other historical sources.

Having said that, some scholars claim that because our view of the world is socially informed—or even socially constructed—we can *only* speak with authority from our point of view. In addition, some cultural theorists contend that personal experience should be considered a highly privileged form of knowledge, one not subject to objective external interrogation or criticism. Understandably, this argument is often asserted in defence of oppressed and marginalized groups whose voices have often been ignored or even distorted in scholarship, which can further their objectification and victimization. At their most extreme, theories such as these imply that historians have no special authority, and perhaps not even the moral right, to study anybody else's past. Needless to say, most historians reject this radical position. The practice of history is predicated on the belief that we have both the competence and the warrant to write about different people who lived in different eras. If we confined ourselves to our own realm of experience, the discipline would collapse. No historian living today flew in the RFC, suffered through slavery in antebellum America, witnessed the upheaval of the Reformation, or gave birth in ancient Rome, but they have to write about such things nonetheless. In our preference for primary sources, however, historians obviously endorse a milder version of these ideas. We already privilege lived experience, even if it comes to us through sources left by long-dead people.

---

76 Note that "stability" does not necessarily mean "accuracy," either, because a story retold over generations can be stable but inaccurate nonetheless. Many societies that cultivate oral historical traditions value highly metaphorical and allegorical versions of the past, where accurate reporting of events is not necessarily the foremost concern.

CHAPTER FIVE

# The Letter: January
# 1918–July 31, 1932

*Your son, my lord, has paid a soldier's debt.*
*He only lived but till he was a man,*
*The which no sooner had his prowess confirmed*
*In the unshrinking station where he fought,*
*But like a man he died.*

—*Macbeth*, 5.8.39–43

Five hundred and sixteen officers and men of the British Empire are believed to have died or been killed on December 28, 1917. They came from every corner of the empire and fought the Great War across a vast expanse of the globe. Among them were Lance Corporal Henry de Bakker of the Auckland Regiment, New Zealand Expeditionary Force, who fell at Polygon Wood in Flanders; Mercantile Marine sailor Cheong Pow of Hong Kong, drowned with 27 of his shipmates when SS *Santa Amalia* was torpedoed by a U-19 submarine 30 miles from Malin Head, Ireland; Private H.H. Fellows of the Royal Welsh Fusiliers, killed in Palestine and buried in the holy city of Jerusalem; Ahmad Khan of the 29th Punjabis, who died in German East Africa and rests in what is now Tanzania; 44-year-old Private John Winfield of the Ordnance Corps, who died of natural causes in England; and Captain Alfred Edwin McKay of London, Ontario, commander of "A" Flight, 23 Squadron, Royal Flying Corps, last seen around noon, diving on a German two-seater southeast of Ypres.[1]

---

1 Number and names of the fallen for December 28, 1917 from the Commonwealth War Graves Commission (www.cwgc.org). The best surviving official account of McKay's last action is NA, Air Ministry: AHB, AIR 1/852/204/5/397, Reports on Aeroplane and Personnel Casualties, Captain A.E. McKay, SPAD No. B6734.

The next day, Charles Bryant attended to one of the most painful duties squadron majors had. Letters of condolence were obligatory and often read as such, with commanding officers at a loss for words about pilots they barely knew. Unable to muster genuine sentiment, they conscripted shopworn clichés about patriotism, courage, and manliness. Some such phrases find their way into the letter Bryant wrote to Joe McKay, but he had known Eddie for two months, a veritable epoch in a scout squadron, and his remarks seem longer and more heartfelt than expected. "Dear Sir," the letter began,

> It is with the very deepest regret that I am writing to tell you about your brother, who failed to return from patrol yesterday. I entertain very little hope that he might be alive. He was diving on an enemy machine when he got into a spinning nose-dive, and I am afraid he must have been killed behind the German lines. The other two pilots with him lost sight of him, as they were both busy with an enemy machine, and never saw him again. All I can think that happened was that he either got shot by the observer in the machine he was diving on or else got his controls jammed and could not regain control of his machine.
>
> I cannot tell you how much I feel his loss, as he was one in a thousand, and by far the best man I had, and one that I could least spare. Gallant and courageous, he hardly ever returned from a patrol without a fight or fights. He was loved and admired by every member of my squadron, officers and men alike, and to me his loss is irreparable. I am afraid there is no chance of his being alive, but as he lived, so he died, a true and gallant soldier, and I know that he would wish for no better death. If I had a squadron of pilots like him it would indeed be a fine fighting force. Men of his calibre and character are hard to find these days, and we can ill afford to lose them. Please accept my deepest sympathy for you in losing so gallant a brother.
>
> Our loss is almost as great, both from companionship and example, for he set the rest of the squadron the best example that any man could, in work or in play. Of course, there is always a small ray of hope that he may be all right, but I fear that it is very small, and to him it would be a very small compensation to spend the rest of the war as a prisoner.[2]

This letter probably arrived in Cobalt some time in the third week of January. Joe McKay kept it all his life. At some point he pasted it into the inside cover of

---

2 Letter: Charles Bryant to Joseph McKay, December 29, 1917. Author's collection via Robert Mackay. The letter subsequently was published in the *London Advertiser*, January 23, 1918, 1.

a handsome, leather-bound antique book called *History of the House and Clan Mackay* that Eddie had sent him as a gift.[3] It remains there today, a further entry in the clan's history.

No doubt the finality of Bryant's news came as a blow, even if it was not entirely unexpected. On New Year's Day, the War Office sent Joe McKay a telegram informing him that Eddie was missing, but that brief message had offered a modicum of hope. Missing, the message explained, "does not necessarily mean killed or wounded." It promised further details as they arrived.[4] The family seems to have clung to some small hope that Eddie might have survived and been taken prisoner. Eddie's brother Garfield, serving as a private with the CEF in France, wrote to RFC headquarters on January 13, inquiring if Eddie had been wounded and whether he could be contacted.[5] It was not impossible: three of the six 23 Squadron pilots shot down in the two months prior to McKay had survived and were in captivity. Just a few weeks earlier, London's newspapers had reported that McKay's friend and fellow pilot, former *London Advertiser* sports writer Bert Perry, was alive in German captivity after having initially been declared missing. The anguish suffered by the McKay family during those days of uncertainty was one experienced by tens of thousands of families over the course of the war. In the vast majority of cases, "missing" meant that a soldiers' remains were either unrecoverable or unidentifiable. Bryant's letter was emphatic that McKay was dead, but officials at the War Office required further confirmation. The opposing sides retained channels of communication concerning prisoners through their legations in the Netherlands and via the International Red Cross, through which a steady flow of queries about the missing passed. On February 2, however, a German machine over the Ypres salient dropped a note into British lines stating that Captain A.E. McKay was dead. In a letter to Joe informing him of the news, the War Office asked specifically that "under no circumstances should the source of this information" (i.e., a dropped message) be "divulged in any obituary or other notices inserted in the press or elsewhere"—it being inadvisable, apparently, to let the public know that the Hun was capable of honourable conduct. The letter stressed that, while the message was unconfirmed, it was "probably correct."[6] In mid-March, McKay's identity discs were returned to the British through the Red Cross in Geneva with no further details. Then, on April 2, his name appeared on an official list of the

---

3  The book, dated 1829, is presently in the author's collection via Robert Mackay.
4  NA (UK), WO Service File, Telegram: War Office to J.D. McKay, January 1, 1918.
5  McKay, WO Service File, Letter: G.M. McKay to War Office, January 13, 1918.
6  McKay, WO Service File, Letter: War Office to J.D. McKay, February 5, 1918. Date of drop from McKay, Casualty Card.

dead from the German Red Cross.[7] A month later, the War Office formally declared him dead.[8]

By then, it was already old news back home. The report that McKay was missing broke in London's papers on January 14. On January 23, the *Advertiser* reprinted Bryant's letter, which apparently had been passed on to the editors by the family. The following day, the *Free Press* published excerpts from it and took a moment to reflect.

> His companions seem to believe that the noble young Canadian has made his final flight. Somewhere behind German lines he sleeps, his soul gone on to an eternal home, while his work for humanity is weaved into the fabric of sacrifice and honor. The white flower of a blameless life was his. He went forth with quiet resolution, and won though to his goal many, many times. A gallant young London gentleman! The name of "Eddie" McKay will never be forgotten while memory of the war lasts.[9]

To the modern reader, sentiments such as these might ring hollow, naïve, and jingoistic. Bryant's suggestion that McKay would have "wished for no better death" may even strike us as callous or cruel. Today, the war is often remembered as having been fought for no good reason by morally equivalent adversaries who cruelly slaughtered a generation of young men in one futile trench battle after another. This perspective took shape during the war and subsequently was adopted by a generation of disillusioned and cynical novelists, poets, painters, and other intellectuals. At their most radical, the artists of what was sometimes called the "lost generation" extended their critique of the war into an indictment of humanity itself.[10] Their condemnation, undoubtedly shared by many who had fought and families who had suffered, was comprehensible. The war had left millions dead and millions more broken in body and mind. It tore apart empires; redrew the map of Europe, the Middle East, and portions of Africa; and unleashed revolutionary forces whose impact is still felt today. Even in the victorious states, the war shook the foundations of the social and political order. In Canada, as elsewhere, the war was at once nation building and dangerously divisive. In particular, the country's

---

7  McKay, Casualty Card; McKay, WO Service File, Telegram, War Office to J.W. McKay, April 16, 1918. The discs were returned to Joe McKay thereafter but subsequently have been lost.

8  McKay, WO Service File, Telegram, War Office to McKay, May 2, 1918.

9  "Captain "Eddie" McKay," *London Free Press*, January 23, 1918, 2.

10  On this, see the enormously influential works by Paul Fussell, *The Great War and Modern Memory* (New York: Oxford University Press, 1975) and Modris Eksteins, *Rites of Spring: The Great War and the Birth of the Modern Age* (Boston: Houghton Mifflin, 1989).

protracted national debate over conscription rent the veneer of patriotic consensus and led to severe recriminations between French and English Canadians.

But Bryant's letter and the articles that appeared in local papers reflecting on McKay's death serve as an important, cautionary reminder to modern readers. We must not assume that our own attitudes about the war, nor those of a select group of intellectuals writing in the decade following the war, were shared universally by the generation that actually fought it. Divisive though the war was, another and perhaps even predominant cultural response emerged during the war and moulded the vast commemorative efforts that followed. As Jonathan Vance has argued, in Canada in particular, the unifying theme of the vast commemorative efforts that followed the war was the search for consolation, in which rational understanding took a backseat. In poetry, fiction, and memoirs; on canvas and in sculpture; in the language and ritual of annual Armistice Day services; in the stone memorials, stained-glass windows, and bronze markers that appeared in nearly every city centre, town square, church, school, and civic building throughout the country, Canadians constructed a mythology of the war in which the dominant themes were not, as Vance put it, ones of

> despair, aimlessness, and futility, but of promise, certainty, and goodness. It assured Canadians that the war had been a just one, fought to defend Christianity and Western civilization, and that Canada's sons and daughters had done all by their country and would not be forgotten for their sacrifices.[11]

Vance argues that whether or not such ideas were accurate reflections of the reality of the war is beside the point: how people perceive the past has a reality of its own, deserving of study as a product and reflection of its historical circumstances.

To many on the home front, the Knights of the Air may have exemplified the virtues of courage, honour, physical prowess, and patriotic self-sacrifice, but they were not uniquely possessed of them. The sentiments found in Bryant's letter can readily be located in countless tributes to others. The high-minded Victorian rhetoric that regarded such virtues as the hallmarks of masculinity had not perished in the trenches—nor did the view, advanced from every corner early in the conflict, that the Great War would decide nothing less than the fate of Christian civilization. McKay's sacrifice, like that of so many others, was, in the words of the *London Free Press*, no less than "work for humanity," never to be forgotten. Two

---

11   Jonathan Vance, *Death So Noble: Memory, Meaning, and the First World War* (Vancouver: UBC Press, 1997), 266. I have been influenced by the work as a whole in this discussion.

years later, an article announcing the dedication, in McKay's name, of a memorial
trophy for grade school hockey, touched on many of the same themes. It, too,
demonstrates that neither prewar conceptions of masculinity, heroism, and the
pure and purifying potential of sport nor their relationship to the "great game"
of war had given way to cynicism and despair. In language that might easily have
been written in 1914, McKay, it said, represented the "finest types of athletic manhood ever connected with London sport."

> What his athletic career taught him of "playing the game" carried him glori-
> ously through to that life's glorious closing in the greatest game of them all,
> with life and death as the even and odd. An ideal of manhood such as the
> Eddie McKay Memorial Cup represents might well for generations of the
> school children of London be one to be maintained, striven, and fought for.[12]

This conception of masculinity may seem deeply sexist at a time when it is no
longer widely accepted that such qualities are the sole province of men, just as the
valorization of McKay's sacrifice might seem callously and even dangerously jingoistic. But there is every reason to think that sentiments such as these continued
to resonate powerfully throughout the combatant nations in the years following
the war.

In 1917, the British government established the Imperial War Graves Commission, with a mandate to bury the dead and find suitable means of memorializing
them. One of the commission's governing policies was non-repatriation: the dead
would be buried as near to where they died as possible. Their cemeteries would
be their monuments, built on or near the very battlefields where they fought and
fell.[13] There was surprisingly little objection to this permanent separation of families from their fallen loved ones, but one consequence was that it heightened
the significance of the local cenotaph. Throughout the British Empire, the local
memorial became a surrogate grave for the dead and the annual Armistice Day
services a surrogate funeral.[14] Like many of the fallen of the Great War, then, Eddie
McKay was commemorated in many places. In addition to stained-glass windows

---

12  C.S. Granton, "The Eddie McKay Memorial Cup," *London Advertiser*, April 10, 1920, 8. The cup
    was donated by William Haddon, former president of Western's athletic association. Its current
    location is unknown.
13  Renamed the Commonwealth War Graves Commission in 1964, the organization extended its
    work in the Second World War. It currently maintains 1.7 million graves or names on memorials to
    the missing in over 150 countries. On the commission and its founder, see David Crane, *Empire of
    the Dead* (London: William Collins, 2013).
14  Jonathan Vance, "Remember Armageddon," in *Canada and the First World War: Essays in Honour of
    Robert Craig Brown*, edited by David Mackenzie (Toronto: University of Toronto Press, 2005), 409–34.

to his memory in churches near his hometown, his name is on the cenotaph in Embro, Ontario, not far from where he grew up; it appears on the roll of honour in his former high school in London and also in First St. Andrew's Church, his congregation in the city. It appears on two commemorative markers at Western University, and, in 2012, it was added to the cenotaph in Stratford, Ontario. With 66,000 others, his name is inscribed in the Book of Remembrance in Canada's most important war memorial—the Peace Tower in the Centre Block of Canada's Parliament in Ottawa—and in similar books at St. Clement Danes Church in London, England, where fliers from both world wars are commemorated. Surprisingly, and perhaps mistakenly, it also appears in the flying services roll of honour in the Scottish National War Memorial in Edinburgh Castle. And he is commemorated in France.[15]

In two ceremonies held a day apart at the end of July and beginning of August 1932, the Imperial War Graves Commission unveiled what the Toronto *Globe* described as the last of the "great circle of commemorative structures for the 1,100,000 dead of the British Empire": the Arras Memorial to the Missing and the immense Thiepval Memorial to the Missing of the Somme.[16] Between them, the two monuments recorded the names of nearly 110,000 of the fallen who had no known grave. The Arras Memorial, unveiled on July 31, enclosed an additional and distinctive commemorative monument: a 25-foot-tall obelisk capped with a globe—the Flying Services Memorial—upon which the names of a thousand missing pilots were engraved.[17] Like many IWGC sites, the memorials were designed by Sir Edward Lutyens, a gifted and prolific English architect who had been one of the principle designers of the city of New Delhi. Apart from designing over half of all IWGC cemeteries and memorials, Lutyens was also the architect of the Whitehall Cenotaph, a scale copy of which serves as the focal point of Remembrance Day services in London, Ontario, down to the present. The graceful, neoclassical Arras Memorial, dedicated to some 35,000 Commonwealth servicemen missing in the Arras sector, is typical of his work. (The red brick Thiepval Memorial, dedicated the following day, is not.) Lutyens was there on July 31 when a large delegation from the United Kingdom, accompanied by representatives of every dominion and dignitaries from France, gathered for the unveiling. Among them were politicians, generals, diplomats, and high-ranking clergy, but occupying the place of honour were the thousands of veterans and their families who had

---

15  In 2007, a marker to McKay's memory was placed on Western's campus. Western had no cenotaph commemorating its student dead until 2009. The author located McKay's name in an honour roll in the Scottish National War Memorial in the summer of 2015.

16  "Memorial Unveiled to British Fliers," *Globe*, August 1, 1932, 10.

17  The globe atop the monument was sculpted by Sir William Reid Dick.

travelled from the UK to attend. Many had arrived in Arras the day before, only to find the local hotels booked. They spent the warm July night sleeping in the city's Grand Place then stormed the cafes before descending on the memorial for the mid-afternoon ceremony.[18]

Hugh Trenchard, now commissioner of the Metropolitan Police, presided over the ceremony. In his brief address, spoken at a podium near the obelisk itself, Trenchard paid special tribute to the men of the flying services. Near the end of his speech, he explained the significance of the finial at the top of the memorial, and then expressed sentiments that would have been familiar to all present from countless other such occasions since the war had ended.

> The globe placed on the obelisk has a significance bridging the years that have passed since November, 1918. It stands exactly, with its north and south points, as our globe hung in space on the morning of Armistice Day, 1918. On every anniversary of that morning, it will recall the sacrifice that these kinsmen of ours made, winning infinite peace for themselves in the struggle to win peace for their country, and it will catch, however faintly, the warmth of the sun that shone down that day on the trenches of the Arras Front, when at last no sound came from the distant guns and Death rode no longer on the airman's wings.[19]

Prayers followed and a reading of Psalm 129 and then the hymn "For All the Saints [who from their labours rest]," which continues "For Martyrs, who with rapture kindled eye, / Saw the bright crown descending from the sky, / And seeing, grasped it, Thee we glorify." The buglers of the Durham Light Infantry sounded the Last Post and the ceremony reached its emotional crescendo as pipers from the Seaforth Highlanders played "Flowers of the Forest." Overhead, five planes droned past in formation—they were, fittingly, from 24 Squadron. As the ceremony concluded and the delegates exited past the French honour guard, veterans lingered to pay tribute to fallen comrades.[20] Among them were many who had served with the RFC, and on the obelisk they found the names of Douglas Gray, Henry Evans, Lanoe Hawker, Edmund Lewis, Eddie McKay, and others in that fellowship of famous knights they knew. Perhaps, as they lingered and wept at the memory of fallen friends, they derived some solace in the words spoken by the officiating chaplain a short time earlier: "Inspired by the example of these our

---

18  "British Arras Memorial," *Glasgow Herald*, August 1, 1932, 11.
19  Trenchard's remarks were reported in "Missing War Dead: Arras Memorial Dedicated," *The Times*, August 1, 1932, 10.
20  "Memorial Unveiled to British Fliers," *Globe*, August 1, 1932, 10.

brothers, we who remain may give our lives in service and sacrifice for the progress of humanity so that we be not ashamed when we meet with them beyond the grave."[21]

That day, a Sunday, the people of Germany voted in their federal election. Adolf Hitler and the Nazis were returned to the Reichstag as its largest party.

## Historians, Historical Ethics, and the End of History

So ends Eddie McKay's story, or at least the version of the story that I wanted to tell and was able to tell based on the sources I had. As we have discussed, another historian with different interests and abilities might have told the story in a different way. And I nearly *did* tell a slightly different story because of a mistake I made early in my research. According to his service file, McKay was posted to 24 Squadron on June 21, 1916.[22] Prior to discovering his logbook, this was the best information I had, and it led me to believe something that was not true. In 1965, Tyrrell Hawker, who served as an officer in the Royal Artillery, wrote an affectionate biography of his brother Lanoe, 24 Squadron's legendary commander. In it, he recounts an uproarious party that the squadron had a week before the Somme offensive began.

> That night there was a "binge" in the mess, during which T. noticed that one of the newly arrived pilots had a medical dressing on his head.... "What's happened to you?" he asked. There an awkward silence as this pilot looked down at his plate, and T. turned enquiringly to Lanoe.
>
> "Serves him right," said Lanoe a little grimly. "He didn't obey orders to keep his head down when passing through the gauge." The "gauge" was a French side-board, with a shelf beneath the usual cupboard which had ornamental finials at each end. Newly arrived pilots, as part of their initiation ceremony, were swung by their comrades and projected face down from one end of the shelf to the other to slide out in a heap if satisfactorily gauged. If the novice, to see where he was going, raised his head, his scalp was split by the sharp point of the finial at the far end, as this youngster's had been.[23]

Hawker threw the party on June 22, so I concluded that the injured newcomer had to be Eddie McKay. I thought this was a tremendous anecdote, funny and

---

21  Reported in *Glasgow Herald*, August 1, 1932, 13.
22  McKay, Air Ministry service record.
23  Hawker, *Hawker VC*, 181. Tyrrell Hawker refers to himself as "T" throughout.

humanizing, exactly the sort of thing my biography needed more of. Months later, however, I discovered McKay's logbook. Reading it, I realized at once that McKay's service file is inexact. McKay *arrived* in France on June 21 but was not posted to 24 Squadron until July 3. So the story could not have been about him after all. From another source I discovered that 2nd Lt. Sidney Pither arrived at Bertangles on June 21, so he is probably the one who came to dinner with the bandaged head.[24] The story is still a very good one, of course. It tells us something about the giddy and reckless off-duty shenanigans of young pilots. McKay probably had to pass through "the gauge" himself, too, especially since the day after he arrived bad weather grounded the squadron, giving the other pilots plenty of time to torment the newcomer. Still, I liked the story better when I thought it was about him. I liked the book better when that story was in it.

Suppose I had never discovered McKay's logbook or that Pither had arrived on the 21st. That story, and my belief that it was about McKay, would have made it into the final work, although prudence would have required me to say that he was "probably" the pilot with the bandaged head. It would have been an honest mistake. Errors are inevitable in any work of history, but we expect historians to keep them to a minimum and to take responsibility for them when they are found. The willingness to do so is one of the ethical responsibilities that we have as a profession. Indeed, there are numerous and very admirable cases of scholars who have revised or even reversed their opinion about their own work because new evidence has come to light. Now let us consider a far more uncomfortable matter of professional ethics. Supposing, for the sake of telling a better story, I had simply concealed the truth about McKay's actual date of arrival. Doing so would have posed no particular difficulty, had I wished it. I could have included the story about the hazing ritual and plausibly claimed that it was about McKay. Needless to say, I never for a moment considered this course of action, but the question of *why* I did not has broader implications worth exploring.

In the early 2000s, the historical profession was rocked by a series of cases of professional malfeasance involving well-known historians. Stephen Ambrose and Doris Kearns Goodwin, two academically trained historians who were also best-selling authors, were found to have committed plagiarism. Michael Bellesiles, recipient of one of the discipline's most prestigious awards, the Bancroft Prize, was found "guilty of unprofessional and misleading work" by a committee investigating his book *Arming America*. As punishment he lost the Bancroft Prize and, more significantly, resigned from his position at Emory University. Joseph Ellis, author of several important and popular biographies of early presidents of the

---

24 Air Ministry Service Records, S.E. Pither, AIR 76/405/186.

United States, was exposed for having tried to bolster his public reputation by lying about his military service.[25] Meanwhile, in the United Kingdom, a libel trial involving the American historian Deborah Lipstadt and the British Holocaust denier David Irving garnered enormous media attention. Irving, whose early works on the Second World War were sometimes praised for their apparent command of German archival sources, had been an open Holocaust denier since at least the early 1980s, but he sued Lipstadt for calling him that in her 1993 work, *Denying the Holocaust*. The subsequent case literally put history on trial as Lipstadt's legal defence team assembled a group of eminent scholars who exposed decades of systematic and willful malpractice in Irving's work and demolished his contention that the Holocaust was a fabrication of wartime propaganda.[26]

These notorious cases coincided with the cresting of a debate that had been raging within academe about the status of historical knowledge, and brought that debate into sharper relief. Rivers of ink have been spilled over acres of forest to define, describe, and argue about the various movements that are often referred to generically as "postmodernism." It is a term that many of those called "postmodernists" would reject, as they represent a variety of related intellectual movements such as "post-structuralism" and "the linguistic turn," each of which defies easy definition. Beginning in the 1970s, these movements threw a series of haymakers at traditional scholarship in the arts and social sciences, including history. In some respects, and in broad ranging ways, they revived very old arguments about epistemology (the philosophy of knowledge) but cloaked them in contemporary academic garb. A thorough analysis of them is well beyond the scope of this book, but, in brief, the postmodernists deny that "historical writing refers to an actual historical past."[27] Their reasons for doing so are many and complex, but in particular they seize upon the fact that historians do not observe the past directly, only the sources that the past leaves behind. From this commonplace observation, however, they draw a radically different conclusion than E.H. Carr did. You will recall that Carr wrote, "It does not follow that, because a mountain appears to take on different shapes from different angles of vision, it has objectively either no shape at all or an infinity of shapes." The postmodernists, at their most radical, argued precisely that—the mountain of objective historical truth does not exist or it has an infinite number of shapes. At the very least, they argued that it is

---

25 For a discussion of each, see Jon Wiener, *Historians in Trouble: Plagiarism, Fraud, and Politics in the Ivory Tower* (New York: The New Press, 2004).

26 There are several works concerning the Irving trial. See, above all, Richard J. Evans, *Lying about Hitler: History, Holocaust, and the David Irving Trial* (New York: Basic Books, 2001). Evans led the team of historians who dissected Irving's work and claims.

27 George G. Iggers, *Historiography in the 20th Century: From Scientific Objectivity to the Postmodern Challenge* (Middletown: Wesleyan University Press, 2005), 118.

meaningless to talk about the mountain itself—we can only discuss the multiple perceptions of the mountain.[28] From their perspective, what mattered was not, to use Carr's metaphor, the mountain but the "different shapes from different angles of vision" themselves, and they held that each had equal merit because there are no objective or fundamentally correct standards by which to judge.[29] Hence, one of the most radical of all postmodernist critics of traditional, evidence-based history, Keith Jenkins, asserted that "the empiricist project of seeking to know a real past in order to seek real truths which can be validated by evidence is ... an illusion."[30] As these debates reached their zenith, historians including Richard Evans, Keith Windschuttle, and Geoffrey Elton wrote powerful and often seething rejoinders to the postmodernists, defending evidence-based approaches to scholarship, but it was difficult for the opposing sides to find common ground on which to have any sort of discussion at all.[31] Their debates, if they can be called that, were often highly intemperate. Keith Jenkins called Richard Evans the intellectual equivalent of a flat-earther and accused him of engaging in "mean-spirited, often rather arrogant and dismissive discourse," while Geoffrey Elton denounced postmodernism as "the intellectual equivalent of crack."[32]

These debates went largely unnoticed outside of academe and began to recede around the mid-2000s. Despite their fervour, it is arguable that they had very little practical impact on the historical discipline.[33] Some historians found inspiration and even liberation in the postmodernists' broadminded approach to methodology, but Evans, writing in the late 1990s, found that postmodernist ideas were on the whole widely opposed throughout the historical community.[34] Postmodernists argued that the epistemic jig was up; most historians merely shrugged and went about their business in much the same way they always had. Jenkins himself admitted as much, noting that most of the history he read was still (nonsensically, in his view) empiricist. One reason that postmodernist ideas failed to find much purchase among historians is obvious: if historians took these ideas seriously, the discipline would simply collapse. In this work, I have unapologetically laid forth a very traditional, evidence-based approach to historiography. I believe

---

28  Carr, *What Is History?* 21.

29  See, for example, Alun Munslow, "Reappraisal of *What Is History?* [book review]," *History in Focus* 2 (Autumn 2001), http://www.history.ac.uk/ihr/Focus/Whatishistory/carr1.html.

30  Keith Jenkins, *Why History? Ethics and Postmodernity* (London: Routledge, 1999), 110.

31  Geoffrey Elton, *Return to Essentials: Some Reflections on the Present State of Historical Study* (Cambridge: Cambridge University Press, 1991); Keith Windschuttle, *The Killing of History* (Sydney: Maclean Press, 1994); Richard J. Evans, *In Defense of History* (London: Granata Publications, 1997).

32  Jenkins, *Why History?* 95; Elton, *Return to Essentials*, 41.

33  Iggers, *Historiography in the 20th Century*, 150.

34  See Evans, *In Defense of History*, "Introduction," 4–14.

that, with sufficient effort, we can discover truths about the past—however provisionally we might agree upon them—for the same reason that aviation pioneers of Eddie McKay's era discovered better ways to build aeroplanes. This view may seem old-fashioned, but it remains the core of the historical profession's approach to research. Historians today are interested in more things than they used to be, and they employ a broader range of methodologies to research them, but, fundamentally, their approach is a Rankean one. Most historians write stories or make arguments about the past based on evidence accumulated from sources, and they usually believe that their arguments and stories are, if not definitively true, better than competing ones, which is why they bother making and telling them in the first place.

One progenitor of the postmodernist critique whose work demands consideration is a brilliant philosopher of history named Hayden White. In the 1970s, White argued that, in its creative use of sources, history resembles the writing of fiction more than many historians would like to admit. White's work is conceptually challenging and, as is the case with the work of many philosophers, probably more often discussed than actually read. Simply put, White argues that, in order to make history intelligible, historians revert, whether knowingly or not, to the use of familiar plots, modes of argument, and ideologies that undermine the profession's pretensions to objectivity. In one frequently quoted passage, he argued, "Historical narratives are verbal fictions, the content of which are as much invented as found and the forms of which have more in common with their counterparts in literature than they have with those in the sciences."[35] Despite being rather defiantly empiricist in my approach, I admit to succumbing to certain literary affectations from time to time in the writing of this work. For example, I began a previous chapter by remarking that McKay and Knight landed at Bertangles "cold, wet, and rattled." Neither of them said so in any surviving document, but I believe I can plausibly infer this from other evidence. For example, I have the weather reports for the day: it was very cold, windy, and rainy. At 8,000 feet, it would have been very frigid indeed, and the cockpit nacelle of the DH 2 offered pilots no protection from the elements at all—the top wing being behind rather than directly above them. As for "rattled," well, they had just survived a six-on-one dogfight against superior enemy machines. It seemed like a reasonable supposition to make, as in their memoirs many other pilots described the inevitable jitters that set in after combat. Historians who write narratives (and there are still a good many who do) may use some of the methods of fiction writers, but their work can

35  Hayden White, "The Historical Text as Literary Artifact," in *Tropics of Discourse: Essays in Cultural Criticism* (Baltimore: Johns Hopkins University Press, 1978), 82.

and should remain firmly grounded in facts derived from evidence nonetheless. I made this brief defensive patrol to the ramparts of the postmodernist movement to illustrate a point, which brings us back to the question of professional ethics I began with. Plagiarism offends historians because doing history is hard, and we believe that people should get credit for their work. Falsification offends historians because, despite it all, despite the linguistic turn, post-structuralism, postmodernism, and all the relativistic hand-wringing of the past generation, most of us still think that the truth matters. "Just tell a good story," I was advised early in my professorial career. It remains the worst advice I ever received about being an historian and a professor. Because if all that matters is good storytelling, then it hardly matters if the story is true or not. Eddie McKay's story would have been a better one with the hazing ritual in it, but to fabricate or suppress important evidence for any reason is to attack the fundamental integrity of the discipline, rendering history precisely what its critics say it is: bunk. So it is worth repeating: Good historians do not knowingly twist the evidence to suit their purposes, they test the validity of sources through triangulation, they do not suppress evidence that undermines their argument, and, above all, good historians do not make things up. Our understanding of the past is socially informed; it is imperfect; it is provisional; it is subject to revision; at times it rests uneasily alongside competing claims for which the evidence is comparably strong. We can never know with certainty what people did or why they did it, so imagination and speculation are inevitably part of the historian's craft. But history cannot simply be whatever we say it is or whatever we want it to be. Either we have evidence for the things we believe to be true or we do not. The evidence can only be pressed so far before the result can no longer be called history.

Throughout this book, I have discussed various skills that historians must cultivate in order to "do" history, at least in the traditional, evidence-based sense. Increasingly, historians are discovering that they must be digitally literate to access and make use of the immense body of source material becoming available on the Internet. Someday, perhaps before too long, nearly all the sources will be available electronically, and historians might never have to leave their offices to conduct their research. Hours once spent sifting through old records will be reduced to seconds of inquiry using keywords. Already, the rapidity with which new resources are becoming available through the Internet is overwhelming. Midway through writing this biography, I learned that the genealogy website Findmypast (www.findmypast. co.uk) had entered into an agreement with the National Archives in the UK to release the personnel files of all British flying services officers from the First World War. Impressive as this seemed, this addition of a quarter million records was a mere bagatelle next to the eight *billion* already available through that site—and the

14 billion available on ancestry.com. The digital revolution offers extraordinary opportunities for historians, but it will require them to develop new competencies, too. The day is fast approaching when historians who have not plumbed the depths of what is digitally available will seem as questionable in their judgements as today's historians who have neglected to visit the archives. Of course, all this refers only to finding sources. Historians will still have to assess them, choose between them, and write histories based on them. If we reach the point where computers can do that for us too, well, what will be the point of using our intellect at all? Perhaps we won't.

In the interim, before all that happens, we may wish to consider that finding sources more easily will not necessarily guarantee better results. Focusing with laser-like speed and precision will have many advantages, but it may deprive us of the most enjoyable and indeed fruitful aspects of historical research: the sense of accomplishment that comes from travelling to archives and digging through them; the incomparable sensation of connectedness that stems from actual physical contact with artefacts; the feeling of immersion into the past that can only result from long hours of studying primary sources; and, perhaps above all, the thrill of the accidental find. Antique buyers might locate in an instant the object of their desire on the Internet, but there is nothing like the satisfaction of rummaging through dusty boxes and finding something precious that you were not looking for in the first place.

As I write these words, we are still at the beginning of the digital revolution. The rapidity of change is astonishing. I suspect that including discussions of this kind will age this book prematurely. I can well imagine future students, reading this section and marvelling that I considered it worth mentioning at all. (Do not discard it—this section, too, is an historical primary document: the past refracted through the mind of its recorder.) Whatever eventually replaces our present system of archival research—and it *will* be replaced—may well be more efficient, cost effective, faster, and perhaps in some ways better. But it will not be the same, and much may be lost. For now, though, researching even a comparatively minor figure such as Eddie McKay could take many years if one were to follow up every potential lead. Some historians actually do make their subject the work of a lifetime. Will and Ariel Durant spent nearly 50 years writing the 11 volumes of their *History of Civilization*, the story "of the contributions that genius and labor have made to the cultural heritage of mankind," as they described it. By 1975, they had sold two million books, collected a Pulitzer Prize, and made it as far as *The Age of Napoleon* when old age and ill health prevented them from writing more.[36]

---

36 "Historian Will Durant Dies: Author of 'Civilization' Series," *New York Times*, November 9, 1981, http://www.nytimes.com/1981/11/09/obituaries/historian-will-durant-dies-author-of-civilization-series.html.

An eminent medievalist named Warren Hollister spent decades researching and writing a biography of England's Henry I, lost his unfinished manuscript and all his research in a house fire, started again, and died just as the work was nearing completion. A gifted and devoted former student, Amanda Clark Frost, finished the work for him.[37] I urge my own students to take note.

Excluding the end of one's life, though, when is the historian's job done? When can a work of history justly be called finished? One perfectly reasonable answer, especially in the emerging age of electronic publication, is "never." Go to any bookstore, and you will find new releases in the history section whose publishers' blurbs boldly proclaim that they are "the last word" or "definitive work" on their topic, but students of history know that they never are. This is true even when we do not expect to find new evidence in a work of history. It is doubtful that new sources remain to be discovered about the Battle of Thermopylae, where the Spartans made their famous last stand against the armies of the Persian Empire in 480 BCE, but this has not prevented new books from being published about it every few years. We have already discussed why, at length: because history and the past can never be merged, because we have both too few and too many sources, because different historians understand their sources in different ways, because our conclusions must necessarily be provisional and subject to revision, and so forth. There may be other reasons, too. For one thing, the incentive to write a new history may be purely financial. Very occasionally, there is gold in historical hills. A good writer can enliven an old topic with an authorial voice attuned to the tastes of modern readers, and retelling famous stories from a slightly different angle can, very occasionally, be lucrative. A glance down the best-seller list reveals that the reading public has a hunger for history and historical fiction, while Hollywood finds history a source of limitless inspiration.

But if a work of history is never really finished, a historian's work at some point must be. It may end when the historian decides that the work is good enough, that it has served to answer the questions he or she set out to ask, or, at the very least, that time has run out. Time has run out? Indeed. An underappreciated aspect of the historian's craft is that it is often *work*, by which I mean paid labour. Many historians are academics, employed by institutions of higher learning. This affords them the luxury to research and write about history for a living, but usually only once their other duties are attended to. Academic historians also teach, an important job that absorbs a large percentage of their time. They also have to slog through all manner of administrative tasks related to the operation of their

---

37 Jeffrey Burton Russell, "Foreword," in *Henry I*, by C. Warren Hollister (New Haven, CT: Yale University Press, 2001), ix.

departments and institutions, an unimportant job that also absorbs a large percentage of their time. For many professors, research and writing are relegated to the end of the teaching term, those supposed "summers off" for which they endure so much ribbing from family, friends, and sniping journalists. Junior professors, looking to establish themselves in their field, can face tremendous pressure to publish, often at a pace that is conducive to neither work-life balance nor good scholarship. Meanwhile, historians outside of academe face a different challenge. Usually they have full time jobs in other fields, so their historical inquiries are hobby projects, labours of love pursued for years. On a related note, all historians have to contend with the costs associated with research. Sometimes the project ends when the money does. Researching Eddie McKay required expensive transatlantic flights and hotel accommodation, as well as paying research assistants and the often exorbitant costs associated with the digital reproduction of material from archives I was unable to visit myself. These are important aspects of the historian's craft. Their impact on the content and character of finished works ought not to be underestimated. With bigger research grants and softer deadlines, I might have told a different and perhaps better story. "Had we but world enough, and time," Andrew Marvell wrote, but we can never have enough of either, as Eddie McKay well knew.

APPENDIX

# The Mysteries

A commonplace cliché says that hindsight is 20/20, but if this were true, there would be no debates about the past and no need for history or historians. Earlier in this book, I discussed how I chose certain sources but rejected others in order to tell the story of Eddie McKay's life and times. I argued further that source criticism is one of the pillars on which the practice of history rests and that deciding to exclude certain sources from consideration is one of the pillars of source criticism. We might reject certain sources because they are inauthentic or unreliable or because we are not interested them. The sources that follow do not quite fit into any of those categories. They forced me to confront mysteries that, despite my best efforts, remained inexplicable. Reluctantly, I chose not to use them as sources.

## The Woman

Eddie McKay failed to return from patrol on December 28, 1917. His squadron-mates believed that he was killed in action that day, although German sources indicate that he might have died of wounds on the 29th.[1] RFC authorities followed the standard practice of listing him as "missing" until they had confirmation of his death. His name appeared on the lists in the first week of January 1918. Days later, an Englishwoman named Maud Palmer initiated a query about McKay through

---

1  Zentral-Nachweise-Büro Nachlassliste Englander, available on the Prisoners of the First World War ICRC Historical Archives site, http://grandeguerre.icrc.org/.

the International Committee of the Red Cross.[2] Queries of this kind usually were made by family members of the missing, in the hopes of finding their loved ones alive in enemy captivity. In addition, in McKay's War Office service file, there is a copy of a letter from the Red Cross to Maud Palmer, dated March 1918. The letter stated that McKay's identity discs (what we would now call "dog tags") had been returned by the Germans with a note indicating that he was dead.[3]

Who was Maud Palmer? Why was she making inquiries about Eddie McKay? My initial thought was the exciting possibility that she might have been McKay's girlfriend in England. He spent roughly two years overseas, half of them in England, so presumably he met civilians and made friends, possibly even a girl-friend. My genealogical investigation, however, revealed that Maud Palmer (nee Moore) was born in California in 1863, making her 30 years older than McKay. She was married to a noted English landscape artist, Harry Sutton Palmer.[4] They were a well-to-do family, and lived with two servants at Heathcliff Terrace in Chiswick, London.[5] So why did she initiate a query about McKay? What was the connection between them? Perhaps he had been billeted with the Palmers at some point and had kept up correspondence with them. But this, too, is unlikely, as none of his postings were nearer than eight miles to Chiswick, and flying officers tended to live on or very near their aerodromes. Were the Palmers and McKays relatives? My genealogical research revealed no relation between them. Nor did the Palm-ers have a son who might have served with McKay at some point. Having failed entirely to find any connection between them, another possibility occurred to me. Palmer may have been making a query about Captain *E.A.* McKay. Evans Alex-ander McKay was a Canadian in the RFC, an exact contemporary of Eddie, with whom he was often confused, even in official correspondence. It was an easy mis-take to make, especially since Eddie went by his middle name and people some-times assumed that "E" was his first initial, too. Indeed, I travelled down many a path in this project, in pursuit of A.E. McKay, only to find E.A. McKay at the end of it, and sometimes, luckily, vice versa. Evans Alexander McKay actually was taken prisoner after being shot down in 1917.[6] So it seemed to me that this was the

---

2  International Red Cross Committee, Query Card, Captain A.E. McKay, Prisoners of the First World War ICRC Historical Archives, http://grandeguerre.icrc.org/en/File/Search/#/3/2/107/o/British and Commonwealth/Military/MAC K. These records are difficult to search, but McKay's card is under the further subheading MAC K (ROYAL) AIR FORCE.

3  McKay, WO Service File, Letter: British Section International Red Cross to Maud Palmer, March 12, 1918.

4  Barbara Lekisch, *Embracing Scenes about Lakes Tahoe and Donner: Painters, Illustrators, and Sketch Artists, 1855–1915* (Lafayette, CA: Great West Books, 2003), 138–39.

5  Ancestry.com, 1911 England Census. Original citation: 1911 England Census, RG 14, Piece 6978, Schedule Number 151.

6  Air Ministry Service Records, Evans Alexander McKay, AIR 76/321/41.

most likely answer to the mystery. I decided that the matter was best left for some future biographer of E.A. McKay.

Then something totally unexpected happened. Months later, I contacted Eddie McKay's great-nephew, who had in his possession McKay's original FAI certificate. It is in pristine condition, still in its original leather case. Tucked inside the case with the aviator's certificate were two unrelated items. One was McKay's membership card in the Royal Overseas Officer's Club in London, England. The other was a folded piece of paper. It turned out to be a legal document, signed by Joe McKay on 24 January 1918, granting power of attorney over the late McKay's overseas affairs to ... Maud Palmer.[7] So the mystery was back. Who was she? What connection did she have to Eddie McKay? Clearly, she must have been someone of some special significance for Joe McKay to have granted her power of attorney over this brother's affairs. What was it? Was she a friend of a friend, perhaps some business associate of Joe's? Or perhaps she was she simply a member of some volunteer organization in the UK that aided overseas families in such instances. The latter seems unlikely, however, as Palmer initiated her query about Eddie McKay only days after Joe himself was informed that his brother was missing.

One charming possibility is that McKay knew Maud Palmer's daughter. In 1917, Camille Sutton Palmer was about 20 and, if the portrait of her by English painter Frank Dicksee does her justice, remarkably striking in appearance.[8] Like thousands of women in the British Isles, she volunteered her time to the war effort, working at one point in the YMCA's popular "Eagle Hut" in Cavendish Square, a large recreational facility for American servicemen overseas. The hut served pancakes and other food familiar to Americans, and Canadians visited it too.[9] Perhaps she met McKay in some similar setting. It is not impossible. Thousands of Canadian servicemen overseas met women, fell in love, even started families. There is no evidence of any relationship between Eddie and Camille, so I cannot plausibly argue that this was the source of the connection between the families. Historians might incorporate fictive elements into their work, but it does not follow that we write fiction. Still, some wistful and perhaps highly romantic part of my imagination compels me to keep McKay's photograph and Camille's portrait together in a folder on my computer.

There is one final point of interest. In July 1918, Camille Palmer married an American serviceman stationed in the United Kingdom. His name was Lieutenant Benjamin Wyatt, and he went on to a long and distinguished military career.[10]
He was a pilot.

---

7  Document in the author's collection via Robert Mackay.
8  Sir Francis Bernard Dicksee, "Portrait of Camille Palmer," 1913. The portrait appeared in *Royal Academy Illustrated*, 1914, 98. It sold at auction in 2010 and can be found online.
9  "Wedding Bells," *Daily Mirror*, June 13, 1918, 6.
10  "London Letter," *Western Mail*, July 4, 1918, 4. The wedding was reported in many UK papers.

## The Advertisement

In 1924, Eddie McKay was named alongside three RFC recipients of the Victoria Cross in a national advertisement for the Hart Battery Company. The illustration depicted a biplane swooping into action above the tag line "The Vital Spark of the Great Battleplanes." The ad went on to boast of the firm's wartime service, trumpeting the great reliability of the engine batteries it had produced for aeroplanes.

> The proudest pages from the history of Hart Batteries are recalled to make plain that in the Allied service this Canadian-made British equipment came through with flying colors in the supreme and most severe test of all.
> Ask Bishop or Barker or McCudden ... or Eddie McKay, if you can find them! And then you will be proud to equip your car, your motor boat, your radio or farm plant with Hart Batteries.

The commercial exploitation of the war might seem unforgivably crass to us today, but it was commonplace at the time. (Given the incessant engine problems that McKay and other pilots encountered, however, the ad writer might have been unwise to assume that they would praise the batteries' performance.) Why was McKay mentioned in this ad? He had a commendable career, but he certainly did not reach the stratospheric heights of the Victoria Cross–winning luminaries Bishop, McCudden, and Barker. Unfortunately, very few records of early twentieth-century advertising agencies in Canada survive, so I have no idea who wrote or illustrated the ad. Was it a friend of McKay's, perhaps a classmate from Western, who went on to a career in advertising? If so, he did he not seem to realize that McKay (or McCudden, for that matter) was dead. Or perhaps McKay's fame, earned after the October 1916 duel with Boelcke, persisted longer than we might think.

## The Envelope

The archives of the University of Western Ontario hold records from the office of the university president back to 1914. President Braithwaite's papers consist mainly of correspondence related to administrative dross such as faculty salaries and even buying books for the library. Among his papers are two direct references to Eddie McKay. One is a copy of a letter of introduction to a member of Western's board of governors, mentioned in Chapter One. The other is a small envelope

FIGURE A.1: Exploiting Patriotic Enthusiasm. *In November 1916, McKay became Canada's first famous military airman. Fame is fleeting, but this 1924 advertisement for spark plugs mentions him alongside several legendary airmen. Even in the 1920s, advertisers were willing to exploit patriotic enthusiasm for commercial purposes.* (Ottawa Journal, April 20, 1917, 17.)

addressed to Captain A.E. *Mac*Kay (a common error), Royal Flying Corps, care of Cox and Co. This firm, Cox and Company, was a highly regarded British financial institution, now part of the Lloyds banking empire, that served as agents to the army, handling such matters as payroll and the like. When I first discovered the envelope, I opened it excitedly, as I have very little correspondence to or from McKay. It was empty. A search of the adjacent items revealed no letter to McKay or anything that might contain clues as to what was once in it. What had been in it? What was intended to go in it? A letter? A cheque? Why was the envelope not sent? Because his name was misspelled? If so, why was it kept? There is simply no way to know. Historical research is often like this: it offers us tantalizing leads that go nowhere. Learning to live with frustration—that, too, is a skill historians must cultivate.

## The Grave

When the First World War ended, the Imperial War Graves Commission, which was renamed the Commonwealth War Graves Commission in 1960, embarked on the immense and often grisly task of burying the empire's dead and building memorials to the missing. Eddie McKay has no known grave, but his name is inscribed on the Flying Services Memorial at Arras. But we know that the Germans *did* recover his body, because they returned his identity discs and dropped a note into British lines indicating that he was dead. At some point, probably late in the war, his grave was lost. This was not uncommon. Temporary or makeshift cemeteries were often hurriedly laid out with inaccurate grave registries. Others were destroyed by shelling or as the front lines moved, making positive identification of the dead very difficult. Even if McKay's remains subsequently were located by crews working for the IWGC, it may not have been possible to identify him without his identity discs.

Today, visitors to CWGC cemeteries—there are hundreds in Belgium and France alone—are often struck by the huge number of headstones engraved with the words, "A Solider of the Great War, Known Unto God." These are the graves of the unknown, those whose remains were unidentifiable, in some cases because there was so little left to identify. Occasionally, the grave of an unknown might offer a few additional details. For example, one might say, "A Canadian Soldier of the Great War, Known Unto God," meaning that there was enough evidence to identify the nationality or unit of the unfortunate soldier in question. McKay's remains might be lost forever, or they could be interned in the grave of an unknown soldier. We cannot know for certain. Here is an interesting fact, however. On McKay's Royal Flying Corps casualty card, held by the Royal Air Force

Museum, there is a handwritten note that says "buried in Moorslede."[11] There is no indication of the source of this claim or who made the note.

Moorslede is a town in Belgium that was occupied by the Germans for much of the war. It is not far from where McKay was on patrol when he was shot down. The main CWGC cemetery in Moorslede is called Dadizeele New British Cemetery. Resting in the cemetery are 1,029 British and Commonwealth soldiers of the First World War, of which 871 are identified.[12] Among the 158 graves of unknown soldiers there is one whose stone bears this inscription: "An Officer of the Great War, Royal Flying Corps, Known Unto God."[13] Is it Eddie McKay? Modern forensics and archival research probably could determine whether it is, but the CWGC is, quite rightly, highly reluctant to undertake investigations of this kind, except when new remains are discovered in the fields of Western Europe. There are hundreds of thousands of unknown soldiers from the Great War alone, and it may be for the best if we permit them to rest in peace. They stand as a powerful symbolic representation of war's cruelty—that it has the power not just to kill but to erase identities, too. This book, as imperfect and tentative in its conclusions as it must be, has been an effort to rescue the identity of one man from oblivion.

11  McKay, Casualty Card.
12  "Dadizeele New British Cemetery," Commonwealth War Graves Commission, http://www.cwgc.org/find-a-cemetery/cemetery/16201/DADIZEELE NEW BRITISH CEMETERY.
13  "Dadizeele New British Cemetery," Find A Grave, www.findagrave.com.

# SELECTED BIBLIOGRAPHY

## Archival Collections

### *Library and Archives of Canada*

Air Ministry (UK), Ministry of National Defence MG 40
Department of External Affairs RG 24
Department of National Defence RG 24
Lloyd Baillie Rochester Fonds
Ministry of the Overseas Military Forces of Canada RG 9
Russell Marshall Smith Fonds

### *Directorate of History and Heritage, Department of National Defence (Ottawa)*

Personal Papers of General G.A.H. Trudeau

### *Leeds University*

Liddle Collection, Lanoe Hawker Papers

### *National Archives (UK)*

Air Ministry and Royal Air Force Records
War Office Armed Forces Services Records

### *RAF Museum, London*

First World War Casualty Cards (www.rafmuseumstoryvault.org.uk/)
Personal Papers of Air Marshal Sir R.H.M.S. Saundby
Personal Papers of S.J. Sibley

### *Imperial War Museum*

Private Papers of Miss H. Gosling
Private Papers of H.H. Heales

Private Papers of Lieutenant J.M. McAlery
Personal Papers of Major V.A.H. Robeson

## Canadian War Museum

Personal Papers of A. Roy Brown
Personal Papers of Lloyd Breadner

## Oxford County Archives

Oxford County Estate Files to 1934

## Archives and Research Collection Centre, University of Western Ontario

No. 10 Stationary Hospital Fonds
President Braithwaite's Papers
UWO Board of Governors Papers
Beatrice Hitchins Memorial Collection of Aviation History
London and Port Stanley Railway Fonds

## University of Texas, Eugene McDermott Library

George H. Williams, Jr. World War One Aviation Library: Ola A. Slater Collection and
    A.E. Ferko Collection

## Contemporary Periodical Literature

*Aero Club of America*, 1917
*Augusta Chronicle*, 1916
*Aviation Age*
*Echo (London Echo)*
*Flight*, 1914–18
*Globe*, 1916
*Lethbridge Herald*, 1916
*London Advertiser*, 1913–20
*London Free Press*, 1913–18
*New York Times*, 1916
*North Bay Nugget (Cobalt Nugget)*, 1916
*Speedy: The Magazine of the Central Flying School*, 1917–18
*Stratford Beacon-Herald*, 1914–18
*The Times* (London, UK), 1916–18
*Toronto Daily Star*, 1916–17
*Vernon's Directory* (Stratford and London), 1901–16
*Western Gazette*, 1914–16
Western University of London Ontario, *Arts Department Calendar 1914–1915*

## Contemporary Accounts, Published Primary Sources, and Memoirs

Bridgman, Leonard. *The Clouds Remember*. London: Gale and Polden, 1938.
Cook, Edward. *Why the Empire Is at War: The Causes and the Issues*. Toronto: MacMillan Company, 1914.
Fry, W.M. *Air of Battle*. London: William Kimber, 1974.
Gardiner, H.W. *London 1914: A Presentation of Her Resources Achievements and Possibilities*. London, ON: London Printing Company, 1914.
Illingworth, A.E., and V.A.H. Robeson. *A History of 24 Squadron*, 1920.
Jones, H.A. *The War in the Air: Being the Story of the Part Played in the Great War by the Royal Air Force*. Vol. 2. Oxford: Clarendon Press, 1928.
Lambert, Bill. *Combat Report*. London: William Kimber, 1973.
Lee, Arthur Gould. *No Parachute: A Fighter Pilot in World War I*. London: Jarrolds, 1968.
—. *Open Cockpit: A Pilot of the Royal Flying Corps*. London: Jarrolds, 1969.
Leed, Eric. *No Man's Land: Combat and Identity in World War One*. Cambridge: Cambridge University Press, 1979.
Lewis, Cecil. *Sagittarius Rising*. London: P. Davies, 1944.
Lewis, Gwilym. *Wings Over the Somme*. 2nd ed. London: Bridge Books, 1994.
Long, Selden. *In the Blue*. London: John Lane, 1920.
MacMillan, Norman. *Into the Blue*. London: Jarrolds Publishers, 1969. (Revised edition of 1929)
Raleigh, Walter, and H.A. Jones. *The War in the Air: Being the Story of the Part Played in the Great War by the Royal Air Force*. Vol. 1. Oxford: Clarendon Press, 1922.
Richardson, Leonard Atwood. *Pilot's Log: The Flying Log, Diaries, Letters Home and Verse of Lt. Leonard Atwood Richardson, Royal Flying Corps, WW1, 1917–1918*. Edited by Elizabeth Richardson-Whealy. St. Catharines, ON: Paul Heron Publishing, 1998.
Slessor, John. *The Central Blue: Memoirs and Reflections*. London: Cassell and Company, 1956.
von Richthofen, Manfred. *The Red Baron*. Barnsley, UK: Pen and Sword, 2009. (Original work published 1917)

## Secondary Sources

Barker, Ralph. *A Brief History of the Royal Flying Corps in World War I*. London: Constable and Robinson, 2002.
Bednarski, Steven. *A Poisoned Past: The Life and Times of Margarida de Portu, a Fourteenth-Century Accused Poisoner*. Toronto: University of Toronto Press, 2013.
Bennett, Alan. *Captain Roy Brown: A True Story of the Great War, 1914–1918*. Vol. 1. New York: Brick Tower Press, 2012.
Boyle, Andrew. *Trenchard*. London: Collins, 1962.
Bruce, J.M. *British Aeroplanes: 1914–1918*. New York: Funk and Wagnalls, 1969.
Bujak, Edward. *Reckless Fellows: The Gentlemen of the Royal Flying Corps*. London: I.B. Taurus, 2015.
Carr, E.H. *What Is History?* London: Macmillan, 1961.
Clark, Alan. *Aces High: The War in the Air over the Western Front, 1914–1918*. New York: G.P. Putnam's Sons, 1973.

Cook, Tim. *At the Sharp End: Canadians Fighting the Great War, 1914–1916*. Toronto: Viking, 2007.

—. *Shock Troops: Canadians Fighting the Great War, 1917–1918*. Toronto: Viking, 2008.

Cossey, Bob. *Tigers: The Story of No. 74 Squadron, RAF*. London: Arms and Armour, 1992.

Dodd, Ronald. *The Brave Young Wings*. Stittsville: Canada's Wings, 1980.

Drew, George A. *Canada's Fighting Airmen*. Toronto: Maclean Publishing Company, 1930.

Dye, Peter. *The Bridge to Airpower Logistics: Support for Royal Flying Corps Operations on the Western Front, 1914–1918*. Annapolis: Naval Institute Press, 2015.

Edwards, John Carver. *Orville's Aviators: Outstanding Alumni of the Wright Flying School, 1910–1916*. Jefferson, NC: McFarland and Company, 2009.

Elton, G.R. *The Practice of History*. London: Methuen, 1967.

—. *Return to Essentials: Some Reflections on the Present State of Historical Study*. Cambridge: Cambridge University Press, 1991.

Eksteins, Modris. *Rites of Spring: The Great War and the Birth of Modern Age*. Boston: Houghton Mifflin, 1989.

Evans, Richard. *In Defense of History*. London: Granata Publications, 1997.

—. *Lying about Hitler: History, Holocaust, and the David Irving Trial*. New York: Basic Books, 2001.

Fussell, Paul. *The Great War and Modern Memory*. New York: Oxford University Press, 1975.

Gaddis, John Lewis. *The Landscape of History: How Historians Map the Past*. New York: Oxford University Press, 2002.

Gray, B.J. *The AMC DH2*. Windsock Datafile 48. 2nd ed. Hertfordshire: Albatros Productions, 2009.

Gunby, David. *Sweeping the Skies: A History of 40 Squadron Royal Flying Corps and Royal Air Force, 1916–1956*. London: Pentland Press, 1995.

Guttman, Jon. *Pusher Aces of World War 1*. Oxford: Osprey Publishing, 2009.

—. *SPAD VII Aces of World War 1*. Oxford: Osprey Publishing, 2001.

Halley, James J. *Famous Fighter Squadrons of the RAF*. Vol. 1. Windsor: Hylton Lacy Publishers, 1971.

Hart, Peter. *Bloody April: Slaughter in the Skies over Arras, 1917*. London: Cassel, 2006.

—. *Somme Success: The Royal Flying Corps and the Battle of the Somme, 1916*. Barnsley, UK: Pen and Sword, 2012.

Harvey, William. *"PI" in the Sky: History of No. 22 Squadron, Royal Flying Corps & R.A.F. in the War of 1914–1918*. Leicester: Colin Huston, 1971.

Hawker, Tyrrel. *Hawker VC, RFC Ace: The Life of Major Lanoe Hawker VC DSO 1890–1916*. Barnsley, UK: Pen and Sword, 2013. (Reprint of 1965 edition)

Henshaw, Trevor. *The Sky Their Battlefield II*. London: Fetubi Books, 2014.

Howell, Colin D. *Blood, Sweat, and Cheers: Sport and the Making of Modern Canada*. Toronto: University of Toronto Press, 2001.

Hudson, James J. *In Clouds of Glory: American Airmen Who Flew with the British During the Great War*. Fayetteville: University of Arkansas Press, 1990.

Hunt, C.W. *Dancing in the Sky: The Royal Flying Corps in Canada*. Toronto: Dundurn Press, 2009.

Iggers, George G. *Historiography in the 20th Century*. Middletown, CT: Wesleyan University Press, 1997.

Jefford, C.G. *RAF Squadrons: A Comprehensive Record of the Movement and Equipment of all RAF Squadrons and Their Antecedents Since 1912.* Shrewsbury: Airlife Publishing, 1988.

Jenkins, Keith. *Rethinking History.* London: Routledge, 1991.

—. *Why History? Ethics and Postmodernity.* London: Routledge, 1999.

Jones, H.A., and Walter Raleigh. *The War in the Air: Being the Story of the Part Played in the Great War by the Royal Air Force.* 6 vols. and appendices. Uckfield: Naval and Military Press and the Imperial War Museum, 2002. (Originally published 1922–37)

Keegan, John. *The Battle for History: Refighting World War II.* Toronto: Vintage, 1995.

—. *The Face of Battle: A Study of Agincourt, Waterloo, and the Somme.* London: Jonathan Cape, 1976.

—. *The First World War.* Toronto: Random House, 1998.

Keshen, Jeffrey. *Propaganda and Censorship During Canada's Great War.* Edmonton: University of Alberta Press, 1996.

Kidd, Bruce. *The Struggle for Canadian Sport.* Toronto: University of Toronto Press, 1996.

Liddell-Hart, Basil. *History of the First World War.* London: Cassel and Co, 1970.

Mackenzie, David, ed. *Canada and the First World War: Essays in Honour of Robert Craig Brown.* Toronto: University of Toronto Press, 2005.

Mackersey, Ian. *No Empty Chairs: The Short and Heroic Lives of the Young Aviators Who Fought and Died in the First World War.* London: Weidenfeld and Nicolson, 2012.

Malinovska, Anna, and Mauriel Joslyn. *Voices in Flight: Conversations with Air Veterans of the Great War.* Barnsley, UK: Pen and Sword, 2006.

Meyer, Jessica. *Men of War: Masculinity and the First World War in Britain.* London: Palgrave-Macmillan, 2009.

Miller, James F. *DH 2 vs Albatros D I / D II: Western Front 1916.* Oxford: Osprey Publishing, 2012.

Moss, Mark. *Manliness and Militarism: Educating Young Boys in Ontario for War.* Toronto: University of Toronto Press, 2001.

Mott, Morris, ed. *Sports in Canada: Historical Readings.* Toronto: Copp Clark Pittman, 1989.

O'Connor, Mike. *Airfields and Airmen: Somme.* Barnsley, UK: Pen and Sword Aviation, 2002.

Philpott, William. *Three Armies on the Somme.* New York: Alfred A. Knopf, 2010.

Revell, Alex. *British Fighter Units: Western Front, 1914–1916.* London: Osprey Publishing, 1978.

Roach, Edward J. *The Wright Company: From Invention to Industry.* Athens: Ohio University Press, 2014.

Ross, W.A. *History of Zorra and Embro: Pioneer Sketches of Sixty Years Ago.* Embro, ON: Embro Courier Office, 1909.

Shores, Christopher. *British and Empire Aces of World War I.* Oxford: Osprey Publishing, 2001.

Shores, Christopher, Norman Franks, and Russell Guest. *Above the Trenches: A Complete Record of the Fighter Aces and Units of the British Empire Air Forces, 1915–1920.* Stoney Creek, ON: Fortress Publications, 1990.

Stevenson, David. *Cataclysm: The First World War as Political Tragedy.* New York: Basic Books, 2004.

Strachan, Hew. *The First World War*. London: Penguin, 2003.

Taylor, John W.R. *Central Flying School: Birthplace of Air Power*. London: Putnam and Co, 1958.

Tidy, Douglas. *I Fear No Men: The Story of No. 74 (Fighter) Squadron, Royal Flying Corps and Royal Air Force (The Tigers)*. London: MacDonald and Co, 1972.

Tredrey, F.D. *Pioneer Pilot: The Great Smith Barry Who Taught the World How to Fly*. London: Peter Davies, 1976.

Werner, Johannes. *Knight of Germany: Oswald Boelcke, German Ace*. Translated by Claude W. Skyes, with an introduction and appendix by Norman Franks. Philadelphia: Casement, 2009. (Originally published 1932)

Winter, Denis. *The First of the Few: Fighter Pilots of the First World War*. London: A. Lane, 1982.

Wise, S.F. *Canadian Airmen and the First World War: The Official History of the Royal Canadian Air Force*. Vol. 1. Toronto: University of Toronto Press, 1980.

Vance, Jonathan. *Death So Noble: Memory, Meaning, and the First World War*. Vancouver: University of British Columbia Press, 1997.

—. *High Flight: Aviation and the Canadian Imagination*. Toronto: Penguin Canada, 2002.

VanWyngarden, Greg. *Jagdstaffle 2 "Boelcke"*. Oxford: Osprey Publishing, 2007.

White, Hayden. *The Tropics of Discourse: Essays in Cultural Criticism*. Baltimore: Johns Hopkins University Press, 1978.

## Documentary

White, Joanna. *DH2—Flying Into History*. Boston, UK: Primetime Video Productions, 2012. Filmed by Simon White and Joanna White. https://vimeo.com/ondemand/dh2.

# INDEX

Figures and maps are indicated by page numbers in italics.

1st Air Depot (St. Omer), 42–43
1st Canadian Division, 10–11
2nd Air Depot (Candas), 42–43
Second Army, 113
3 Reserve Squadron, 26
Third Army, 44, 118
Third (Corps) Wing, 44, 45, 49, 55
Fourth Army, 44, 45, 55, 56, 86
IV Brigade, 44–45
Fifth Army, 93, 112
Sixth Army (French), 44
Ninth (HQ) Wing, 45
Fourteenth (Army) Wing, 44–45
22 Squadron, 44, 54, 71, 86, 102
23 Squadron, 112, 113–15, 117–19, 133
24 Squadron
    accounts of Jan. 25, 1917 dogfight,
        121–24, 123n67
    aeroplanes in, 44–45, 91–92
    as air raid escorts, 71
    at Arras Memorial dedication, 138
    "B" Flight, 41–42
    in Bloody April (1917), 105
    Canadians in, 51
    casualty and fatality rates, 67, 78, 87
    first major aerial battle at Somme,
        56–58
    flight schedule, 59
    Hawker as leader, 53, 56, 66–67, 67n109,
        68, 88–89
    A History of 24 Squadron (Illingworth
        and Robeson), 100–104
    initiation into, 49–50, 53, 139–40
    loss of air supremacy, 67–68, 87–88
    McKay in, 53–54, 56, 87
    McKay's arrival at, 48–49, 49n31, 52–53
    McKay's departure from, 94

Rabagliati as leader, 90–91, 91n63, 92
    recreation by, 61–63, 92
    replacement of lost members, 48
    in Somme offensive, 52–53, 55–56, 67,
        68–69
    time off in Amiens, 62–63
    victories by, 65
    winter of 1916/1917, 91, 92–93
28 Squadron, 31, 50
33rd Huron Regiment (militia), 11–12,
    13, 36
54 Squadron, 122–23
74 Training Squadron, 109–10, 110n21

aces, use of term, xxiv, xxivn17
Addison, Doug, 109
aerial combat
    24 Squadron first big dogfight, 56–58
    accounts of Jan. 25, 1917 dogfight,
        121–24
    Boelcke's death in, 69–70, 79–82
    Boelcke's rules for, 66, 80
    calculation of victories, xxv–xxvi,
        58–59, 123
    casualties, 42
    development of, 19, 22–23
    Hawker on, 56, 66–67
    Hawker's death, 88–89
    psychological impact, 59, 111
    romantic notions about, xvi, xvii–xviii
    See also airpower; aviators; McKay,
        Eddie, at front
aerobatics (stunting), 29
aeroplanes
    early history, 3–4, 19–20
    first demonstration in London (ON), 4
    terminology, xxiv, xxvi–xxvii

*See also* De Havilland scout (DH 2) aeroplane; *names of specific aeroplanes*
air depots, 42–43
*Air of Battle* (Fry), 113–14
airpower
    archival sources, xxii–xxiii, xxviii–xxix
    ground attacks by, 115–16
    purpose of, xix, xxiv–xxv, 21–22, 90
    *See also* aerial combat; aeroplanes; aviation schools; aviators; Royal Flying Corps
air raids, 71, 115–17
Albatros DI aeroplane (German), 66
Albatros D2 aeroplane (German), 66
Albatros DIII aeroplane (German), 93
Ambrose, Stephen, 140
Amiens (France), 62–63, 63*n*91
Andrews, J.O., 62, 88, 89, 93
Annales school, 96, 96*n*86
anti-aircraft guns (Archie), 47–48, 47*n*26, 54, 67
antiquarians, 98–100
archival fetishism, 39–40
Armée de l'air (France), 21. *See also* France
Arras Memorial to the Missing, 137–39
Ashmore, Edward "Splash," 44
*Augusta Chronicle*, 37–39
aviation schools, 14–15. *See also* Central Flying School; Wright Brothers School of Aviation
aviators
    casualty and fatality rates, 78–79
    celebrity status, 3–4
    certification, 13, 14*n*51, 23, 24, 26, 26*n*105
    contrast with life in trenches, 60–61, 115
    fascination with, xix
    flight schedule followed by, 59
    life of, 60, 61–62, 63–64, 65
    luck experienced by, 77–78
    psychological effects of combat, 59, 111
    romantic notions about, xvi–xviii, 85
    social backgrounds of, 50–51
    terminology, xxiv
    uniform, 51, 52
    views on war by, 111–12
    *See also* aerial combat; aeroplanes; airpower; aviation schools
Avro 504 aeroplane, 28

Bakker, Henry de, 131
Ball, Albert, 51, 110
BE 2c reconnaissance aeroplane (British), 28
Begg, Henry "Bernie," 88
Bellesiles, Michael, 140
Bertangles aerodrome (France), 49, 55, 61
"B" Flight, 24 Squadron, 41–42. *See also* 24 Squadron
Bishop, Billy, xix, xxiv, xxvi, 77, 110, 152
Blériot monoplane (French), 28, 29
Bloch, Marc, 40, 96, 96*n*86
Boelcke, Oswald
    death, 69–70, 79–82
    Manfield shot down by, 41
    reactions to death of, xviii, 82
    rules of aerial combat by, 66, 80
    victories by, 67, 79, 79*n*14
Böhme, Erwin, 79–80, 81–82
bombing and ground attacks, 71, 115–17
Borton, "Biffy," 47
Boulogne-sur-Mer (France), 42
Braithwaite, Edward Ernest, 152
Breadner, Lloyd, 16, 16*n*64, 17
British Expeditionary Force (BEF), 21, 42, 63. *See also specific armies and battles*
Brock, Mel, 73
brothels, 43, 65
Brown, Roy, 16, 17, 18, 20, 26
Bryant, Charles, 114, 117, 118, 119, 132
Bujak, Edward, 29*n*116, 50, 51
Burke, C.J. "Percy," 13, 14

Cambrai, Battle of, 118
Canada
    battles fought in, 10–11, 113
    commemorative efforts, 135
    conscription debate, 134–35
    enlistment for war, 6, 11
    identity in, 1–2
    RFC recruitment in, 12–14, 14*n*57, 51
    university graduates, 9
    at Wright aviation school, 16
Canadian Corps, 113
Canadian Expeditionary Force (CEF), 11, 12, 13, 65
Canadian Militia, 11–12, 13, 36
Candas (2nd Air Depot), 42–43
Carr, E.H., 32–33, 35, 39, 72, 76, 128, 141

cenotaphs, 136–37. *See also*
   commemoration, of dead
Central Flying School (CFS)
   accidents and deaths, 29, 29n116
   development during WWI, 26–27,
      29–30, 106
   instruction at, 27, 108–9
   life at, 107–8
   McKay as instructor, 106, 107–8, 109–10
   McKay's training experience, 26, 28–29,
      30, 31
   prewar purpose, 13, 26
   selection of instructors, 94
   standardized exams, 31
certification, 13, 14n51, 23, 24, 26, 26n105
Chapman, Charles, 41–42, 56, 57
Cheong Pow, 131
Cody, Samuel, 4, 21
Combats in the Air reports, xxv, xxvn19, 75
commemoration, of dead, 135–36, 136–39, 154
commercial exploitation, of war, 152
Commonwealth War Graves Commission,
   *see* Imperial War Graves Commission
condolence, letters of, 132
Connor, Ralph (Charles William Gordon), 5
conscription, 134–35
conspiracy theories, 34
contact patrols, 44n15, 46
Cox and Company, 154
crisis of masculinity, 5–6
Cross, Ronald, 117
Curtiss School (Hammondsport flight
   school), 15
Curtiss School (Long Branch flight
   school), 14

Dadizeele New British Cemetery, 155
*Daily Nugget* (Cobalt, ON), 84
Dayton (OH), 16
death
   commemoration of, 135–36, 136–39, 154
De Havilland scout (DH 2) aeroplane
   advantage, 80
   design, 22, 46
   Gray's research on, 99
   perceptions of, 48, 67
   problems, 68, 71, 87, 88
   replacements for, 91–92
   terminology, xxvi

De Havilland scout (DH 5) aeroplane, 92
digital literacy, 144–45
Drewitt, Herbert, 115

Edwards, John, 18
Ellis, Joseph, 140–41
Elton, Geoffrey, 33, 142
envelope, mystery of, 152, 154
epistemology, 141–42
equipment, military, 98–100
errors, in works of history, 140
ethics, 140–41, 144
Evans, Henry Cope, 41, 51, 56, 60, 67, 138
Evans, Richard, 142

facts
   acceptance of, 35–36
   conspiracy theories and, 34
   cost-benefit analysis in finding, 36–37
   definition, 33
   difficulties with establishing, 74
   errors in sources, 37–39
   history as engagement with, 34, 39–40
   honest use of, 144
   interpretation of, 35
   triangulation for accuracy, 39, 128–29
   *See also* sources
FE 2 aeroplane (British), 22
FE 2B aeroplane (British), 44
Febvre, Lucien, 96, 96n86
Fellows, H.H., 131
fiction techniques, 143–44
fighters (single-seat aircraft), use of
   term, xxiv
First World War
   British deaths on Dec. 28, 1917, 131
   commemorative efforts, 135–36,
      136–39, 154
   consensus on origins, xxix
   lost generation on, 134–35
   support for in British Empire, 6
   transatlantic travel, 25–26
   views on by soldiers, 100–102, 111–12
   *See also* airpower; Canada
First World War, battles
   Cambrai, 118
   Flanders offensive, 112–13, 118
   Passchendaele, 112–13, 115–16
   Pozières, 69

Verdun, 44
Vimy Ridge, 113
Ypres, Second Battle of, 10–11
    See also Somme, Battle of the
Flanders offensive, 112–13, 118. See also
    Passchendaele, Battle of
flight schools, 14–15. See also Central
    Flying School; Wright Brothers
    School of Aviation
Flying Services Memorial, 137–38
Fokker monoplanes (German), 22
France
    airpower, 21, 22, 45
    fatality rate of aces, 78
    Somme offensive, 44, 45
    temptations for soldiers, 64–65
Frost, Amanda Clark, 146
Fry, Willie, 30, 64, 113–14, 117, 118, 119

Galbraith, Daniel, 16
Gatecliffe, Roy Leonard, 73
Gazette (UWO newspaper), 7, 25
George, David Lloyd, xvi
Germany
    airpower, 45, 66, 67, 68, 70
    fatality rate of aces, 78
    Nazis, 139
Globe (Toronto), 11, 14, 84, 137
Goodwin, Doris Kearns, 140
Gordon, Charles William (Ralph Connor), 5
Gough, Michael, 112, 116
Gould, Stephen Jay, 33, 34
Grands Salons Godbert, 63, 64
Gray, Barrington, 91n63, 99
Gray, Douglas, 48, 48n28, 138
ground and bombing attacks, 71, 115–17
Gunn, Murray, 119

Haig, Douglas
    on airpower, 21, 90, 90n60
    criticisms of, 21, 126
    Flanders offensive, 113
    McKay's presentation with, 82, 86
    operational vision, 55
    Somme offensive, 44
Harrington (ON), 1
Hart, Peter, 21–22
Hart Battery Company, 152, 153
Hartley, L.P., 127

Haven, Beckwith, 4
Hawker, Lanoe
    age, 60
    on Arras Memorial, 138
    death, 80, 88–89
    on first big 24 Squadron dogfight, 58
    flying and combat instructions, 56, 66–67
    inspirational role, 67n109, 68
    leadership by, 53, 64
    on McKay's dogfight with Boelcke, 81
    on weather, 61
Hawker, Tyrell, 54, 139
Henshaw, Trevor, 47n26, 91n62
Hindenburg Line, 89, 93
historians, xxvii, 145–47
history
    antiquarians and, 98–100
    archival fetishism, 39–40
    change resulting from, xxvii
    conclusions as provisional, xxviii, 146
    constructed nature of, xxix–xxx
    difficulty comprehending past
        worldviews, 127–28
    digital literacy for, 144–45
    as engagement with facts, 34, 39–40
    errors in works of, 140
    ethics, 140–41, 144
    evidence-based approach, 142–43, 144
    fallacy of authority only coming from
        experience, 128, 129
    fallacy of imposing own views on past,
        95, 135
    literary techniques in telling, 143–44
    methodology, xx–xxii, 96
    microhistory, xx, 97–98
    objectivity debate, 32–33
    operational military, 95, 124
    oral, 128–29
    origin of term, xxvii
    vs. past, xxvii–xxviii
    philosophy of, xxi
    postmodernist debate, 141–42
    public interest in, 98, 146
    reason for study, xix
    relativism, xxx, 32, 128, 141–42, 144
    theories in, 40, 74
    understanding past thought, 125–26
    war and society studies ("new" military),
        95–96, 97–98, 100, 124, 125

war focus, 95–96, 95n85
*See also* facts; historians; *mentalité*;
reading against the grain; sources;
triangulation
*A History of 24 Squadron* (Illingworth and
Robeson), 100–104
*History of Civilization* (Durant and
Durant), 145
*History of the House and Clan of Mackay*, 133
Hoare, Cuthbert, 86
Hollister, Warren, 146
Holocaust, 141
Hughes, Sam, 7
Hughes Chamberlain, Robin, 41, 53, 56–57,
65, 87

*The Idea of History* (Collingwood), 125–26
Imperial War Graves Commission, 136,
137, 154
Irving, David, 141

Jaffray, William, 93, 103–4, 123–24
*Jagdstaffels* ("hunting squadrons"), 66, 70.
*See also* Jasta 2
jargon, 121
Jasta 2, 67, 79, 88. See also *Jagdstaffels*
Jenkins, Keith, 142
Joffre, Joseph, 44
Jones, Ira "Taffy," 108, 108n17, 109

Keegan, John, 97, 98
Kemp, Norman, 117
Kendall, Sidney, 119
Kennedy, Patrick Sylvester, 38
Khan, Ahmad, 131
Knight, Arthur Gerald, 51, 69–70, 79, 80,
81–82, 86

Langan-Byrne, Patrick, 60, 67, 67n112, 68
Lee, Arthur Gould
on aviators, xix
on contrast between flying and trenches,
60–61
on flight training, 27
on ground attacks, 116
luck experienced by, 77
memoirs on war, xvii
on squadrons, 49
Lee, Cecil, 61

Lees, Alan, 123, 123n67, 124
*Lethbridge Daily Herald*, 84
letters of condolence, 132
Lewis, Cecil
on aerial combat, xvii–xviii, 59
on flight training, 108–9
on leisure for aviators, 61, 63, 65
on Somme offensive, 45, 46
Lewis, Edmund, 43, 91n64, 92, 138
Lewis, Gwilym, 42–43, 48, 106, 107
Lewis gun, 29, 57
Lipstadt, Deborah, 141
literary techniques, 143–44
London (England), xxiii
London (ON), xxiii, 3, 4
London Advertiser
on first flight in London, 4
on McKay and rugby, 8
on McKay's death, 134
on McKay's four-day adventure, 70–72, 76
on McKay's victory over Boelcke, 82–83,
84, 85
on Western's rugby team, 10
London Free Press
on horrors of war, 11
letter from McKay republished in, 19
on McKay's death, 134
on McKay's stove fire, 101
on McKay's victory over Boelcke, 83, 85
on McKay's visit to England, 72–73
Long, Selden, 63, 102, 123n67
Longhorn aeroplane (French), 28
Loraine, Robert, 31, 31n124, 53
lost generation, 134–35
Löwenhardt, Erich, 79
luck, 77–78, 104
*Lusitania* (ship), 11
Lutyens, Edward, 137

MacLean, Archibald, 94
Macmillan, Norman, 60, 78, 115
Manfield, Philip, 41, 56, 67
Mannock, Edward Corringham "Mick," 78,
108, 108n17, 110n21
Marvell, Andrew, 147
masculinity, crisis of, 5–6
Mathers, Frank, 111
Maurice Farman "Shorthorns" and
"Longhorns" aeroplanes (French), 28

McAlery, J.M., 114, 114*nn*40–41, 115, 116–17, 117*n*50
McCudden, James, 67–68, 79, 152
McCurdy, John, 14
McKay, Angus (brother), 2
McKay, Eddie
  approach to, xv–xvi, xxii
  archival sources, xxiii, xxviii, 34–35, 36–37, 113–14
  description of, xxiii
  as hero, xviii, 84–85
  mistaken anecdote about, 139–40
  reason for study, xix–xx
  response to acclaim, 85–86
  *See also* McKay, Eddie, as CFS instructor; McKay, Eddie, at front; McKay, Eddie, death of; McKay, Eddie, in RFC; McKay, Eddie, prewar life
McKay, Eddie, as CFS instructor
  Addison on, 109
  arrival at, 105
  life at, 107–8
  positions within, 109–10
  promotion while at, 107, 109
  records on, 106
  return to France from, 110–11, 112
  selection for, 94
McKay, Eddie, at front
  in 23 Squadron, 112, 113–14, 114–15, 114*n*41, 117–18
  in 24 Squadron, 48–49, 49*n*31, 52–53, 93, 94
  account of Jan. 25, 1917 dogfight, 121–22, 124
  bombing raid experience, 116
  calculation of victories, xxv
  crash prior to death, 99, 119
  departure to France, 31–32, 42, 43
  on DH 2 replacements, 92
  dogfight and death of Boelcke, 69–70, 79–82, 85
  dogfights, 56–58, 66, 67, 68–69, 86*n*47, 87–88, 87*n*49, 115
  engine problems, 68
  first dogfight, 56–58
  as flight commander, 117–18
  flight schedule, 59, 72
  four-day adventure claim, 70–72, 76
  leave to England claim, 72–74
  on life at front, 60, 63
  logbook, 99
  missed decoration opportunity, 86
  nickname, 93, 124
  "petty bosch" shoot-up, 54
  Somme offensive, 46–47, 52–53, 56, 87
  stove fire in hut, 101
  venereal disease, 64–65, 65*n*104, 75
  winter of 1916/1917, 91, 93
McKay, Eddie, death of
  chivalrous gesture at, xviii
  circumstances of, 42, 131, 149
  commemoration of, 2*n*5, 134, 135–36, 136–37, 137*n*15, 138
  confirmation of, 133–34
  grave of, 154–55
  letter of condolence by Bryant, 132–33
  "missing" status, 133
McKay, Eddie, in RFC
  departure for England, 23–26
  enlistment, 16–17
  flight instruction in England, 28–29, 30, 31
  overview of career, xix, 119–21
  promotion, 107, 109
  uniform, 51, 52
McKay, Eddie, prewar life
  in 33rd Huron Regiment (militia), 11–12, 13, 19, 36
  birth, 1, 1*n*1
  certification as pilot, 23, *24*
  childhood, 2–3
  family background, 1
  first exposure to aeroplanes, 4
  in sports, 4, 7–8, 9, 19, 35
  at Western University, 6–9
  at Wright Brothers Aviation School, 15–16, 17–19, 18*n*73, 20, 23, 37–39
McKay, Evans Alexander (E.A.), 150
McKay, Garfield (brother), 61, 133
McKay, Joe (brother), 9, 15–16, 84, 132–33, 151
McKay, Mary (mother), 1, 2, 3
McKay, Sandy (brother), 3, 19, 23
McKay, Sidney (brother), 2, 25, 36, 61
McKay, William (father), 1, 2–3
McLeod, Alan, xvi
memoirs, WWI pilot, xvii
memorials, *see* commemoration, of dead

memory, 128–29
*mentalité*, 96, 100–102, 124–25
methodology, xx–xxii, 96
microhistory, xx, 97–98
militia, 11–12, 13, 36
*Missanabie*, SS, 25
missing, use of term, 133
mistakes, in works of history, 140
Moorslede (Belgium), 155

"new" military history (war and society
    studies), 95–96, 97–98, 100, 124, 125
newspapers, Canadian, 11. See also *London
    Advertiser; London Free Press*
*New York Times*, 84
Nieuport scout aeroplane (French), 22
non-repatriation, 136
*No Parachute* (Lee), xvii. *See also* Lee,
    Arthur Gould

objectivity, 32–33, 35
Ontario Temperance Act, 64
OOC (drive down out of control), xxv, xxvi
*Open Cockpit* (Lee), xvii. *See also* Lee,
    Arthur Gould
operational military history, 95, 124
oral history, 128–29

Palmer, Camille Sutton, 151
Palmer, Maud, 149–51
parachutes, 126–27
Paris, 65
Pashley, Eric Clowes, 78*n*5, 103
Passchendaele, Battle of, 112–13, 115–16
Paulhan, Louis, 20
pedagogical microhistory, xx
Perry, Bert, 8, 133
Perth Regiment (militia), 36–37
pilots, *see* aviators
Pither, Sidney, 140
plagiarism, 140, 144
Plumer, Herbert, 113
von Poelnitz (pilot), 103
postmodernism, 141–42, 143. *See also*
    relativism
Pozières, Battle of, 69
*The Practice of History* (Elton), 33
Provisional School of Instruction, 12, 19
public interest, in history, 98, 146

quantitative methodology, 96

Rabagliati, Euan Cuthbert, 90–91, 91*n*63,
    92, 122
RAF, *see* Royal Air Force
Raleigh, Walter, 50
Ranke, Leopold von, 33
RE 8 aeroplane (British), 112
reading against the grain, 76, 104
relativism, xxx, 32, 128, 141–42, 144
reserve squadrons, 26, 26*n*106
RFC, *see* Royal Flying Corps
Richthofen, Manfred von (Red Baron)
    under Boelcke's command, 66
    on Boelcke's death, 80, 81–82
    death, xviii, 16, 78
    death of Hawker, 80, 88–89
Rinehart, Howard, 19, 37
Ritchie, Joseph "Rico," 73
RNAS, *see* Royal Naval Air Service
Robeson, V.A.H., 100, 101, 104
Ross, James Kenneth, 94
Ross, Vivian, 25–26, 77–78
Ross-Hume, Alec, 12–13
Royal Aero Club, 13, 26
Royal Air Force (RAF)
    Canadians in, 51
    formation of, xxiv
    on parachutes, 126–27
    resources used by, 22
Royal Flying Corps (RFC)
    Bloody April (1917), 105
    establishment, xxiv, 21
    fatality rate of aces, 78
    Haig's expansion proposal, 90, 90*n*60
    IV Brigade in Somme offensive, 44–45
    offensive patrolling policy, 54–55,
        54*n*50, 90
    purpose of, 21–22, 90
    recruitment, 12–14, 14*n*57, 26*n*105, 106
    relationship with RNAS, xxiv
    replacement of lost members, 48
    social backgrounds of members, 50–51
    in Somme offensive, 89–90
    uniform, 51, 52
    *See also* 24 Squadron; Central Flying
        School
Royal Naval Air Service (RNAS)
    personnel and aeroplanes, 21

recruitment by, 12, 13, 14, 14*n*57, 26*n*105
relationship with RFC, xxiv
reputation, 16
rugby, xxiii, 7–8, *10*
Rumey, Fritz, 79

*Sagittarius Rising* (Lewis), xvii–xviii. *See also* Lewis, Cecil
*Santa Amalia*, SS, 131
Sassoon, Siegfried, 63, 64
Saundby, Robert, 27, 27*n*107, 30, 49–50, 69, 88
School of Military Aeronautics, 30
scouts (single-seat aircraft), use of term, xxiv
SE 5A aeroplane (British), 68, 112
seatbelts, 127
Second World War, 22, 141
service squadrons, 26–27
Shaw, James Alexander, 38
Shores, Christopher, xix*n*10, xxiv
Shorthorn aeroplane (French), 28
Slessor, John, 94
Smith, Russell, 117
Smith-Barry, Robert, 29
social history, 96
Somerville, Cavanagh N., 38
Somme, Battle of the
    air offensive, 44–45, 46, 52–53, 55–56, 66–67, 89–90
    artillery bombardment in preparation, 43–44, 45
    beginning of, 45–46
    first major aerial battle, 56–58
    outcome of, 89
    preparation for, 44
Sopwith Camel aeroplane (British), 108, 112
Sopwith Pup aeroplane (British), 91, 108, 122
source criticism, xxx, 34, 36–39, 71, 149
sources
    authority of creator, 72
    digital literacy for, 144–45
    enjoyment of research, 145
    first-hand accounts preferred, 75
    gaps in, xxix
    importance of multiple, 74–75
    locating, xxviii, 102–4
    *mentalité* from, 100–102
    record-keeping errors, 94*n*83

rejection of, 149
reliability, 71–72
for RFC, xxviii–xxix
theft of, 122–23
types, xxviii
*See also* facts; source criticism
SPAD VII aeroplane (French), 112, 117, 118
SPAD XIII aeroplane (French), 112, 119
*Speedy* (CFS newspaper), 107, 107*n*13, 111
sports, 4–5, 7–8, 19
Stacey, C.P., xvii
St. Omer (1st Air Depot), 42–43
stunting (aerobatics), 29
synchronization technology, 22

tanks, 118
Taylor, Stewart, 65, 75, 86, 93, 110, 117, 119*n*61
temperance movement, 64
theories, 40, 74
Thiepval Memorial to the Missing of the Somme, 137
thought, history of, 125–26
Tidmarsh, David, 41, 56
*Toronto Daily Star*, 38, 84, 109
transatlantic travel, 25–26
Trenchard, Hugh
    air depots, 42
    at Arras Memorial dedication, 138
    offensive patrolling policy, 54, 55, 90
    pilot replacement policy, 48
    on pilot training, 30, 53
    on squadron leaders flying patrol, 53, 88
triangulation, 39, 73–74, 128–29
Trudeau, George, 119, 119*n*61

university graduates, 9
University of Western Ontario, *see* Western University

Vance, Jonathan, 135
venereal disease, 64–65, 75
Verdun, Battle of, 44
Verey lights, 117
Vimy Ridge, Battle of, 113

war, history focus on, 95–96, 95*n*85
war and society studies ("new" military history), 95–96, 97–98, 100, 124, 125

Welch, J.W., 101
Wellesley, George, 50
Western University
    archives, 152
    history of, 6
    McKay at, 6–9
    rugby at, 7–8, 10
    support for First World War, 9–10
    use of name, xxiii
West Zorra Township (ON), 1
*What Is History?* (Carr), 32–33. *See also*
    Carr, E.H.
Whitaker, William, 119
White, Hayden, 143
Whitehall Cenotaph, 137
Wilkinson, Alan, 68, 89, 104
Wilson, R.E., 66
Windschuttle, Keith, 142
Winfield, John, 131
Winter, Denis, xxii, 12, 29$n$116, 97–98
Wise, S.F., xxii
Wood, Arthur Holroyd O'Hara, 109–10
Wood, Harry
    account of Jan. 25, 1917 dogfight,
        121–22, 124

in diary entry, 103
flight training of, 30
as instructor at CFS, 94, 109, 110, 110$n$22
relationship with McKay, 51, 86$n$47,
    93, 107
on time off in Amiens, 62, 65
Woollett, Henry, 122, 124
Wright, Orville, 15, 17, 20, 20$n$83
Wright, Wilber, 15, 17, 20$n$83
Wright Brothers School of Aviation
    advantages of, 15
    examination, 23
    instruction, 17–19
    life at, 16, 16$n$64
    sources on arrival in Augusta, 37–39
Wright Flyer aeroplane, 17, 19, 23, 26
Wright Model B, 28
Wyatt, Benjamin, 151

Yeates, Victor, 28
"The Young Aviator Lay Dying" (song),
    61–62
Young Men's Christian Association
    (YMCA), 5
Ypres, Second Battle of, 10–11